AF531524

AQUATIC BIODIVERSITY AND POLLUTION

Edited by

Dr. Pawan Kumar 'Bharti'

Environmental Scientist
Centre for Agro-Rural Technologies (CART-India)
20, Jamaalpur Maan, Raja Ka Tajpur, Bijnore (UP) – 246 735
(India)

Dr. Avnish Chauhan

Assistant Professor
Department of Applied Science, College of Engineering
Teerthanker Mahaveer University, Moradabad (UP) – 244 001
(India)

&

Prof. H.A.H. Kaoud

Professor
Department of Animal, Poultry, Aquaculture and Environmental Pollution
Faculty of Veterinary Medicine, Cairo University, Cairo, Egypt

Associate Editors

Dr. Kumar Satish Chandra

Lanco Infratech Ltd., Gurgaon – 122 016 (Haryana)
(India)

&

Dr. Pawan Kumar

J.M. Envirotech Pvt. Ltd, Gurgaon (Haryana)
(India)

DISCOVERY PUBLISHING HOUSE PVT. LTD.
NEW DELHI-110 002

Published by:
Tilak Wasan

DISCOVERY PUBLISHING HOUSE PVT. LTD.
4383/4B, Ansari Road, Darya Ganj
New Delhi-110 002 (India)
Phone : +91-11-23279245, 43596064-65
Fax : +91-11-23253475
E-mail : discoverypublishinghouse@gmail.com
sales@discoverypublishinggroup.com
parul.wasan@gmail.com
web : www.discoverypublishinggroup.com

***First Edition:* 2013**

ISBN: 978-93-5056-359-5

Aquatic Biodiversity and Pollution

© 2013, Editors

All rights reserved. No part of this publication should be reproduced, stored in a retrieval system, or transmitted in any form or by any means: electronic, mechanical, photocopying, recording or otherwise, without the prior written permission of the author and the publisher.

This book has been published in good faith that the material provided by authors is original. Every effort is made to ensure accuracy of material, but the publisher and printer will not be held responsible for any inadvertent error(s). In case of any dispute, all legal matters are to be settled under Delhi jurisdiction only.

Printed at:
Aditi Fine Art Press
Delhi

Preface

Aquatic biodiversity can be defined as the variety of life and the ecosystems that make up the freshwater, tidal, and marine regions of the world and their interactions. Declining biodiversity worldwide is a major and ongoing environmental dilemma. Although aquatic biodiversity has been declining continually, species extinction rates have gone from about one species per year over the past 600 million years to hundreds of species per year in recent times.

Human activities are causing species to disappear at an alarming rate. Aquatic species are at a higher risk of extinction than mammals and birds. Losses of this magnitude impact the entire ecosystem, depriving valuable resources used to provide food, medicines, and industrial materials to human beings. Runoff from agricultural and urban areas, the invasion of exotic species, and the creation of dams and water diversion have been identified as the greatest challenges to freshwater environments. Overexploitation of aquatic organisms for various purposes is the greatest threat to marine environments. Other threats to aquatic biodiversity include urban development and resource-based industries, such as mining and forestry that destroy or reduce natural habitats. Beside these, air and water pollution, sedimentation and erosion, and climate change also pose threats to aquatic biodiversity.

This book provides comprehensive coverage of the fundamental principles and current practices and trends in the field of aquatic biodiversity, conservation and environmental pollution. This book updates the subject matter, illustrations and problems to incorporate new concepts and issues related to aquatic biodiversity, conservation, aquaculture and environmental pollution.

Particularly thanks are due to all contributors from Egypt, Nigeria, India; and publisher also for their contribution and assistance.

I hope this book will be of benefit to researcher/academia who is working in the field of environment, ecology, freshwater ecology, aquatic ecosystem, environmental pollution, fisheries and agriculture.

Dr. Pawan Kumar 'Bharti'

Contents

List of Contributors

1. **A.K. Prusty**, Project Directorate of Farming System Research, Meerut-250 110, India
2. **Amir Khan,** Department of Biochemistry, Division of Life Science, Sardar Bhagwan Singh Post Graduate Institute of Biomedical Sciences & Research Balawala, Dehradun, INDIA.
3. **B. K. Behera,** Central Inland Fisheries Research Institute, Barrackpore- 700 120, India
4. **C.N. Ariole,** Department of Microbiology, University of Port Harcourt, P.M.B. 5323, Port Harcourt, Nigeria
5. **D.K. Belsare,** Society for Natural Resources, Culture and Human Environment, Bhopal (MP), India
6. **D. Panda,** Central Inland Fisheries Research Institute, Barrackpore-700 120, India
7. **Dharmendra Kumar Meena,** Central Inland Fisheries Research Institute, Barrackpore-700 120, India
8. **Fouzia Ishaq,** Limnological Research Lab, Department of Zoology and Environmental Science, Gurukula Kangri University, Haridwar, India
9. **G.C. Okpokwasili,** Department of Microbiology, University of Port Harcourt, P.M.B. 5323, Port Harcourt, Nigeria
10. **Hussein A. Kaoud,** Prof. of Animal, Poultry, Aquaculture Hygiene and Environmental Pollution; Head, Department of Veterinary Hygiene and Management, Faculty of Veterinary Medicine, Cairo University, Egypt
11. **Habeeba Ahmad Kabir,** Limnology Research Laboratory, Department of Zoology, Aligarh Muslim University, Aligarh, (UP)- 202002, India.
12. **Kanti Meena**, Central Research Institute for Jute and Allied Fibers, Barrackpore- 700 120, India

13. **Md. Shahbaz Akhtar,** Directorate of Coldwater Fisheries Research, Bhimtal- 263 136, India

14. **Pronob Das,** Central Inland Fisheries Research Institute, Barrackpore- 700 120, India

15. **Saltanat Parveen,** Limnology Research Laboratory, Department of Zoology, Aligarh Muslim University, Aligarh, (UP)- 202002, India.

16. **Satendra Kumar,** RHS Krishi Vigyan Kendra (Jawaharlal Nehru Krishi Vishwa Vidyalaya) Badgaon, Balaghat-481115 (MP), India

17. **Shailendra Sharma,** Department of Biotechnology, Adarsh Institute of Management & Science, Dhamnod (M.P.), India

Aquatic Biodiversity and Pollution

—*Hussein A. Kaoud, Egypt*

ABSTRACT

Aquatic biodiversity can be defined as the variety of life and the ecosystems that make up the freshwater, tidal, and marine regions of the world and their interactions.

Human activities are causing species to disappear at an alarming rate. Aquatic species are at a higher risk of extinction than mammals and birds. Losses of this magnitude impact the entire ecosystem, depriving valuable resources used to provide food, medicines, and industrial materials to human beings.

Air and water pollution are widespread threats that can directly poison threatened and endangered species, reduce their numbers, and diminish their available habitat. Coastal and estuarine ecosystems have been, and still are, heavily influenced by the human species through pollution and habitat loss throughout the world. This coastal pollution and its impacts have resulted in a number of environmental issues including the enrichment of enclosed waters with organic matter leading to eutrophication, pollution by chemicals such as oil, and sedimentation due to land-based activities or sea level rise due to the global change.

Keywords: *Aquatic Biodiversity, environmental pollution, aquatic ecosystem.*

INTRODUCTION

Biodiversity' can be used as a synonym for living nature, with an emphasis on its complexity, at genetic, species and ecosystem levels. This complexity is vital in the maintenance of healthy ecosystem functioning, and it is important to recognize this when developing policies to protect the natural environment (UNEP-WCMC, 2012).

The variety of life on Earth, its biological diversity is commonly referred to as biodiversity. The number of species of plants, animals, and microorganisms, the enormous diversity of genes in these species, the different ecosystems on the planet, such as deserts, rainforests and coral reefs are all part of a biologically diverse Earth. Appropriate conservation and sustainable development strategies attempt to recognize this as being integral to any approach. Almost all cultures have in some way or form recognized the importance that nature, and its biological diversity has had upon them and the need to maintain it. Yet, power, greed and politics have affected the precarious balance.

Estimated Number of Described Species	Number of Species Evaluated by 2010 (IUCN Red List ver. 2010.3)	Number of Threatened (IUCN Red List (UCN Red List ver. 2010.3)	Number Threatened in 2010 (% of Species Evaluated
Mammals	5.490	1.142	21%
Birds	10.027	1.223	12%
Repties	9.084	469	28%
Amphibians	6.638	1.895	30%
Fishes	31.600	1.414	26%
Subtotal	**62.839**	**6.143**	**21%**
Insects	1,000.000	711	24%
Moluscs	85.000	1.036	42%
Crustaceans	47.000	606	28%
Corals	2.175	236	27%
Arachnids	102.248	18	58%
Valvet Worms	165	9	82%
Horseshoe Crabs	4	0	0%
Others	68,658	24	46%
Subtotal	**1,305,250**	**2,639**	**31%**
Mosses	16,236	82	79%
Ferms and Allies	12.000	139	61%
Gymnosperms	1.052	322	40%
Flowering Plants	268,000	7,948	70%
Green Algae	4,242	0	0%
Red Algae	6.144	9	16%
Subtotal	307,674	8,500	68%
Lichens	17,000	2	100%
Mushrooms	31,496	1	100%
Brown Algae	3,127	6	40%
Subtotal	**51,623**	**9**	**50%**

Fig. 1.1: Numbers of described species by taxonomic group (IUCN Red List version 2010.3)

The genetic diversity inherent in most species provides the raw material to respond rapidly to changed circumstances. Change is, of course, the normal state of affairs in the living world. What makes our present situation unique is the rapidity and scale of the change. Our fragmentation and destruction of habitats constitutes a massive uncontrolled experiment in ecology and genetics. Knowledge of population structures, i.e. the distribution and amount of genetic variation, of a wide range of organisms is necessary, as is a much deeper understanding of the biological significance of different sorts of variation.

Although much debate on biodiversity focuses on 'species', it is important to note that this is not a standard unit. The way species are defined differs between groups and between taxonomists. However, despite these ambiguities, measures of species richness and distribution are important tools in assessing the state of the environment and the direction and speed of change. The number of described species is now around 1.7 million. The estimated total number of species in existence ranges in order of magnitude from around 10 million to 100 million.

Species are unevenly distributed over the Earth's surface. Most vertebrate species have small ranges, and these narrowly-distributed species tend to co-occur in "centers of endemism", which are concentrated in the tropical regions. This means there are some areas of the world, and some countries, with much higher levels of species richness than others. Although patterns of terrestrial diversity are better understood than those in the aquatic realm, it is clear that there are also areas of high marine biodiversity such as coral reef ecosystems.

MATERIALS AND METHODS

Why is Biodiversity Important?

Biodiversity boosts ecosystem productivity where each species, no matter how small, all have an important role to play. For example, a larger number of plant species means a greater variety of crops; greater species diversity ensures natural sustainability for all life forms; and healthy ecosystems can better withstand and recover from a variety of disasters. And so, while we dominate this planet, we still need to preserve the diversity in wildlife.

At least 40 per cent of the world's economy and 80 per cent of the needs of the poor are derived from biological resources. In addition, the richer the diversity of life, the greater the opportunity for medical discoveries, economic development, and adaptive responses to such new challenges as climate change.

Aquatic Biodiversity

Aquatic biodiversity can be defined as the variety of life and the ecosystems that make up the freshwater, tidal, and marine regions of the world and their interactions.

Aquatic Biodiversity Encompasses

- **Freshwater ecosystems**, including lakes, ponds, reservoirs, rivers, streams, groundwater, and wetlands.

Lakes are inland bodies of freshwater ranging in size from less than one acre to several thousands of acres. Simply stated, lakes are the bodies of water that fill depressions in the earth's surface. Lakes may be further described by their origin and classified by trophic status according to their characteristics.

Reservoirs are lakes, often man-made, that control water flow for hydroelectric power generation, flood control, and/or municipal water supplies.

Rivers and streams are the general terms used to describe natural and man-made bodies of moving water. Rivers are larger than streams and empty into large water bodies such as oceans and lakes. River and stream systems consist of numerous tributaries joined together to form a main channel. The tributaries (streams) are identified by their stream order, denoted by its position in the system. There are three main types of streams:

Ephemeral streams regularly exist for short periods of time, usually during a rainy period, and may have defined channels even when they are dry. *Intermittent streams* flow at different times of the year, or seasonally, when there is enough water from rainfall, springs, or other surface sources such as melting snow or even discharge from a wastewater treatment facility. *Perennial* streams are those that flow year-round.

Fig. 1.2: Nile allows Egypt to continue today as one of the largest and most powerful nations of Africa and the Middle East

A wetland is a place where water is the primary factor controlling the immediate environment. Wetlands can be as small as a child's wading pool or as large as a lake.

Wetlands generally occur where land and water meet and underground water is at or near the surface, or where land is covered water less than six feet deep. The water level in a wetland rises and falls. This shift may depend on location, weather, climate, or surrounding ecosystems. The area may be temporarily saturated, then dry up until another watery inundation. Meanwhile, a wetland provides a rich home to many animals and plants.

Fig.1.3: Wetlands generally occur where land and water meet and underground water is at or near the surface, or where land is covered water less than six feet deep

Ground Water

When rain falls to the ground, the water does not stop moving. Some of it flows along the land surface to streams or lakes, some is used by plants, some evaporates and returns to the atmosphere, and some seeps into the ground. Water seeps into the ground much like a glass of water poured onto a pile of sand.

As water seeps into the ground, some of it clings to particles of soil or to roots of plants just below the surface. This moisture provides plants with the water they need to live. Water not used by plants moves deeper into the ground. The water moves downward through empty spaces or cracks in the soil, sand, or rocks until it reaches a layer of rock through which water cannot easily move. This is called the ***saturation zone.*** The water then fills the empty spaces and cracks above that layer. The topmost layer of an aquifer is known as the ***water table.*** Water tables can be above ground, barely below the surface, or hundreds of feet underground. Other aquifers that are enclosed beneath this are called ***confined aquifers***. Instead of flowing as an underground river, ground water is held in tiny crevices between soil or rock much like water is held in a sponge.

Aquifer is the name given to underground soil or rock through which ground water can easily move. The amount of ground water that can flow through soils or rock depends on the size of the spaces in the soil or rock and how well the spaces are connected. The amount of spaces is the porosity. ***Permeability*** is a measure of how well the spaces are connected.

Aquifers typically consist of gravel, sand, sandstone, or fractured rock such as limestone. These types of materials are permeable because they have large connected spaces that allow ground water to flow through. The spaces in the gravel aquifer are called ***pores.*** The spaces in a fractured rock aquifer are called ***fractures.*** If a material contains pores that are not connected, ground water cannot move from one space to another. These materials are said to be impermeable. Materials such as clay or shale have many small pores, but the pores are not well connected. Therefore, clay or shale usually restricts the flow of groundwater. Understanding these properties enables land use planners to determine the best methods of extracting ground water for human use.

Ground water can become unusable if it becomes polluted and unsafe to drink. It can become polluted by seepage through landfills, septic tanks and sewage systems, hazardous waste sites, landfills, underground storage tanks, road salt, waste oil disposal, and fertilizers or pesticides used on farms and homes. However, with careful use and by reducing sources of pollution, ground water can continue to be an important natural resource in the future.

- Marine ecosystems are a part of the largest aquatic system on the planet, covering over 70% of the Earth's surface. The habitats that make up this vast system range from the productive near shore regions to the barren ocean floor. Some examples of important marine ecosystems are: including oceans, estuaries, salt marshes, sea grass beds, coral reefs, kelp beds, and mangrove forests.

Marine ecosystems are home to a host of different species ranging from tiny planktonic organisms that comprise the base of the marine food web (i.e., phytoplankton and zooplankton) to large marine mammals like the whales, manatees, and seals. In addition, many fish species reside in marine ecosystems including flounder, scup, sea bass, monkfish, squid, mackerel, butterfish, and spiny dogfish. Birds are also plentiful including shorebirds, gulls, wading birds, and terns. Some marine animals are also endangered including whales, turtles, etc. In summary, many animal species rely on marine ecosystems for both food and shelter from predators.

(A) (B)

Fig. 1.4 (A-B): Coral reefs provide food and shelter to the highest levels of marine diversity in the world.

Marine ecosystems contain several unique qualities that set them apart from other aquatic ecosystems, the key factor being the presence of dissolved compounds in seawater, particularly salts. This total gram weight of dissolved substances (salts) in one kg of seawater is referred to as salinity. In general 85% of the dissolved substances are Sodium (Na) and Chlorine (Cl) in seawater. On average seawater has a salinity of 35 parts per thousand grams (ppt) of water. These dissolved compounds give seawater its distinctive "salty" taste, affect species composition of particular marine habitats, and prevent oceans from freezing during the winter. Daily changes in factors such as weather, currents, and seasons as well as variations in climate and location will cause salinity levels to vary among different marine ecosystems. In areas such as *estuaries,* tidal marshes, and mangrove forests, tidal and freshwater influences from river and streams makes it necessary for marine organisms to adapt to a wide range of salinity levels. These organisms such as mussels, clams, and barnacles, are called euryhaline (salt tolerant) organisms. Other organisms, in particular finfish, are unable to tolerate such changes in salinity. These organisms are considered to be stenohaline (salt intolerant). These species require more constant levels of salinity, forcing them to either migrate to new areas when fluctuations in salinity levels occur or to seek out areas where salinity change is minimal (e.g., the deep ocean).

Like other aquatic ecosystems, marine ecosystems require nutrients and light to produce food and energy. However, both nutrients and light are limiting factors in marine ecosystem productivity. Like many other aquatic plants, photosynthetic marine organisms (i.e., phytoplankton) rely upon sunlight and chlorophyll *a* to absorb visible light from the sun as well as nitrogen (N), phosphorus (P), and silicon (Si) to generate food and promote growth and reproduction. However, the amount of light penetrating the ocean surface tends to decrease with increasing water depth, therefore photosynthesis can only take place within a small band near the surface of the water (called the photic zone). In addition, nutrient availability often varies significantly from place to place. For example, in the open ocean, nutrient levels are often very poor causing primary production to be very low. In contrast, nearshore waters such as estuaries and marshes are often rich in nutrients, allowing primary production to be very high. In some instances, nearshore ecosystems have an excess of nutrients due to runoff and other terrestrial sources. Excess nutrients can cause an over-stimulation of primary production, depleting oxygen levels and causing eutrophic conditions to occur in coastal habitats.

Marine ecosystems are very important in to the overall health of both marine and terrestrial environments. According to the World Resources Center, coastal habitats alone account for approximately 1/3 of all marine biological productivity, and estuarine ecosystems (i.e., salt marshes, sea grasses, mangrove forests) are among the most productive regions on the planet. In addition, other marine ecosystems such as coral reefs provide food and shelter to the highest levels of marine diversity in the world.

Aquatic biodiversity includes all unique species, their habitats and interaction between them. It consists of phytoplankton, zooplankton, aquatic plants, insects, fish, birds, mammals, and others.

The greater the biodiversity, the greater the stability of an environment, and vice versa. For example, large tracts of undisturbed forest modify their own environments by stabilizing air temperatures, capturing rainfall, recycling water vapor, and preventing the accumulation of carbon dioxide and greenhouse gases. Habitat fragmentation (isolation) and destruction are the leading threats to aquatic biodiversity. Aquatic habitats are being drained, channeled, or polluted at increasing rates. Freshwaters are the most threatened ecosystems and aquatic animals are at the greatest risk. The destruction of wetlands is largely the result of human population increases and development pressure. For example, riversides are premium development properties, attracting large numbers of people and houses that threaten erosion and water pollution.

Declining biodiversity worldwide is a major and ongoing environmental dilemma. Although aquatic biodiversity has been declining continually, species extinction rates have gone from about one species per year over the past 600 million years to hundreds of species per year in recent times.

Effects on Biodiversity

It is now well established that there are anthropogenic chemicals released to the environment that can disrupt the endocrine systems of a wide range of wildlife species. The reproductive hormone-receptor systems appear to be especially vulnerable. Indeed, changes in sperm counts, genital tract malformations, infertility, an increased frequency of mammary, prostate and testicular tumors, feminization of male individuals of diverse vertebrate species and altered reproductive behaviors, have all been reported (Sharpe & Skakkebaek, 1993; Colborn et al., 1996). With regard to environmental management, the problem of endocrine disrupting chemicals is extremely difficult to address. Basic research is required to strengthen the scientific foundation for risk assessment: e.g., baseline studies on endocrine dysfunction across classes of animals to reduce the uncertainty associated with species extrapolations (NSTC, 1996).

An extensive list of chemicals which are thought to be capable of disrupting the reproductive endocrine systems of animals has been assembled. They fall into the following categories:

1. Environmental oestrogens (oestrogen receptor mediated) (e.g., methoxychlor, bis¬phenolic compounds);
2. Environmental antioestrogens (e.g., Dioxin, Endosulphan);
3. Environmental antiandrogens (e.g., Vinclozolin, DDE, Kraft mill effluent);
4. Toxicants that reduce steroid hormone levels (e.g., Fenarimol and other fungicides; endosulphan);
5. Toxicants that affect reproduction primarily through effects on the CNS (e.g., dithiocarbamate pesticides, methanol); and
6. Other toxicants that affect hormonal status (e.g., cadmium, benzidine-based dyes).

Threats to Aquatic Biodiversity

Human activities are causing species to disappear at an alarming rate. Aquatic species are at a higher risk of extinction than mammals and birds. Losses of this magnitude impact the entire ecosystem, depriving valuable resources used to provide food, medicines, and industrial materials to human beings (Tewari and-Bisht, 1991). Runoff from agricultural and urban areas, the invasion of exotic species, and the creation of dams and water diversion have been identified as the greatest challenges to freshwater environments (Allan and Flecker 1993; Scientific American 1997). Overexploitation of aquatic organisms for various purposes is the greatest threat to marine environments, thus the need for sustainable exploitation has been identified by the Environmental Defense Fund as the key priority in preserving marine biodiversity. Other threats to aquatic biodiversity include urban development and resource-based industries, such as mining and forestry that destroy or reduce natural habitats. In addition, air and water pollution, sedimentation and erosion, and climate change also pose threats to aquatic biodiversity.

- **Population growth**

  Increasing population leads to increasing pressure on aquatic resources. The impact of development and human changes to aquatic landscapes has caused massive reductions in aquatic species biodiversity. Certain fish, snails, mussels, crayfish, and other aquatic creatures have completely disappeared. Others have been substantially and continually reduced in numbers over the years. Tragically, many species are lost before we even know that they existed.

  1. Humans live near water sources for a variety of reasons
  2. Transportation
  3. drinking water supply
  4. recreation.

- **Climate change**

  1- Some forests in some coastal habitats vulnerable to changes in sea levels.

  - During the past 100 years, sea levels have risen by 4-8 inches. 2

- **Air and water pollution**

Air and water pollution are widespread threats that can directly poison threatened and endangered species, reduce their numbers, and diminish their available habitat. Acid rain is poisoning and global warming is heating our surface waters, resulting in dramatic declines in aquatic biodiversity.

Pollution is the introduction of contaminants into an environment that causes instability, disorder, harm or discomfort to the ecosystem i.e. physical systems or living organisms. Pollution can take the form of chemical substances or energy Pollutants, the elements of pollution, can be foreign substances or energies, or naturally occurring; when naturally occurring, they are considered contaminants when they exceed natural levels. The most important type of environmental pollution is **Water pollution**:

Pollution load — Four forms of pollutants can be distinguished-

(*a*) Poisonous pollutants — Agrochemicals, metals, acids and phenol cause mortality, if present in a high concentration and affect the reproductive functionality of fish (Kime, 1995).

(*b*) Suspended solids — it affects the respiratory processes and secretion of protective mucus making the fish susceptible to infection of various pathogens.

(*c*) Sewage and organic pollutants — They cause deoxygenation due to eutrophication causing mortality in fishes.

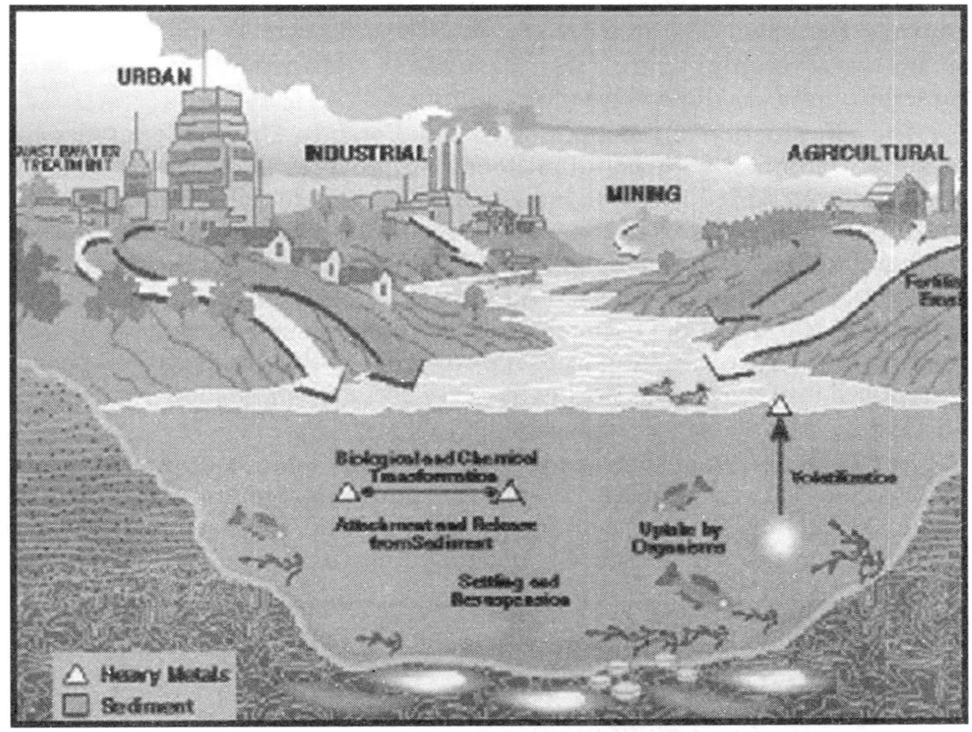

Fig. 1.5: Sources of water pollution.

(d) Thermal pollution — It cause increase in ambient temperature and reduce dissolved oxygen concentration leading to death of some sensitive species.

RESULTS AND DISCUSSION

Freshwater Ecosystems

Freshwater Species Population Index

Between 1970 and 1999, the Freshwater Species Population Index fell by nearly 50%, which constitutes a very rapid decline in population indices. The Freshwater Species Population Index measures the average change over time in the populations of some 194 species of freshwater birds, mammals, reptiles, amphibians and fish. The index represents the average of six regional indices, which measure freshwater species populations in Africa, Asia-Pacific, Australasia, Europe, Latin America and the Caribbean, and North America. There has been a much smaller decline over the past 30 years in the freshwater species of North America and Europe than those in the other regions. Much of the loss and degradation of freshwater ecosystems in the industrialized world took place prior to 1970.

The harvest of freshwater fish is likely to increase either through **capture fisheries** or **aquaculture** (otherwise known as 'fish farming'). In many developing countries, freshwater fish provide a significant contribution to the diets of local communities.

The introduction of the non-native Nile Perch to Africa's Lake Victoria in 1954, combined with pollution loading and increased water turbidity resulting from agriculture and industrial development, has greatly reduced indigenous fish populations. Kenya for example, reported only 0.5% of its commercial fish catch as Nile Perch in 1976. Five years late, the proportion was 68%. Lake Victoria, the second largest lake in the world, has lost an estimated 200 different endemic species found nowhere else, while the remaining 150 are endangered. Two-thirds of the freshwater species introduced into the tropics worldwide have become established (Revenga et al., 1998)

In Africa and Asia, fish provide 21% and 28% of all animal protein, respectively (Revenga et al., 1998). The figures are more significant in landlocked countries, where data on the fish caught are often not formally recorded, and their importance is not fully known.

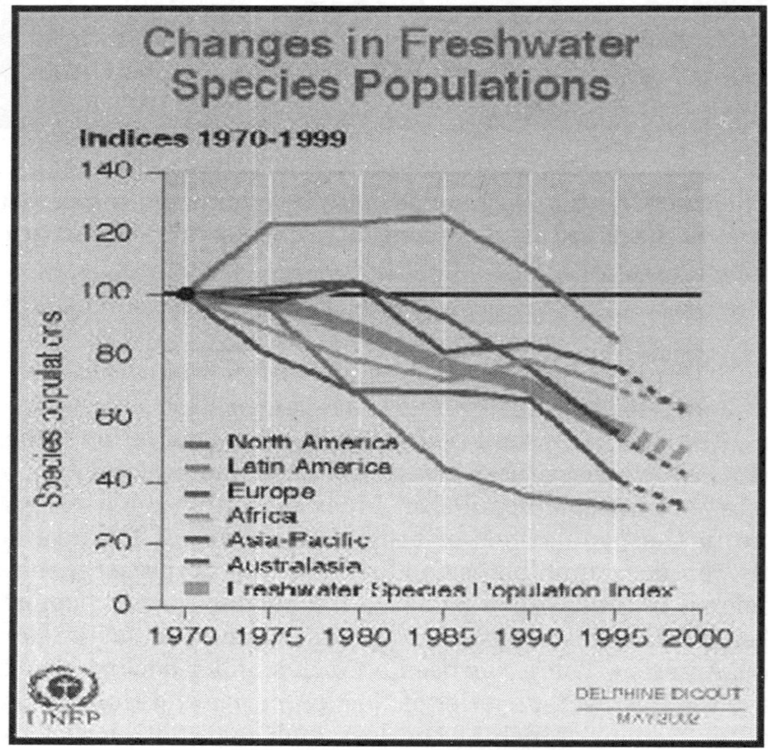

Fig.1.6: Freshwater Species Population Index

In 1999, the reported fish production form inland waters totaled 28 million tonnes, with contributions of 8.2 and 19.8 million tonnes from capture fisheries and aquaculture, respectively. With major under-reporting from subsistence fisheries, these figures could be twice as high (FAO, 2000).

Reasons of Declining Fresh Water Aquatic Biodiversity

Habitat loss

Aquatic habitats are the areas where water plants and animals live and obtain shelter, water, nutrients, and food for survival. Loss of habitat is the major reason why aquatic biodiversity is declining. Many of our native aquatic habitats were lost as early pioneers cleared the land, drained and filled wetlands, and cleared streamside forests.

Dams isolate upstream and downstream populations of fish, mussels, crayfish, snails, and other aquatic animals. They also alter water quality and flows, changing rivers into reservoirs and sediment basins that will not support native stream life. Our natural biodiversity is lost through many careless human activities including: the large-scale cutting of streamside forests, the overharvest of native plants and animals, the indiscriminate use of pesticides, draining and filling of wetlands, mining, stream gravel dredging, water pollution, flood control, dams, irrigation and water diversions, road construction, and the conversion of wetlands to agricultural and city development. Preventing habitat loss is the first important the first important step to take in protecting native species, and restoring important degraded habitat is the second step.

Introduced Species (Aquatic exotics)

Alien species (nonnative, introduced, or non-indigenous species) are animals or plants that have been accidentally moved or intentionally introduced into areas beyond their native, natural geographical range. Why are invasions of exotic species a problem for native aquatic life forms? Introduced aquatic plant and animal species can disrupt the balance of natural ecosystems. Exotic species threaten to out compete (for food or space) native species, lowering biodiversity and the abundance of our native species.

In their new habitats, these exotics have no natural predators, and can eliminate native species directly or indirectly. They may carry diseases and parasites that can infect native plants and animals. Invasive organisms can potentially reproduce with native species and alter the gene pool, leading to hybridization and homogeneity, and reducing genetic diversity. In many places, native species are on the brink of extinction because of competition with exotic species.

Introduced nonnative species cause widespread destruction by reducing or eliminating economically important native species. Exotic species may cause economic damage by:

- reproducing with valuable species and producing worthless hybrids and crossbreeds;
- carrying or supporting harmful pests;
- reducing recreational boating, swimming, commercial fishing; and
- importing diseases that affect related native plants, animals, and even humans.

Human Activities

Human activities are causing species to disappear at an alarming rate. It has been estimated that between 1975 and 2015, species extinction will occur at a rate of 1 to 11 percent per decade. Aquatic species are at a higher risk of extinction than mammals and birds. Losses of this magnitude impact the entire ecosystem, depriving valuable resources used to provide food, medicines, and industrial materials to human beings.

While freshwater and marine ecosystems face similar threats, there are some differences regarding the severity of each threat. Runoff from agricultural and urban areas, the invasion of exotic species, and the creation of dams and water diversion have been identified as the greatest challenges to freshwater environments (Allan and Flecker 1993; Scientific American 1997). Overfishing is the greatest threat to marine environments, thus the need for sustainable fisheries has been identified by the Environmental Defense Fund as the key priority in preserving marine biodiversity.

Reclamations

Land reclamations can destroy nursery grounds of juvenile fish and the habitats of shellfish. Many coastal cities e.g. Wellington, Auckland and Lyttelton, have reclaimed shallow marine areas for extra land. Reclamation is still continuing around New Zealand, but now environmental Impacts Reports are required as part of the consent process. Regional coastal plans are also required to be prepared by regional councils, setting out what activities and effects are allowed in the coastal marine are. The impact or reclamation on fisheries resources is more likely to be taken into account.

Mineral Exploitation

Oil production, with its associated pollution risks, and mining of the seabed and beach sands can disrupt marine habitats, Mining companies are now much more aware of environmental impacts than in the past.

Rubbish, such as plastic and bits of fishing nets dumped at sea or on the foreshore is a menace to fish, marine mammals and birds. Fishers are often blamed for this, and while some probably are still irresponsible.

Enhancement (Reseeding)

Enhancement is another more positive human impact. It involves releasing hatchery-reared young into the wild or providing additional protection to naturally spawned juveniles. This is not done on a wide scale, because of cost, the exceptions in New Zealand being scallops and salmon. Research is being done on snapper and rock lobster enhancement.

Marine Ecosystems, Including Oceans, Estuaries, Salt Marshes, Sea Grass Beds, Coral Reefs, Kelp Beds, and Mangrove Forests

Coastal and estuarine ecosystems have been, and still are, heavily influenced by the human species through pollution and habitat loss throughout the world. This **coastal pollution and its impacts** have resulted in a number of environmental issues including the enrichment of enclosed waters with organic matter leading to eutrophication, pollution by chemicals such as oil, and sedimentation due to land-based activities or sea level rise due to the global change. Over 80% of all marine pollution originates from land-based sources which are primarily industrial, agricultural and urban. Pollution accompanies most kinds of human activities, including offshore oil and gas production and marine oil transportation.

The effects of contaminants on coastal ecosystems are very difficult to assess. In the estimation of possible effects, the actual concentrations are compared with the levels that can cause effects. Results of laboratory experiments give only limited information in relation to the field situation, due to the complexity of natural systems and (in general) the co-occurrence of a multitude of contaminants in the field. Actual changes in the sea are often very difficult to discern from the large variability, which occurs naturally.

Measurement of marine pollution using biological indicators provides information on the bio-availability of contaminants and the integration of the effects of multiple exposures and exposure over time. Multiple exposures is the combined action of all chemical contaminants. Even if the contaminants are present at concentrations too low to cause gross harmful effects, they can cause a suite of biochemical reactions in marine organisms generally called stress. Amongst the result of prolonged stress is the suppression of the immune system, thus increasing sensitivity towards the impact of infectious agents and parasites.

Natural factors such as temperature extremes and fluctuations of salinity or anthropogenic activities, such as fisheries, can aggravate these reactions. A suite of biochemical reactions in marine organisms may occur as a response increasing sensitivity towards the impact of infectious agents and parasites.

The composition and structure of the fauna, flora and habitats of coastal seas has been changing at an unusual rate in the last few decades, due to changes in the global climate, invasive species and an increase in human activities. The unusual rapid rate of change, rather than the nature of the change itself, is the reason for the deterioration of many environments;

over the last 50 years the rate and extent of this deterioration has been unprecedented, as were the consequences on biological diversity. The term biodiversity is used by the Convention on Biological Diversity (1992) to refer to all aspects of variability evident within the living world, including diversity within and between individuals, populations, species, communities, and ecosystems. The term is commonly used loosely to refer to all species and habitats in some given area, or even on the Earth overall. In fact, it relates to environmental attributes, often species or species groups, which can be sampled and whose modification is supposed to reflect a change of biological diversity.

Beaches are important areas for tourism. However, the increasing population and standard of living push many areas to their sustainable limits, both from a tourism and environmental point of view. In beach tourism there are clear feedback mechanisms, nice beaches attract people, and too many tourists on the beach decrease the attractiveness. Tourism, a major source of income for many coastal communities, can have major effects on coastal environments unless the scale and type of activities are controlled. Biodiversity reduction, resource depletion, and human health problems may result from the accumulated environmental effects. Setting maxima to tourist numbers is a proper managerial measure, however, once these maxima are reached, pressure to relax the restrictions increase. Clear definitions of maxima, and scientifically adopted calculation methods are necessary.

With the increasing standard of living, the recreational boating increases, and in some countries harbors and marinas built primarily for recreational use by small boats may disturb more of the coastal zone than commercial and industrial use. The environmental impacts of marinas and small harbors depend on site location, design, construction methods, and 'house-keeping'. Careful site planning can help avoid or minimize many of the impacts.

While freshwater and marine ecosystems face similar threats, there are some differences regarding the severity of each threat. Runoff from agricultural and urban areas, the invasion of exotic species, and the creation of dams and water diversion have been identified as the greatest challenges to freshwater environments (Allan and Flecker 1993; Scientific American 1997). **Overfishing is the greatest threat to marine environments**, thus the need for sustainable fisheries has been identified by the Environmental Defense Fund as the key priority in preserving marine biodiversity.

Overfishing

Reefs are suffering directly and indirectly from the increasing pressure of mans' resource exploitation (Reef Education Network). Overfishing is one driving pressure that has had devastating impacts on coral reefs (Aquatic Biodiversity and Environmental Pollution Web, 2012). Aggressive fishing methods have hurt coral reefs sometimes beyond repair. However, overfishing in general is also a damaging problem to many coral reefs around the world. Specifically to the Great Barrier Reef, overfishing has caused a shift in the reef ecosystem. Overfishing of certain species near coral reefs can easily affect the reef's ecological balance and biodiversity (Reef Education Network, 2012).

Impacts of Overfishing

- Destructive fishing techniques can have direct physical impacts on reef environments or create a deceit of certain species in the ecosystem.
- Unauthorized fishing occurs in areas that are not supposed to be fished causing even further destruction to coral reefs (Great Barrier Reef Marine Park Authority).
- The vulnerability of coral-reef species is partly because of their life-history adaptations to uncertainty in survival of recruits and juveniles in diverse communities where predation and competition are intense.

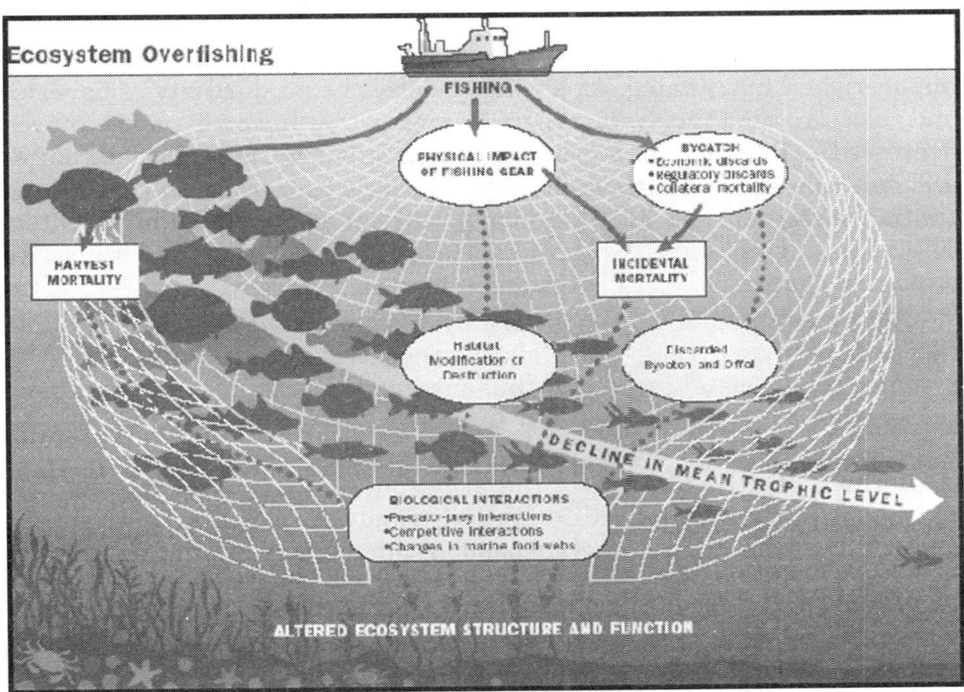

Fig. 1.7: Overfishing is one driving pressure that has had devastating impacts on coral reefs

- With low rates of survival of recruits, multiple attempts at reproduction are favored through longevity and large size. These traits lead to low rates of population turnover and special vulnerability to overfishing.
- Ecosystem overfishing occurs when overfishing affects multispecies assemblage composition, food-web dynamics, or ecosystem function
- Overfishing can devastate the marine ecology of the Great Barrier Reef because of the specific needs of the coral reef. Since certain amounts of nutrients, oxygen and salt content the fishes in the coral reef ecosystem help maintain the balance needed by the corals, without these fishes the coral reef will collapse (Coral Reef).

There are many causes to losses of marine biodiversity, especially in the coastal waters of industrialized countries. Direct habitat destruction through the erection of engineering and drainage works which disturb the physical integrity of coastal and marine systems is the most drastic, as the habitat itself is changed to a point where the ecosystem loses its identity and fulfils a completely different function as before. Poor fisheries management, including the uncontrolled exploitation of corals and mollusks and the by-catch of large numbers of non-target species in fisheries is another important aspect of the detrimental exploitation of marine living resources due to the lack of an integrated approach to coastal zone management, leading to impoverished functioning. As a consequence, the productivity of fisheries and such important ecosystems such as mangroves and coral reefs has been depressed, and local human communities are suffering. In general, estuaries and salt marshes, mangrove forests, and sea grass beds near cities and towns are severely degraded worldwide with many species being threaten. The increasingly observed worldwide bleaching of corals could lead to massive ecological changes for coral reefs and other marine ecosystems.

Most contaminants enter the sea by flows from the surrounding land, in particular via rivers, the highest concentrations are often found in estuaries and coastal areas and thus maximal effects of contaminants on the ecosystem could be expected to occur. This general picture can be influenced by additional inputs from sources at sea - ships, off-shore platforms - and by inputs via the atmosphere. After entering the sea, contaminants are usually diluted and widely dispersed. However, the adsorption of contaminants to suspended solid material in the sea leads to the occurrence of elevated concentrations in the seabed in areas where this material settles. These substances are of varying origin and composition, but they are together classed as stable or persistent, and have decisive properties in common. They are not readily degradable, or not at all degradable, toxic to living organisms, and bio-available (living organisms can take them up and accumulate them). The persistence of certain groups of contaminants, recognized as "toxic" in the marine environment, varies:

- **Organic synthetic substances**

In common, POCs all have the following characteristics: they are stable and toxic, and share a similar structure. It has emerged that some highly stable organic compounds - chiefly halogenated hydrocarbons - can have serious environmental effects in the sea. Such substances have in common the presence of a halogen in their molecule (chlorine, iodine, fluorine, astatine), have a low polarity and low water solubility. Aromatic compounds are more reactive and susceptible to chemical and biochemical transformation and include pesticides (chlorinated such as DDT – DDE, Polycyclic Aromatic Hydrocarbons, Hexa Cyclo Hexan, and organometallics such as tributyltin). There are 209 congeners of Poly Chloro Biphenyls, all with different properties. This variety makes both analysis and effect studies complicated. The metabolic pathways of polychlorinated biphenyls (PCBs) congeners are complex. Though the use of PCBs has been prohibited for a long time, emissions from unidentified sites still occur. For example, re-circulated waste paper used as raw material for new pulp was discovered downstream from a paper mill. It is unclear how organic synthetic organic chemicals affect marine organisms but PCBs, for instance, are frequently found in fish liver, seal blubber, bird eggs, and human fat. Organochlorines have been associated with impaired reproductive ability in seals and whales. For instance, octachlorostyrene (OCSs) have been found in benthic organisms. OCS concentrations can be taken as an indication of incomplete combustion resulting in the accumulation of chlorinated hydrocarbons in marine organisms.

Organometallic compounds such as tributyltin have been used extensively as antifouling agents and are now banned in many countries because of its effect known as *imposex*. Imposex refers to a change of sexual characteristics in invertebrates, female gastropods growing a penis, for instance. Compounds in alternative antifouling products form a special field of interest, since these compounds are especially applied to display their toxic effects in the marine environment. Their use is expected to increase in the near future due to the total ban on tributyltin-based antifouling chemicals by the *International Maritime Organization* IMO in 2003.

- **Oil and gas and offshore installations**

Oil is at the heart of the modern economy in providing a cheap source of energy and as a raw material for making plastics, etc. It is a mixture of hydrocarbons and up to 25% non-hydrocarbons such as sulphur, vanadium, and metals. Environmental impacts occur at all stages of oil and gas production and use. They result from prospecting activities (including seismic techniques), physical impact due to the installation of rigs, operational discharges when production starts, accidental and routine spills, and finally combustion. Nihoul & Ducrotoy (1994) have estimated the input of oil to the North Sea, due to the offshore industry, at 29% of the total input of oil.

Offshore installations may disturb the environment through the placement of structures on the seabed, which disturb benthic organisms, acoustic disturbances and light emission. An increasing number of installations are currently reaching the end of their productive life and will need to be dismantled or removed throughout the world's seas.

Overall, coastal ecosystems remain largely affected by direct discharges of oil from offshore activities and illegal discharges from ships. Operational discharges consist of production water and drilling cuttings. Although the amount of oil discharged via production water is increasing as platforms are getting older, cuttings still account for 75% of the oil entering the sea as a result of normal operations. The effects on the marine environment have been extensively studied by national authorities as well as by the industry.

• **Radioactive substances**

Present day levels of radioactive substances found in coastal waters are the result of natural [radioactivity]] (cosmic rays, earth's crust), and possibly released radioactivity due to human activities such as oil exploration and combustion, phosphate production and use, land-based mining, managed discharges from nuclear power and reprocessing facilities, fallout from atmospheric nuclear weapons testing and accidents, medical diagnosis and therapy, and food conservation. The world's oceans have been a sink for radioactive waste from the production of nuclear weapons and electric power since 1944. Radioactive waste enters the ocean from nuclear weapon testing and the resulting atmospheric fallout, the releasing or dumping of wastes from nuclear fuel cycle systems, and nuclear accidents (for example Chernobyl in 1985). Dumping of high-level radioactive waste is no longer permitted in the ocean, but dumping of low-level wastes is still permitted. Low-level waste contains fewer radioactivities per gram than high-level waste. High-level wastes usually have longer half-lives. For example, one common high-level waste that is produced by spent nuclear fuel has a half-life of 24,100 years.

• **Metals**

Heavy metals are naturally occurring and do not degrade. They are not particularly toxic as the condensed free elements (except Mercury (Hg) vapor) but they are dangerous to living organisms in the form of cations and when bonded to short chains of atom carbon. In particular cations have a strong affinity for sulphur. For example, sulfhydril groups in enzymes attach themselves to cations or molecules and so the enzyme is blocked. They are a problem in the marine environment because they bioaccumulate in marine organisms and despite measures taken to combat pollution, they are still concentrating year after year. Pollution above background levels in the environment can cause serious effects. For instance, copper is a useful oligoelement bit in excess it affects trophic levels. As a free element, mercury has hundreds of applications, for example in electrical switches. Despite

Fig.8A: Some kinds of fish in Red sea.

emissions of vapor from the industry have been curtailed, there are still releases from unregulated burning of fuel or wastes. This human source of

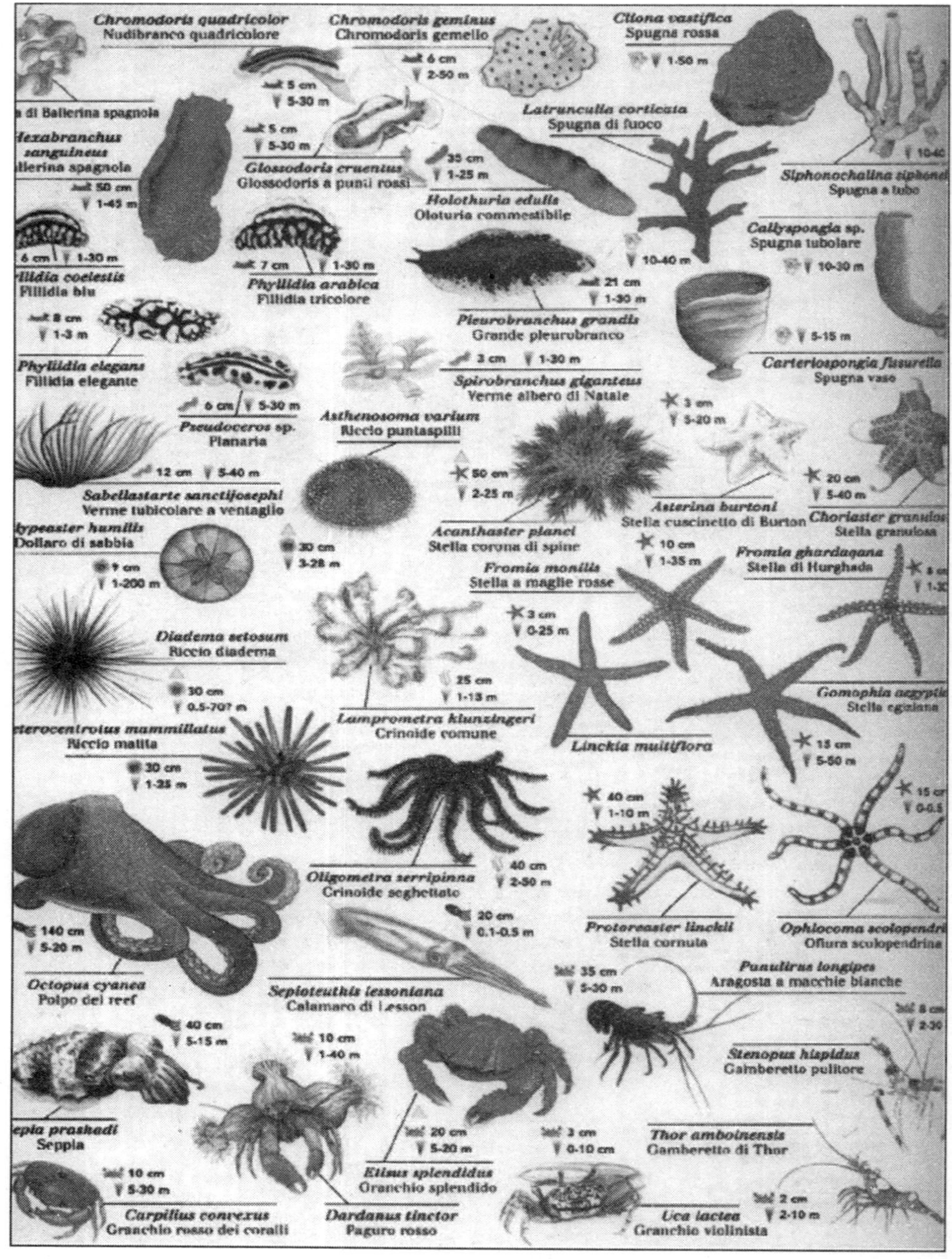

Fig.8B: Some kinds of biodiversity life's in Red sea.

pollutant is added and its atmospheric inputs rival volcanoes. The ultimate sink for metals and many organic compounds is the sediment. Processes involved include deposition and burial as heavy metals are retained by:

- adsorption onto the surface of mineral particles;
- complexation by molecules in organic particles, and
- Precipitation reactions.

CONCLUSION

Coastal pollution and its impacts have resulted in a number of environmental issues including the enrichment of enclosed waters with organic matter leading to eutrophication, pollution by chemicals such as oil, and sedimentation due to land-based activities or sea level rise due to the global change.

Protecting and restoring fresh water aquatic biodiversity through: 1) maintain the important functions of wetlands, state and federal governments have implemented plans to mitigate wetland loss, 2) When a wetland is lost, one should be created in its place, 3) Managing invasive species, 4) Because of the environmental impacts of dams, there has been a push to rehabilitate rivers by removing dams where possible.

REFERENCES

Aquatic Biodiversity and Environmental Pollution, Web (2012): http://nptel.iitm.ac.in/courses/120108002/2

Coetser, S.E., Heath, R.G., and Ndombe, N. (2007): Diffuse pollution associated with the mining sectors in South Africa: A first–order assessment. *Water Sci.Technol.* 55, 9–16.

Crossland C.J., Bairn D. and Ducrotoy J.P. (2005): *The coastal zone: a domaine of global interactions.* In: Crossland,C.J. (Ed.), Coastal Fluxes in the Anthropocene, Springer, Berlin, pp. 1-37.

Ducrotoy J.P. and Elliott M. (2006): Recent Developments in estuarine ecology and management. *Marine Pollution Bulletin* 53, 1-4.

French J. (2006): Tidal marsh sedimentation and resilience to environmental change: Exploratory modelling of tidal, sea-level and sediment supply forcing in predominantly allochthonous systems. *Marine Geology* 235, 119-136.

Global Issues. http://www.globalissues.org

Gren I.M., Turner and Wulff F. (2000): *Managing a Sea*, Earthscan Publications Ltd, London.

Grant A. and Briggs A.D. (2002): Toxicity of sediments from around a North Sea oil platform: are metals or hydrocarbons responsible for ecological impacts? *Marine Environmental Research* 53, 95-116.

Kemper, K.E. (2004): Groundwater – from development to management. *Hydrogeology J.* 12 3–5.

Marine Biodiversity Wiki-http://www.marbef.org/wiki/Imag

Nihoul C., Ducrotoy, J.P. (1994): Impact of oil on the marine-environment - policy of the paris commission on operational discharges from the offshore industry", *Marine pollution bulletin*, 29(6-12), pp. 323-329

Ofiara D. and Seneca,J. (2006): Biological effects and subsequent economic effects and losses from marine pollution and degradations in marine environments: Implications from the literature. *Marine Pollution Bulletin*.

Talen M. (1991): *Ocean Pollution*, Lucent Books, Gale Group, Farmington Hills, MI, U.S.A.

Tewari G and Bisht A.(2012): Aquatic Biodiversity: Threats and Conservation. Aquatic Fish Database. Est. 2012 Ascot International

Thomas K.V. and Hilton M.J. (2004): The occurrence of selected human pharmaceutical compounds in UK estuaries. *Marine Pollution Bulletin*, 49: 436-444.

UNEP-WCMC (2012): The UNEP World Conservation Monitoring Centre (UNEP-WCMC)

U.S. Environmental Protection Agency (2012): Aquatic Biodiversity - the Variety of Life. http://www.epa.gov/bioiweb1/aquatic/index.html

Yanagi T. and Ducrotoy J.P. (2003): Towards coastal zone management that ensures coexistence between people and nature in the 21st century. *Marine Pollution Bulletin* .47 :1-4.

Seasonal Dynamics of Microbial and Physico-Chemical Characteristics of *Clarias Gariepinus* Hatchery Systems

—C.N. Ariole, Nigeria
—G.C. Okpokwasili, Nigeria

ABSTRACT

Seasonal changes in microbial and physico-chemical characteristics of three Clarias gariepinus *hatchery systems were studied. Analysis of the hatchery tank water showed seasonal variation in total heterotrophic count, total coliforms,* Salmonella sp., Staphylococcus sp., Aeromonas hydrophila *and fungi counts with higher counts during the dry season months and lower counts during the rainy months. Higher temperature, BOD, ammonia, nitrate, phosphate and sulphate concentrations were associated with the hatcheries during the dry season months than rainy months while higher dissolved oxygen levels were recorded during the rainy season than dry season. There was in apparent seasonality in pH. Low levels of metals Na (2.3-36.80ppm), K (0.0-46.80ppm), Ca (0.4-16.80ppm), Mg (0.37-11.81ppm), Zn (0.09-1.25ppm) and Fe (0.0-0.61ppm) were detected in the hatchery systems with no obvious seasonality in their occurrence. Multiple linear correlation analyses revealed significant ($p<0.05$) positive correlations between total heterotrophic bacteria counts, total coliforms and fungi and temperature, BOD, NH_3, NO_3^-, PO_4^{3-} and SO_4^{2-} values, and significant ($p<0.05$) negative correlation between these microbial counts and dissolved O_2 concentration.*

Keywords: *Physico-chemical characteristics, Total coliform, Fungi,* Clarias Gariepinus, *Hatchery Systems.*

INTRODUCTION

Fish is the primary source of animal protein in many countries and for many millions, particularly in poorer sections of the community; it far exceeds meat or milk (Higgins and Kolbye, 1984). Clariid catfishes constitute a major family of food fish of economic value in sub-Saharan African (Adebayo,

2006). The African catfish (*Clarias gariepinus*) is rapidly gaining status as prime aquaculture species in a number of African, Asian and European countries (Areerat, 1987); Hecht *et al.*, 1988). The fish has been reported as the most commercially important among about ten species of *Clarias* which occur in the Rivers State of Nigeria (Akiri, 1987) and is in high market demand as table fish, being tasty and scale less (Ezechi and Nwuba, 2007).

Various bacteria and fungi which grow on fish and its environment pose a potential threat to aquaculture by occasionally assuming-epidemic proportions without warning (Shah *et al.*, 1977; Okaeme, 1989). Mortalities in hatcheries and fish pond/tanks have been attributed to a number of factors such as poor water quality, environmental stress, low resistance to diseases and infection by parasites, bacteria, fungi and viruses (Delince *et al.*, 1987; Ogbondeminu and Madu, 1989; Chibunda *et al.*, 2010). These factors can cause decreased activity of the immune system of fish species and fry and fingerlings are most vulnerable as they are yet to build up immunity.

The effects of temperature (Ajuzie and Appelbaum, 1996), salinity (Oladosu *et al.,* 1999) and water hardness (Molokwu and Okpokwasili, 2002a) on the embryonic development and larval survival of *Clarias gariepinus* have been reported. The microbial flora in farmed *Clarias gariepinus* hatchery systems have been established (Molokwu and Okpokwasili, 2002b).

Seasonal changes in physico-chemical parameters are known to influence fish disease in tropical freshwater culture ponds (Okpokwasili and Obah, 1991). There is no documented reported on the influence of water quality and environmental (seasonal) factors on the microbiology of tropical hatchery systems. Information about the microbiology and physico-chemistry of Nigeria hatcheries is essential if conditions such as adverse water quality or the onset of disease states are to be recognized and corrected.

This study was, therefore, designed to establish the relationship between physico-chemical characteristics and microbial groups in *Clarias gariepinus* hatchery systems and also to determine the effect of seasons on them.

Materials and Methods

Sample Collection

Hatchery tank water samples used for this study were collected from fish hatcheries located at African Regional Aquaculture Centre (ARAC), Aluu, Ellah Lakes PLC, Obirikom and Fawumi Fish Rumuokoro-all in Rivers State. Samples were collected from January to December. All samples were collected using sterile glass containers and were analyzed within two hours of collection.

Microbial Enumeration, Isolation and Identification

Water samples were enumerated after preparing ten-fold serial dilutions of the samples using 0.85% (W/V) NaC1 as diluent. Counts of culturable aerobic bacteria, total coliforms, *Salmonella* sp., *Aeromonas hydrophila* and fungi were obtained after plating 0.1ml of appropriate dilutions of the samples in triplicate plates of sterile tryptone soya agar (TSA), MacConkey agar, bismuth sulphite agar, mannitol salt agar, Rimler-Shotts agar (Shotts and Rimler , 1973) and acidified potato dextrose agar (PDA) respectively using spread plate technique (APHA, 1985). With the exception of PDA plates which were incubated at 25^0C for 5-7 days, plates were counted after 48 hours incubation at 30^0C.

Characterization of the bacteria isolates was performed according to the methods describes by Gerhardt *et àl.* (1981) This involved colonial morphology and cell micromorphology, Gram reaction, catalase, indole, methyl red, Voges-Proskauer and citrate utilization tests, motility tests and oxidation/fermentation (O/F) test for glucose utilization. Additional tests performed include hydrogen sulphide production, urea utilization, nitrate reduction, starch hydrolysis, gelatin liquefaction and sugar fermentation. Identification of the isolates to generic level followed the scheme of Kaper *et al.* (1979), Sakata (1989) and Holt *et al.* (1994).

Physico-Chemical Analysis

All the chemical reagents used were of analytical grade and were purchased from sigma chemical company. St. Louis, Missouris, USA.

A number of physico-chemical parameters of the hatchery tank water were determined using standard procedures (APHA, 1985). They include temperature, pH, dissolved oxygen (DO) and biological oxygen demand (BOD). Others include ammonia, nitrate, sulphate and phosphate.

The temperature was directly measured on the hatchery site by the use of a mercury thermometer. The pH was determined using pH meter (Jenway model 3015). Dissolved oxygen was determined using the azide modification of Winkler method. Specific methods employed in the analyses for other parameters were: ammonia and nitrate (distillation), sulphate (tudidimetry) and phosphate (Ascorbic acid method).

Determination of Metals

The atomic absorption spectrometric method for metal determination as described in APHA (1985) was adopted. The concentrations of Fe, Mg, K, Ca, Na and Zn in Nigerian fish hatchery systems were evaluated.

Statistical Analysis

Multiple linear correlation coefficients were calculated for the mean $\log_{10}$ microbial counts and the measured physico-chemical parameters using IBM XT computer.

RESULTS

Seasonal changes in the microbial counts of hatchery tank water from ARAC, Ellah and Fawumi Fish Farms are presented in Figures 1-3 respectively. Generally, apparent seasonality was shown by all the microbial counts with higher counts during the dry season months and lower counts during the rainy months in all the farms except in Ellah farm were high counts of the microbial groups were obtained in the rainy month of July. The lowest counts of all the microbial groups were obtained in month of June for Ellah and Fawumi farms and the month of May for ARAC.

The result of the seasonal changes in the physcio-chemical parameters of hatchery tank water is shown in Figure 4. There was no apparent seasonal variation in pH in the three hatcheries. The pH fluctuated between the range of 5.48-7.50 throughout the monitoring period in the three hatcheries. A seasonal variation in temperature of the hatchery system was apparent. Higher water temperatures were recorded during the dry season months than rainy months except in December where the lowest temperatures were observed with the least (24.5°C) recorded in Ellah hatchery.

The result indicated a higher BOD value in the dry season month of March than in the rainy season months for ARAC and Fawumi hatchery water. The same trend was followed in Ellah hatchery with a higher BOD value in the dry season months of April and November than in the rainy season months.

Seasonality in the dissolved oxygen level was apparent. A higher value was recorded during the peak of the rainy season months than during the late rainy season and dry season months for all the hatchery systems.

Low levels of ammonia were encountered in the hatcheries. Relatively higher values were recorded in the dry season months except in August where the highest value of 6.08×10^{-2} mg/L was observed in Fawumi farm.

The highest nitrate value recorded for each hatchery system was observed in the dry season months of December (for ARAC and Ellah) and April (for Fawumi farm).

Higher values of sulphate were recorded in the dry season months of January and February than in the rainy months for ARAC farm. However, in Fawumi and Ellah farms, higher values were observed in the rainy months of May and August than in the dry season months.

Although low levels of phosphate were observed in the hatchery systems, relatively higher values were observed in the dry season months of January-March (for ARAC hatchery) than in the rainy months.

Seasonal changes in the metal levels of the hatchery system are presented in Tables 1-3. All the metals analysed were detected in the hatchery systems except ferrous ions (Fe^{2+}) which was not detected in some months and potassium ion which was not detected in May in Fawumi farm. The influence of season in their occurrence was not apparent. Fluctuations in the concentrations of Na^+, K^+, Ca^{2+},Mg^{2+}, Zn^{2+} and Fe^{2+} occurred in all the hatcheries throughout the monitoring period. Very low levels of zinc and ferrous ions were detected in the hatcheries.

The results of multiple linear correlation analysis of the measured microbiological and physico-chemical parameters of the hatchery systems are presented in Tables 4-6. Generally, significant ($p<0.05$) positive correlations were observed between all the microbial groups and temperature while significant ($p<0.05$) negative correlations were observed between these groups and dissolved oxygen in all the hatcheries. In ARAC hatchery (Table 4), significant positive correlations at 95% confidence limit were observed between aerobic THC, total coliforms and fungi and temperature, BOD, NH_3, NO_3^-, PO_4^{3-} and SO_4^{2-} while significant ($p<0.05$) negative correlations were observed between the microbial groups and pH and DO. In Ellah hatchery (Table 5) significant ($p<0.05$) positive correlations were observed between aerobic THC and total coliform and temperature, NH_3, NO_3^-, PO_4^{3-} and SO_4^{2-} while significant ($p<0.05$) negative correlations were observed between the microbial groups and pH and DO. In Fawumi hatchery (Table 6) significant ($p<0.05$) positive correlations were observed between aerobic THC and fungi and pH, temperature, BOD, PO_4^{3-} and NH_3 while ($p<0.05$) negative correlations were observed between the microbial groups and DO and NO^-_3.

DISCUSSION

The results of the seasonal variation in microbial counts of hatchery tank water from the hatcheries presented in Figures 1-3 revealed the occurrence of higher microbial counts during the dry season months and lower counts in the rainy months. These results corroborate the report of other workers (Okpokwasili and Obah, 1991; Okpokwasili and Ogbulie, 1993) who worked in pond system. In the tropical environment, airborne droplets, nuclei and dust particles which carry airborne microorganisms are on the increase during the dry season. These dust particles are known to be disseminated widely by conventional air current, contaminating every conceivable type of substratum (Cruikshank *et al.*, 1980). This could be why higher microbial counts were obtained in the hatchery system during the dry season and the corresponding lower counts during the rainy months. Furthermore, the higher microbial loads during the dry season months may also be attributed to decrease in groundwater level following extended period of sunshine and no rainfall which resulted in increased concentration of nutrients in groundwater (source water).

A general evaluation of the physico-chemical parameters revealed an apparent influence of seasonal changes on the physico-chemical quality of the tropical hatchery culture systems (Figure 4). The fluctuation in pH of the hatchery system has been reported in pond system (Okpkwasili and Obah, 1991) and river system (Odokuma and Okpkwasili, 1993). The maximum acceptable pH range recommended for domestic water by WHO (2004) is 7.0 - 8.5. Results from this study suggested that the pH of the hatchery water from the three farms, in most of the months during the sampling period, were slightly below the acceptable limits. This could be part of the reason why these hatcheries experienced lots of eggs and larval mortalities during the monitoring period.

The observed higher water temperatures in the dry season and lower temperature in the rainy season were due to higher ambient temperatures in dry season and lower ones in the rainy season that is associated with tropical climate. This pattern of seasonal variation in temperature has been reported in pond systems (Okpokwasili and Obah, 1991). Furthermore, the low temperatures observed in the hatcheries in the dry season month of December may be attributed to the humid climatic condition associated with tropical environment during harmanttan period.

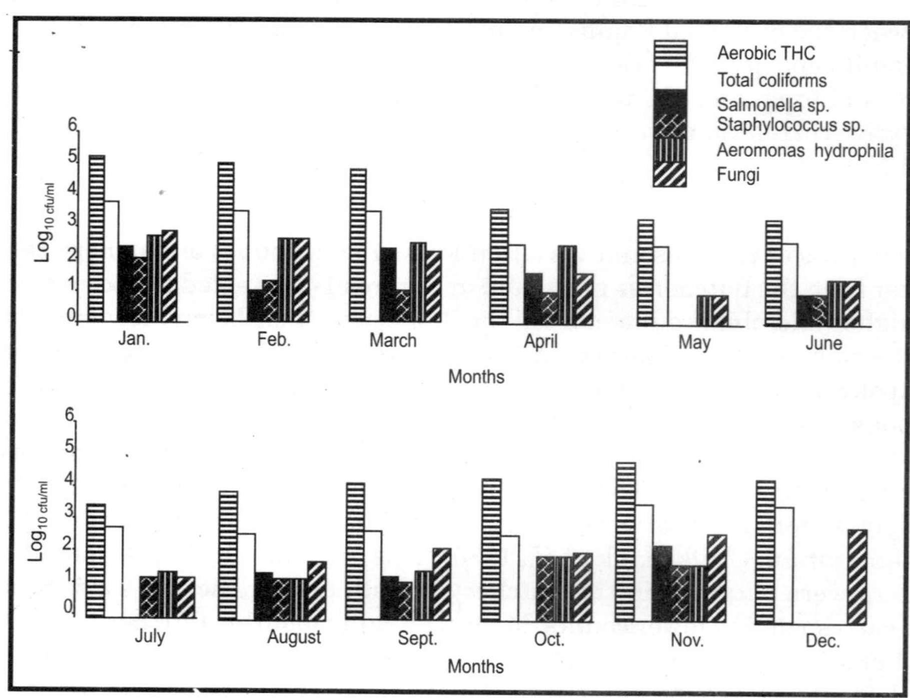

Fig. 2.1: Seasonal changes in microbial counts of hatchery tank water from ARAC fish farm, Aluu

Dissolved oxygen concentration was found to be higher during the rainy season and lower during the dry season. Similar result was observed in pond system (Okpokwasili and Obah, 1991). The low dissolved oxygen concentration during dry season may be as a result of the corresponding high water temperature, since the solubility of oxygen in water is inversely related to temperature (Boyd, 1979).

Generally, BOD, ammonia, nitrate, phosphate and sulphate concentrations were higher in the dry season months in the hatchery system. This pattern of seasonal influence in BOD, NH_3, NO^-_3, PO_4^{2-} and SO_4^{2-} values may be attributed to increased microbial and organic load with consequent greater microbial activities associated with dry season in hatchery system as previously reported in this study. The relatively higher value observed in August in Fawumi farm may be due to the period of no rainfall in the month of August usually known as August break period. Increase in NH_4^+-N and NO^-_3-N levels as a result of increase in organic substance, supplied by fish feed, in pond and culture flask systems have been reported by (Okpokwasili and Eleke, 1996). The concentrations of these parameters in the hatchery system were found to be low and within the acceptable limits for water to be used for domestic purposes (WHO, 2004).

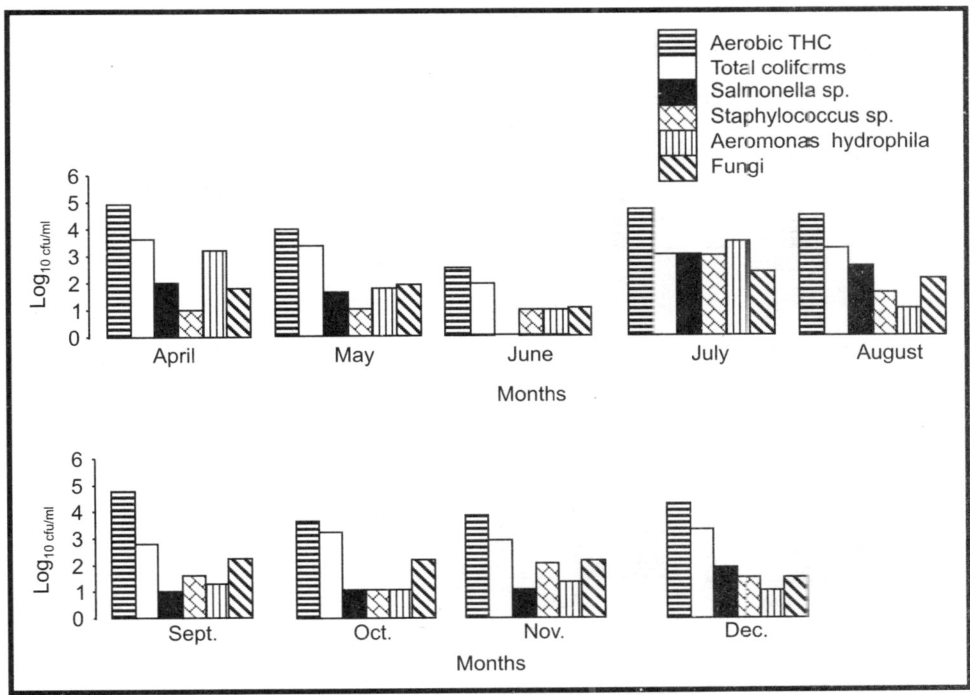

Fig. 2.2: Seasonal changes in microbial counts of hatchery tank water from Ellah fish farm, Obirikom

Seasonal variation was not apparent in the metal levels of the hatchery systems. Okpokwasili and Ogbulie (1993) reported similar result of inconsistent seasonality in metal concentrations in pond system. The non-detection of ferrous ion, in some months, in the hatchery water may be attributed to the geochemical nature of the soil where the hatcheries and their source water (borehole) were sited. This may also explain why fluctuations in metal concentrations occurred. Low concentrations of these metals were detected in the hatchery system. The recorded concentration fall within the acceptable limits recommended for water to be used for domestic purposes (WHO, 2004). This suggests that the hatchery waters were not polluted.

Generally, the total heterotrophic bacteria counts, total coliforms and fungi correlated positively ($p<0.05$) with temperature, BOD, NH_3, NO^-_3, PO_4^{3-} and SO_4^{2-} values and negatively with dissolved oxygen in the hatcheries. These results are consistent with the high microbial counts obtained during the dry season when temperature and concentrations of these chemical parameters were high and dissolved oxygen low.

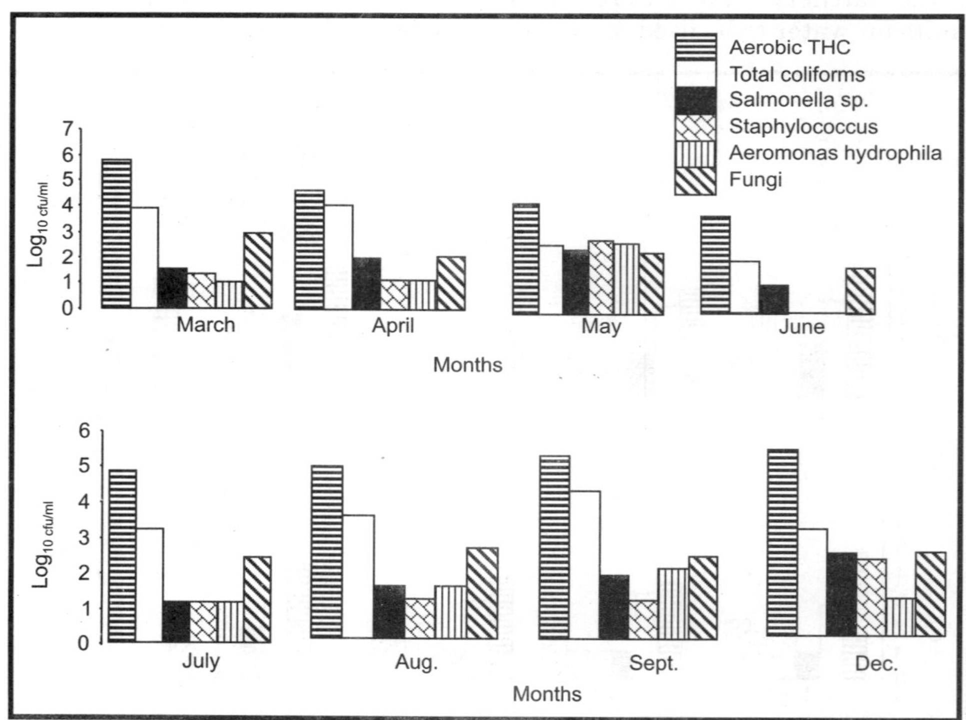

Fig. 2.3: Seasonal changes in microbial counts of hatchery tank water from Fawumi fish farm, Rumuokoro.

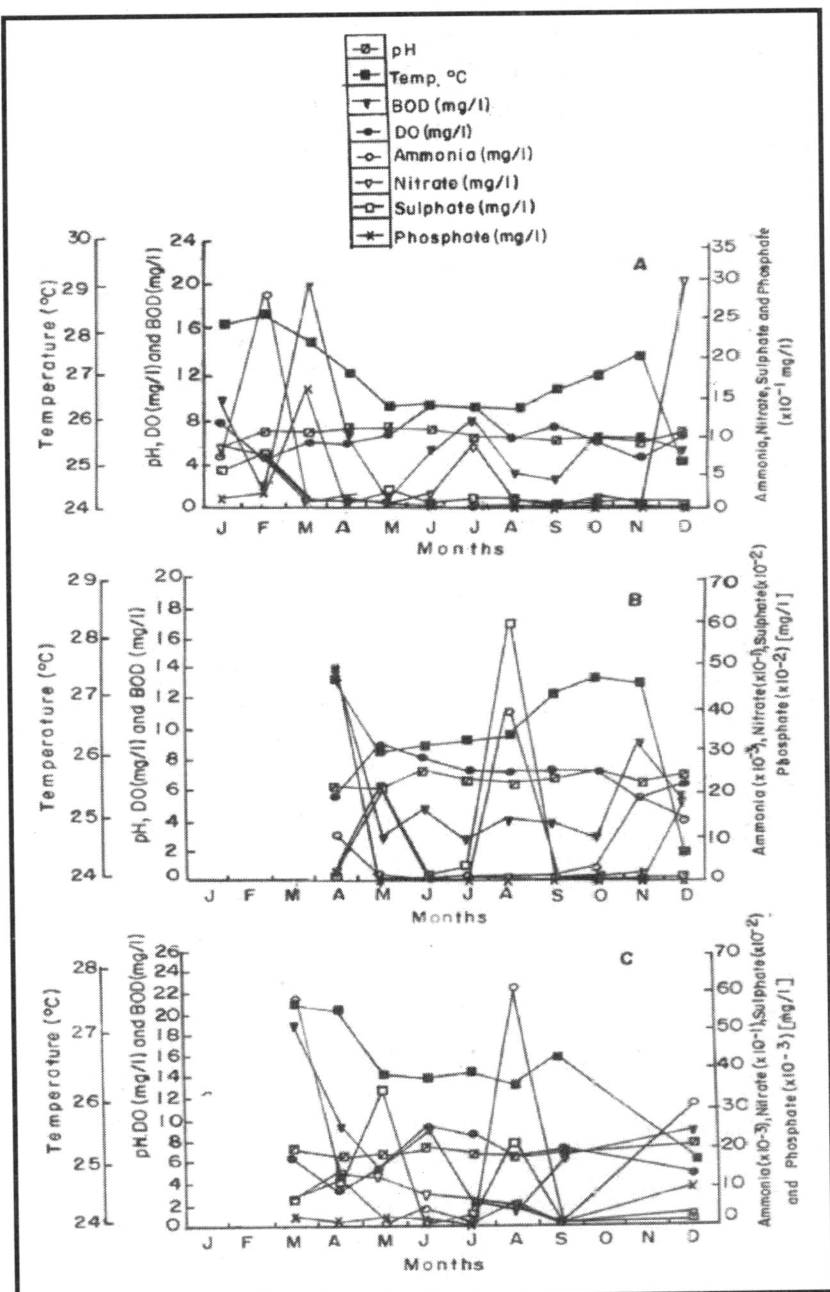

Fig. 2.4: Seasonal changes in physico-chemical properties of hatchery tank water samples from ARAC fish farm (A), Ellah fish farm (B), and Fawumi fish farm (C).

Table 2.1: Levels of Metals in ARAC Hatchery Tank Water

Months	Metal Concentrations (ppm)					
	Na^+	K^+	Ca^{2+}	Mg^{2+}	Zn^{2+}	Fe^{2+}
January	2.30	7.80	5.4	2.54	0.36	ND
February	4.60	3.90	8.28	5.00	0.41	ND
March	9.20	3.90	6.6	3.95	0.71	0.04
April	2.30	3.90	5.4	3.27	0.36	0.03
May	4.60	7.80	12.8	8.00	0.55	ND
June	18.40	7.80	8.4	5.86	0.15	ND
July	36.80	23.40	6.4	4.40	0.88	0.01
August	4.60	7.80	4.0	1.45	0.44	0.02
September	11.50	7.80	4.8	2.03	0.09	0.05
October	18.40	19.50	6.8	4.96	0.37	0.02
November	9.20	7.80	5.2	2.72	0.37	ND
December	4.60	3.90	6.8	3.09	0.53	ND

ND = not detected

Table 2.2: Levels of Metals in Ellah Hatchery Tank Water

Months	Metal Concentrations (ppm)					
	Na^+	K^+	Ca^{2+}	Mg^{2+}	Zn^{2+}	Fe^{2+}
April	2.30	7.80	3.20	1.93	1.01	ND
May	9.20	15.60	0.40	0.83	0.39	ND
June	2.30	5.85	2.40	1.62	0.51	ND
July	2.30	23.40	2.00	0.79	0.55	0.08
August	2.30	11.70	1.60	0.37	0.56	0.12
September	2.30	3.90	3.20	1.00	0.42	ND
October	2.30	7.80	4.80	2.57	0.37	0.06
November	32.20	19.50	2.00	1.19	1.25	0.01
December	2.30	7.80	8.40	3.99	0.53	0.54

ND = not detected

Table 3: Levels of Metals in Fawumi Hatchery Tank Water

Months	Metal Concentrations (ppm)					
	Na^+	K^+	Ca^{2+}	Mg^{2+}	Zn^{2+}	Fe^{2+}
March	34.50	23.40	16.80	11.45	0.39	ND
April	18.40	11.70	6.40	4.27	0.68	0.04
May	23.00	ND	16.00	11.81	0.32	0.02
June	18.40	19.50	12.00	8.75	0.41	ND
July	23.00	15.60	12.00	6.62	0.47	0.03
August	21.85	23.40	10.00	4.49	0.20	ND
September	23.00	11.70	7.20	3.11	0.56	ND
December	34.50	46.80	10.40	9.19	0.38	0.06

ND = not detected.

Table 2.4: Correlation matrix of physico-chemical parameters and microbial groups associated with *Clarias gariepinus* hatchery tank water in ARAC fish farm, Aluu

Microbial Groups	Physico-Chemical Parameters							
	pH	Temp.	BOD	DO	NH_3	NO_3^-	SO_4^{-2}	PO_4^{-3}
Aerobic THC	-0.552	0.7084	0.3775	-0.54	0.4795	0.0974	0.414	0.3669
Total coliforms	-0.523	0.4674	0.4385	-0.356	0.4083	0.4064	0.3871	0.3834
Salmonella sp.	-0.535	0.64	0.4788	-0.268	0.0711	-0.395	0.0589	0.4242
Staph. sp.	-0.584	0.6637	0.2377	-0.114	0.1917	-0.39	0.1674	-0.013
Aer. hydrophila	-0.331	0.8784	0.4002	-0.241	0.4786	-0.483	0.4764	0.4107
Fungi	-0.423	0.3882	0.2079	-0.461	0.3676	0.4172	0.2076	0.152

Table 2.5: Correlation matrix of physico-chemical parameters and microbial groups associated with *Clarias gariepinus* hatchery tank water in Ellah fish farm, Obirikom

Microbial Groups	Physico-Chemical Parameters							
	pH	Temp.	BOD	DO	NH_3	NO_3^-	SO_4^{-2}	PO_4^{-3}
Aerobic THC	-0.513	0.0859	0.2526	-0.41	0.2155	0.1905	0.193	0.4289
Total coliforms	-0.561	0.0132	0.2901	-0.338	0.3002	0.1581	0.2643	0.5104
Salmonella Sp.	-0.457	-0.215	-0.017	-0.215	0.3618	0.4086	0.4418	0.187
Staph. sp.	-0.039	-0.063	-0.176	-0.274	0.0686	0.3965	-0.013	-0.297
Aer. hydrophila	-0.506	0.185	0.3498	-0.203	-0.272	0.0874	-0.221	0.5823
Fungi	-0.392	0.4751	-0.163	-0.247	0.1143	-0.123	0.1774	-0.099

Table 2.6: Correlation matrix of physico-chemical parameters and microbial groups associated with *Clarias gariepinus* hatchery tank water in Fawumi fish farm, Rumuokoro

Microbial Groups	Physico-Chemical Parameters							
	pH	Temp.	BOD	DO	NH_3	NO_3^-	SO_4^{-2}	PO_4^{-3}
Aerobic THC	-0.2594	0.2538	0.6515	-0.268	0.6171	-0.339	-0.189	0.2427
Total coliforms	-0.339	0.6053	0.3721	-0.526	0.3665	-0.15	-0.129	-0.181
Salmonella sp.	-0.056	-0.206	0.1168	-0.752	-0.049	0.2147	0.489	0.0996
Staph. sp.	-0.064	-0.255	-0.032	-0.514	0.0255	0.203	0.6306	0.3241
Aer. hydrophila	-0.459	0.0291	-0.3	-0.395	-0.148	0.1089	0.6977	-0.124
Fungi	-0.1152	0.2633	0.4657	-0.119	0.6633	-0.171	0.1811	0.1988

Acknowledgement

The authors wish to thank the management and staff of African Regional Aquaculture Centre (ARAC), Aluu, Dr. J.S. Fawumi and Staff of Fawumi Fish Farm and Management and staff of Ellah Lakes Plc for their hospitability during the sampling period.

REFERENCES

Adebayo, O.T. (2006): Reproductive Performance of Africa Clarriid Catfish *Clarias gariepinus* Broad stocks on varying Material stress. *Journal of Fisheries International*, **1** (1-2): 17-20.

Ajuzie, C.C. and Appelbaum, S. (1996): Best temperature for African catfish eggs and larvae. *Fish Farmer International file,* **10** (1): 14-15.

Akiri, J. (1987): Studies on *Clarias* species in Rivers State. Ph.D. Thesis, Rivers State University of Science and Technology, Port Harcourt, Nigeria.

APHA. (1985): *Standard Methods for Examination of Water and Wastewater* 15th ed. American Public Health Association, Washington, D.C.

Areerat, S. (1987): *Clarias* culture in Thailand. *Aquaculture,* **63**:355-362.

Boyd, C.E. (1979): Water quality in warm water fish ponds. Agricultural Expansion Station, Auburn University, Auburn, Alabama.

Chibunda, R.T., Pereka, A. E., Phiri, E. C. J. and Tunaraza, C. (2010): Ecotoxicity of mercury contaminated sediment collected from Mabubi River (Geita District, Tanzania) to the Early life stages of African Catfish *(Clarias gariepinus). International Journal of Environmental Research,* **4** (1):49-56.

Cruickshank, R., Duguid, J. R., Maimion, B. P. and Swain, R. H. A. (1980): Medical Microbiology. 12th Edition. Vol. 11: The Practice of Medical Microbiology. Churchill Livingstone, Edinburgh.

Delince, G. A., Campbell, D., Jansen, J. A. L. and Kutty, M. N. (1987): Seed Production. African Regional Aquaculture Centre (ARAC), Aluu, Port Harcourt.

Ezechi, C.U. and Nwuba, L. A. (2007): Effect of Different Dietary items on the Growth of African Hybrid Heterobranchus Bidorsalis x *Clarias gariepinus. Animal Research International*, **4**(12): 662-665.

Gerhardt, P., Murray, R. G. E., Costilow, R. N., Nerster, E. W., Wood, W. A., Krieg, N. R. and Phillips, B. B. (eds.). (1981): Manual of Methods for General Bacteriology, American Society for Microbiology Washington, D.C.

Hecht, T., Vys, W. and Britz, P. J. (1988): The Culture of the African Sharptooth Catifsh (*Clarias gariepinus)* in Southern African National Scientific Programmes Report No. 153.

Higgins, B. C. and Kolbye, A. C. (1984): Risks and Benefits of Seafood. In: Regelis, E. P. (ed). Seafood Toxins. America Chemical Society Symposium Series, **262**:59-67.

Holt, J.G., Krieg, N. R., Snealth, P. H. A., Stanley, J. T. and Williams, S. T. (eds). (1994): Bergey's Manual of Determinative Bacteriology, 9th ed. Williams and Wilkins, Baltimore, Maryland, USA.

Kaper, J., Seidler, R. J., Lockman, H. and Colwell, R. R. (1979): Medium for Presumptive Identification of *Aeromonas hydrophila and* Enterobacteriaeae. *Applied Environmental Microbiology,* **38**:1023-1026.

Molokwu, C.N. and Okpokwasili, G. C. (2002a): Effect of water hardness on egg hatchability and larval viability of *Clarias gariepinus. Aquaculture International,* **10**(1):57-64.

Molokwu, C.N. and Okpokwasili, G. C. (2002b): Microbial flora of *Clarias gariepinus* in the early stages of development. *Tropical Freshwater Biology,* **11**: 91-100.

Ogbondeminu, F.S. and Madu, C.T. (1989): Preliminary Studies on Bacterial Microflora Associated with farmed *Clarias* in NIFFR/DFFRI Hatchery Complex at different stages of fish development. *Annual Report of National Institute of Freshwater Fisheries Research of Nigeria,* pp: 95-103.

Okaeme, A.N. (1989): Bacteria Associated with Morality in Tilapias, *Heterobrancus bidorsalis* and *Clarias lazera* in indoor hatcheries and outdoor ponds. *Journal of Aquaculture in the Tropics,* **4:**143-146.

Okpokwasili, G. C. and Eleke, F. N. (1996): Effects of fish feeds on the activity and survival of *Aeromonas hydrophila and nitrifying* bacteria in a tilapia fish pond. *Tropical freshwater Biology,* **5**:67-83.

Okpokwasili, G.C. and Obah, O. O. (1991): Relationship between Water Quality and Bacteria Associated with the "Brown Patch" Disease of Tilapia Fingerlings reared in Tropical Freshwater Culture Ponds. *Journal of Aquaculture in the Tropics,* **6**: 157-172.

Okpokwasili, G.C. and Ogbulie, J. N. (1993): Bacteria and Metal Quality of Tilapia (*Oreochromis nilotica)* aquaculture systems. *International Journal of Environmental Health Research,* **3**:190-202.

Oladosu, G.A., Busar, A. N., Uka, A., Oladosu, O.O. and Ayiala, O. A. (1999): Influence of Salinity on the Developmental stages of African Catfish (*Clarias anguillaris). Journal of Applied Sciences and Environmental Management* **2** (1): 29-34.

Sakata, T. (1989): Microflora of Health Animals. In: Austin, B. and Austin, D. A. (eds.). *Method for the Microbiological Examination of Fish and Shellfish.* Ellis Horwood Ltd. Chichester pp: 141-163.

Shah, K. L., Jha, B. C. and Jhingran, A. G. (1977): Observations on some aquatic Phycomycetes Pathogenic to eggs and fry of Freshwater Fish and Prawn. *Aquachultur,* **12**:141-147.

Shotts, E. B. and Rimler, R. (1973): Medium for Isolation of *Aeromonas hydrophila. Journal of Applied Microbiology,* **26**: 550-553.

WHO. (2004): Guideline for Drinking Water Quality. 3rd edition, Vol.1. Recommendations. World Health Organization, Geneva, pp: 210-220.

Effect of Copper Intoxication on Survival and Immune Response in Tropical Freshwater Prawn, *Macrobrachium Rosenbergii*

— H.A. Kaoud, Egypt

ABSTRACT

The aim of this study was to investigate LC_{50} and toxic effect of Cu^{2+} on some defense functions of tropical freshwater prawn, Macrobrachium rosenbergii *[including total hemocyte count (THC), hyaline cell count (HCC), and phagocytic activity] as well as survivability of the prawn.*

The tests were conducted to determine LC_{50} and the toxic effect of copper sulphae (Cu^{2+}) on THC, HCC, phagocytic activity % and survival rate for 72 and 96 hours exposure. The 72-h LC_{50} was 0.45 mgL^{-1} while, the 96-h LC_{50} was 0.35 mgL^{-1}. Survival of prawns exposed to more than 0.20 mgL^{-1} of Cu^{2+} was sig-nificantly ($P< 0.05$), reduced and resulted in great reduction in THC, HT, phagocytic activity %, and histopathological alterations in gills (hyper mucus, congestion, swelling , edema , hyperplasia, haemolymph cell infiltration as well as thickened and enlarged gill chambers & lamellar sinuses) & hepatopancreas (dissolving of the hepatocytes, haemolysis, haemocytic infiltration in the interstitial sinuses, thickening and ruptures of the basal laminae).

Keywords: *Copper;* Macrobrachium rosenbergii*; Immunity; Toxicity*

INTRODUCTION

In decapod crustaceans, 3 types of circulating hemocytes are recognized: hyaline, semi-granular and large granular cells (Tsing et al. 1989). They are involved in cellular immune responses that include phagocytosis and constitute the primary method of eliminating microorganisms or foreign particles (Bayne 1990). In addition to phagocytosis, hemocytes are involved in coagulation and in the production of melanin via the prophenoloxidase system (Johansson & Söderhäll1989, Söderhäll et al. 1996). Several physico-chemical parameters and environmental contaminants have been reported to affect the immune response in crustaceans and these have been reviewed by Le Moullac & Haffner (2000).

Copper toxicity for fish is primarily related to structural damage to the gills (Wilson and Taylor 1993) but in crustaceans the physiological effects of copper toxicity are not as clearly understood.

Circulating hemocytes can be affected by extrinsic factors in several species of decapods crustaceans (Truscott & White 1990, Le Moullac et al. 1998, Le Moullac & Haffner 2000, Cheng & Chen2001).

Environmental toxicants have been reported to cause a reduction in hemocyte count in the common shrimp *Crangon crangon* (Smith & Johnston 1992).

Copper salts (copper hydroxide, copper carbonate and copper sulphate) are widely used in agriculture as fungicide, algaecide and nutritional supplement in fertilizers. They are also used in veterinary practices and industrial applications. Copper sulphate is released to water as a result of natural weathering of soil and discharge from industries, sewage treatment plants and agricultural runoff. Copper sulphate is also intensively introduced in water reservoirs to kill algae. Thus excessive amount of copper accumulates in water bodies and cause toxicity to aquatic fauna and flora and ultimately to man. Copper and its compounds have been designated as priority pollutants by EPA (1975).

Present study was carried out on the fresh water prawns *Macrobrachium rosenbergii* (Crustacean - Decapods) to evaluate the LC_{50} values of copper sulphate and its effect on immunity as well as the histo-pathological alterations in this tropical prawn.

MATERIALS AND METHODS

Experimental Designs

In tests, freshwater was adjusted with the desired temperatures of 20-28 °C. and the desired pH, freshwater was adjusted with 1 N HC1 or 1 N NaOH solutions (pH; 7-7.8, dissolved oxygen; 5-8, salinity; 12-15‰,hardness; 100-150 ppm Ca(CO)3, total ammonia; less than 10 ppm, nitrate; 20 ppm,nitrite 1ppm).

Stock Copper Solution

Stock solution of copper sulphate (CuSO4.5H2O: AR grade: Elgomhoria laboratories, chemical division-Cairo, Egypt) was prepared by dissolving 100 mg of salt in 100 ml double distilled water. Two drops of glacial acetic acid was added to stock solution so as to prevent the precipitation.

Macrobrachium rosenbergii

Were obtained from a commercial farm in Egypt, and acclimated in the laboratory for 7 days before experimentation. For experiments, test and control groups comprised 10 prawns each in triplicate. After treatment, each group of 10 prawns was kept in a separate 30 L glass aquarium containing 25 L aerated water.

Acute Toxicity Test

The acute toxicity test was performed according to the USEPA procedure for the static non-renewal technique (USEPA, 1993). After an acclimatization period, 7 days .Prawn [6.7 to 7.5 g, averaging 8.10 (±0.15) g in weight] were transferred from the stock tank to the experimental aquaria. Ten fish were randomly placed in each glass aquarium filled with 25 liter of water and were not fed for 48 hr before starting and for 96 hr during the experiment. The tests consisted of a control and at least five concentration groups (0.20, 0.40, 0.50, 0.60 and 0.80 mg L^{-1}), five replicates per group, with ten prawns in each replicate. At the beginning of the test and every 24 hr, the symptoms and the number of dead prawn were recorded. The results of the median lethal concentration (LC_{50}) at 24 hr, 48 hr, 72 hr and 96 hr were computed.

Immune Activity

For immune activity assays, tests were carried out in triplicate or quadruplicate test groups consisting of 2 prawns each in separate 30 L glass aquaria containing 25 L aerated water. In all tests, prawns were fed twice daily with a formulated prawn diet. During experiments, water temperature was maintained at 20-28°C, pH; 7-7.8, dissolved oxygen; 5-8, salinity; 12-15‰, total hardness; 100-150 ppm Ca(CO)3, total ammonia; less than 10 ppm, nitrate; 20 ppm, and nitrite 1ppm.

The wet weight of prawn in the intermolt stage ranged from 6.7 to 7.5 g, averaging 8.10 (±0.15) g (mean SD) with no significant difference among various treatments (Peebles, 1977). Immune activity assays were carried out in quadruplicate with test groups consisting of two prawns each in separate glass tanks (30 L) containing 25 L of aerated test solution- The prawns were exposed to each treatment for 96 hrs.

Cells Count

Hemolymph (100 ìl) was sampled individually at the beginning of each test and at 72 h. It was withdrawn from the ventral sinus of each prawn into a 1 ml sterile syringe (25 gages) containing 0.9 ml anticoagulant solution (trisodium citrate 0.114 M, sodium chloride0.1 M, pH 7.45, osmolality 490 mOsm kg–1). A drop of the anticoagulant-hemolymph mixture was placed on a hemocytometer to measure THC and HC using an inverted-phase contrast microscope.

Culture of L. garvieae

The bacterial strain *L. garvieae* isolated from diseased (artificial infection) of *Macrobrachium rosenbergii* was used in this study. The bacterium was cultured on tryptic soy agar (TSA) for 24 h at 28. °C before being transferred to 10 ml of tryptic soy broth (TSB) for 24h at 28 °C as a stock culture. The stock cultures were then centrifuged at 7155 x g for I5 min at l4 °C. The supernatant fluid was removed and the bacterial pellet was resuspended in saline solution (0.85 NaCL) at 10^{10} cfu mL^{-1} as stock bacterial suspensions for testing.

Phagocytic Activity of M. rosenbergii to L. garvieae

After exposure in each treatment, prawns were injected in the cephalothoraxes with 20 µL of the bacteria suspension (10^{10} cfu mL^{-1} in 0.85% NaCI) resulting in 2 x 10^{8} ' cfu $prawnl^{-1}$ .After injection the prawns were held in their respective solutions for 3h. Hemolymph (200 µl) was collected from the ventral sinus and mixed with 200 µl of sterile anticoagulant containing sodium citrate, 0.8 g; EDTA, 0.34 g; Tween 80, 10 µl; distilled water, 100 ml; pH, 7.45; 490 mOsM kg^{-1}.This mixture was used to measure phagocytic activity.With two prawns in each of three replicates, a total of 6 measurements $parameter^{-1}$ existed for each treatment.

Phagocytic activity was measured using the method described by Weeks-Perkins et al. (1995). Where 200 µl *of* diluted hemolymph sample was mixed with 0.2 ml of 0.1% paraformaldehyde for 30 min at 4 °C to fix the hemocytes. They were then centrifuged at 800x g at 4 °C, washed and resuspended in 0.4 ml of sterile phosphate buffer solution. The suspension (50 µl) was spread onto a slide glass and air-dried and stained with Diff-Quick stain. 200 hemocytes were counted using light microscope and the phagocytic rate was estimated as follows:

PR = [(phagocytic hemocytes) / (total hemocytes)] x?100.

Histopathological Examination

Tissue specimens from fresh *Macrobrachium rosenbergii* were taken (gill and hepatopancreas) and fixed in 15 % buffered neutral formalin. They were processed to obtain five micron thick paraffin sections then stained with Hematoxylin and Eosin (Bancroft *et al.*, 1996) and examined under light microscope.

Statistical Analysis

Data were analyzed by analysis of variance and Pearson's correlation, which calculated the relationships between metal concentration and survival rate of prawn.

RESULTS

Acute Toxicity

(LC_{50})

The 24 hr, 48 hr, 72 hr and 96 hr LC50 values for copper sulphate in *Macrobrachium rosenbergii* were 0.60, 0.55, 0.45 and 0.35 mg L^{-1}, respectively.

A regression analysis of prawn survival (%) on Cu concentration was highly significant ($P < 0.001$; $r^2 = 0.982$). Using the re-sulting regression equation, the 72-hr LC_{50} for copper was calculated to be 0.45 mgL^{-1} While, it was 0.35 mgL^{-1} for 96-hr.

Survival rate

There were significant differences ($P < 0.05$) in the survival among different treatments. After 72 hours, mean *(±SD)* survival of prawns in control tanks (0 Cu) was 100 % and significantly higher ($P < 0.05$) than that of prawns in all other treatments (Table 1). At 72 hours, survival of prawns ex-posed to 0.20 mg/L and 0.40 mg/L concentrations of copper were significantly greater *($P < 0.05$)* than for prawns exposed to higher doses, but were not significantly different from each other ($P < 0.05$). Survival of prawns exposed to 0.6. , and 0.8 mg/L of copper were sig-nificantly lower ($p < 0.05$), with means *of (±SD)* 40±3.0, and 30 ±0.10 %, respectively, but at concentration 1, 0 mgL^{-1} it was 0% (Table 1).

After 96 hr, mean *(±SD)* survival of prawns in control tanks (0 Cu) was 100 % and significantly higher ($P < 0.05$) than that of prawns in all other treatments (Table 1). At 96 hr, survival of prawns ex-posed to 0.20 mgL^{-1} (92±1.62) was significantly greater *($P < 0.05$)* than for prawns exposed to higher doses. Prawns exposed to 0.40, 0.50, 0.60 and 0.80 mgL^{-1} showed sig-nificantly reduction of survival rate *($P < 0.05$)*, with means *of (±SD)* 60± 2.70, 50±3.0, 30 ±0.10 and 10± 0.2 %, respectively, while at concentration 1, 0 mgL^{-1} it was 0 % (Fig. 1).

Immune Activity

72-hr Cu-exposure, of 0.40, 0.5, 0.6 and 0.8 mgL^{-1} concentrations were significantly *($P < 0.05$)*, had greater reduction in THC, HC and Phagocytic activity % than for prawns exposed to lower concentrations (0.20 mgL^{-1}).

Concerning 96-hr ex-posure to 0.20 mgL^{-1} Cu, THC, HC and phagocytic activity % were showed no significant reduction *($P < 0.05$)*, but, at concentrations 0.40, 0.5, 0.6 and 0.8 mgL^{-1} they were showed great significant *($P < 0.05$)* reduction .

Histopathological Alterations

Gills: showed hyper mucus, mild congestion, swelling and edema at low doses of Cu intoxication. Severe edema, hyperplasia, haemolymph cell infiltration as well as thickened and enlarged gill chambers & lamellar sinuses at highest doses were observed.

Hepatopancreas: showed dissolving of the hepatocytes, haemolysis, haemocytic infiltration in the interstitial sinuses, thickening and ruptures of the basal laminae (Table 2).

DISCUSSION

Copper toxicity for fish is primarily related to structural damage to the gills (Wilson and Taylor 1993) but in crustaceans the physiological effects of copper toxicity are not as clearly understood.

Circulating hemocytes can be affected by extrinsic factors in several species of decapods crustaceans (Truscott & White 1990, Le Moullac et al. 1998, Le Moullac & Haffner 2000, Cheng & Chen2001).

Mandelli (1971, c.f. Couch 1979) found Cu to be toxic to *P. aztecus* and *P. duorarum* larvae at 0.05 mgL^{-1} (50 ppb) while normal growth occurred at 0.025 mg/l. Inhibition of reproduction in the brine shrimp *Artemia salina* has also been shown after exposure to extremely low levels of CuS04. While the 48-hour LD50 for this *Artemia* species was~25 ppt, adverse effects on reproduction were found at levels 24,000 to 156,000 times lower (Browne, 1980). Cu at 1.3 mgL^{-1} was lethal in 24 h(s) to 100% of *P. stylirostris* larvae (Lawrence *et al.*, 1981, c.f. Bray and Lawrence, 1992) and was toxic at 0.1 mg/l to adult lobsters (McLeese1974, c.f. Bray and Lawrence, 1992). Concentration of 0.14 mg/l Cu reduced survival of *Mysidopsis bahia* while 0.077 mgL^{-1} Cu reduced reproduction in *M. bahia* (Gentile *et al.*, 1982; c.f. Bray and Lawrence, 1992). Freshwater prawns appear to be more sensitive to copper than most other species of crustaceans that have been studied. Na et al. (2008) studied the toxic effects of water-borne copper on the giant freshwater prawn *Macrobrachium rosenbergii*, they recorded that, exposure to elevated copper levels might damage the ultrastructure of the gills and hepatopancreas of *M. rosenbergii* and might further weaken their normal physical activities

The LC_{50} values obtained in present study are mainly closure to the findings of Murti and Shukla, 1984 ; Lodhi et al. (2005) (*Macrobrachium lamarrei* and *Macrobrachium dayanum* exposed to Cu^{2+} (the 24, 48, 72 and 96 hr LC_{50} values of copper sulphate for *M. lamarrei* were 0.38, 0.361, 0.343 and 0.300 mg/l and for *M. dayanum* were 1.634, 0.988, 0.532 and 0.418 mg/l respectively) and Shuhaimi-Othman et al,2011 (LC_{50} 96 hr of Cu^{2+} value for *Macrobrachium lanchesteri* was 32 3 μgL^{-1}).

The structural alterations observed in gills in the present study were similar to those of *Macrobrachium lamarrei* and *Macrobrachium dayanum* exposed to Cu^{2+} (Lodhi et al, 2005), *Macrobrachium kistenensis and Caridina sp.* (Ghate and Mulherkar ,1979), profused secretion of mucous on whole body parts and more pronounced in gill region , *Puntius conchonius* (Pant et al., 1980) and *S. gairdneri* (Miller and Mackey, 1982) after exposure to copper and in the reviews of Atchison et al. (1987) and Weber and Spieler (1994).

Furthermore, the hisological structures of gill and hepatopancreas in the present study were similar to those of *Charybdis japonica* (**Luqing** et al, 2008), filaments of *Charybdis japonica* exposed to 2 mg/L Cu^{2+}were thickened irregularly and enlarged gill chambers in which haemolymph cells appeared much more, hepatopancreas dissolved and only an envelope of collected tissue was left around the hepatopancreas duct.

Frías-Espericueta et al. (2008) studied the effect of three concentrations of Cu^{2+} (3.512, 1.756 and 0.877 mg L^{-1}) on juvenile *Litopenaeus vannamei* and found that there were severe time- and dose-dependent structural damages, such as necrosis, loss of regular structure and infiltration of haemocytes in the gill tissues, as well as atrophy, necrosis and irregular tubular structure in the hepatopancreas.

All these lesions may impair respiratory function. Hyperplasia of epithelium increased the diffusion distance thus affecting the exchange of gases, and the fusion of lamellae causes a decrease in the total respiratory area of the gills, resulting in a decreased oxygen-uptake capacity of fish gills (Nowak, 1992). Fish fail to get adequate oxygen for total metabolic activities. Increased thickness of the epithelial layers has been reported to result from hyperplasia following experimental exposure to pesticides (Nowak, 1992). Inflammatory changes, such as swelling and lifting of lamellar epithelium and hyperplasia have also been noted in the gill lamellae of various species of fish following exposure to insecticides (Sunitha and Sahai, 1983; Roy and Munshi, 1991; Nowak, 1992).

MacFarlane et al. (2000) reported that copper was accumulated and regulated in the hepatopancreas of the Semaphore crab, *Heloecius cordiformis.* Gunter and Quinitio (1994) demonstrated the ability of white shrimp to detoxify copper by granule formation in the hepatopancreas tubules and excretion through the feces. Cheng et al. (2001) indicated that hymolymph protein and hemocyanin levels were lower during the post-molt than during the pre-molt stage in prawns due to water and Ca uptake during the molt. Crustaceans that have recently molted may be more sensitive to copper due to changes in hemolymph osmolality.

According to Huner and Dupree (1984), copper sulfate concentra-tions of 1.0 mgL^{-1} or more are needed to kill most algae in water with alkalinities higher than 100 mg/L. In the study of Osunde et al, (2003), the 0.03 mgL^{-1} copper sulfate treatment in water resulted in 100% juvenile prawn mortality. According to our data, the Copper sulfate is not a suitable compound for use as an algaecide in prawn-production ponds unless lower than 0.20 mgL^{-1}. Copper sulfate is also com-monly used to control species of blue-green algae that are responsible for off-flavor in fish and marine shrimp (Chen and Lin 2001). Boyd (1990) reported that copper sulfate is effective at a rate of 0.084 mgL^{-1} for use in controlling blooms of *Microcystis* and other blue-green algae responsible for “off-flavor” in ponds. Toxicity of copper sulfate on ad-vanced juvenile sizes and adult freshwater prawns needs to be deter-mined so that the potential for using copper sulfate for controlling blue green algae in ponds can be established.

Chen (1979) tested Cu in *P. monodon* and found that Cu^{2+} was toxic. Kuo *et al* (1984) suspected that Cd^{+2} and Cu^{2+} were the cause of mortalities in hatchery farms in Taiwan in 1980-1981, with the heavy metals coming from the waste water discharged by nearby industries.

Table 3.1: Effect of Copper on survival, THC (total hemocyte count), HC (hyaline cell count) and phagocytic % of freshwater prawns, *Macrobrachium rosenbergii,* exposed to copper at different concentrations for 96 hours post-treatment. Values are means± SD (n = 3 prawns in each case)

H.meta[1]	Survival%	Ilmmune response		
		THC[2]	HC[2]	Phagocyic%
0	100	222±72	206±38	95±1.20
0.20	82±1.62	196±19	200±22	86±1.20
0.40	60±2.70*	182±25*	185±20*	60±0.60*
0.50	50±3.00*	120±12*	120±12*	40±0.10*
0.6	30±0.10*	110±7.0*	110±11*	30±0.12*
0.80	10±0.10*	110±8.0*	110±22	10±1.20

: Cu^{2+} mg/l^{-1} , [2]:x 10^5ml^{-1}, *Significant ($P < 0.001$), **Significant ($P < 0.05$).

Table 3.2: Semiquantitative scoring of gill and hepatopancreas in freshwater prawn *Macrobrachium rosenbergii* during acute copper exposure (0.20 mgL^{-1}. Copper sulfate)

Histopathology	Exposure Time (hr)			
	24	48	72	96
Gill				
Hypermucus	++	+++	+++	+++
Congestion	+	++	+++	+++
Swelling and edema	+	++	+++	+++
Hyperplasia	-	+	++	+++
Thickened and enlarged	-	+	++	+++
			Hepatopancreas	
Haemocytic infiltration	+	++	++	+++
Hepatocytes Degeneration	–	+	++	+++
Rupture basal laminae	–	–	+	+++

- = none, + = mild, ++ = moderate, +++ = sever. Score value:

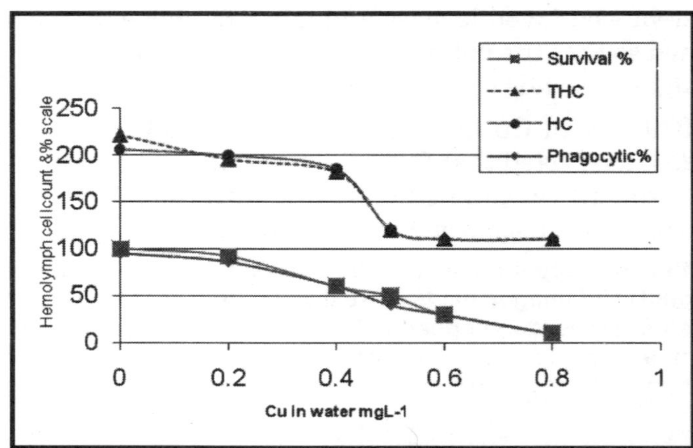

Fig. 3.1: Effect of copper sulphate on survival and immune response in Macrobrachium rosenbergii

CONCLUSION

This study reveals an important precaution for prawn cultivation. Knowledge of the toxicity of copper will be helpful to water quality management in fish farms with specialty to prawn cultures. It affects the immune response and resistance in *Macrobrachium rosenbergii* due to reduction in hemocyte count and phagocytic activity that make it susceptible to infectious agents and death. Caution should be exercised against water source contamination and exposure to fertilizer and industrial pollution.

REFERENCES

Alcivar-Warren, A. (2006): Primavera J.H., Leobert D. de la Pena L.D., Pettit P. and Xu Z.(2006): Heavy Metals, Pcbs And Pahs In *Penaeus Monodon* Shrimp From The Philippines: Indicators Of Environmental Contaminants Exposure

Atchison, G.J., M.G. Henry and M.B. Sandhenrich. (1987):Effects of metals on fish behavior. Environ. Biol. Fish, 18, 11-25

Bayne CJ (1990): Phagocytosis and non-self recognition in invertebrates. Phagocytosis appears to be an ancient line of defense. Bioscience 40:723–731

Boyd, C.R. (1990): Walcr Quality in Ponds for Aquaculture. Alabama Agricultural Ex-periment Slalion. Auburn University, Aubum, Alabama.

Bray, W. A and Lawrence, A. L. (1992): Reproduction of Penaeus species in captivity. In: Marine Shrimp Culture: Principles and Practices; A. W. Fast and L. J. Lester, eds., Elsevier Science Publishers B. V.

Cheng, W., Liu C., and Chen J. (2002): Effect of nitrite on interaction between the giant freshwater prawn *Macrobrachium rosenbergii* and its pathogen *Lactococcus garvieae*. Dis Aquat Org. Vol. 50: 189–197.

Chen, J., C. and C.-H., Lin. (2001): Toxicity of copper sulfate for survival, growth, molt-ing and feeding of juveniles of the tiger shrimp, *Penaeus monodon*. Aquaculture 192 (I): 55-65.

Chen S.C, Lin, Y.D., Liaw LL, Wang, P.C. (2001): *Lactococcus garvieae* infection in the giant freshwater prawn *Macrobrachium rosenbergii* confirmed by polymerase chain reaction and 16S rDNA sequencing. Dis. Aquat. Org., 45: 45–52

Chen, J.C., Lee, Y. (1997): Effects of nitrite on mortality, ion regulation and acid-base balance of *Macrobrachium rosenbergii* at different external chloride concentrations. Aquat Toxicol 39:291–305

Chen JC, Chen SF (1992): Effects of nitrite on growth and molting of *Penaeus mondon* juveniles. Comp. Biochem. Physiol. C 101: 449–452

Cheng W, Chen JC (2001): Effect of intrinsic and extrinsic factors on the haemocyte profile of the prawn, *Macrobrachium rosenbergii*. Fish Shellfish Immunol 11:53–63.

Cheng, H.C. (1979): Acute toxicity of heavy metals to some marine prawns. China Fish. Mon. 316:3-10. In Chinese with English abstract.

Couch, J. A. (1978): Diseases, parasites, and toxic responses of commercial penaeid shrimps of the Gulf of Mexico and South Atlantic coasts of North America. Fish. Bull. 76:1-43.

EPA (Environmental Protection Agency). (1975): Methods for Acute Toxicity Tests with Fish, Macroinvertebralcs, and Amphibians. EPA-660/3-75-009, National Tech-nical Information Service, Washington, DC.

FDA (1981): Action levels for poisonous or deleterious substances in human food and animal feed. Washington, D.C.: Food and Drug Administration.

Fletcher TC, Smith SA, Zelikoff JT, Kaattari SL, Anderson RS, Söderhäll K, Weeks-Perkins BA (eds) Techniques in fish immunology-4. SOS Publications, Fair Haven, NJ, p 223–231

Ghate, H.V. and L. Mulherkar. (1979) : Histological changes in the gills of two fresh water prawn species exposed to copper sulphate. Indian J. Exp. Biol., 17, 838-840

Gunter, V., and E.T. Quinitio. (1994): Accumulation and excretion of metal granules in the prawn, *Penaeus monodon,* exposed to water-borne copper, lead, iron and cal-cium. Aquatic Toxicology 2.S (3-4): 223-241.

Hernández-López J, Gollas-Galván T, Vargas-Albores F (1996): Activation of the prophenoloxidase system of the brown shrimp (*Penaeus californiensis* Holmes). Comp. Biochem. Physiol. C 113:61–66.

Johansson MW, Söderhäll K (1989): Cellular immunity in crustaceans and the proPO system. Parasitol. Today. 5:171–176.

Kuo, GH, Lin, YS, Chen, HC, Lo, CF. (1984): Diseases and mortalities of cultured marine fish and shellfish in Taiwan. Liao IC and Hirano R, eds. Proceedings of ROC-Japan symposium on mariculture; 1981 December 14-15, Taipei, Taiwan. Pingtung, Taiwan: Tungkang Marine Laboratory: 173-192. (TML Conference Proceedings, No. 1).

Le Moullac G, Haffner P (2000): Environmental factors affecting immune response in Crustacea. Aquaculture 191: 121–131

Le Moullac G, Soyez C, Saulnier D, Ansquer D, Avarre JC, Levy P (1998): Effect of hypoxia stress on the immune response and the resistance to vibriosis of the shrimp *Penaeus stylirostris*. Fish Shellfish Immunol 8 621–629

Lodhi,H.S., Khan, M. A., Verma R. S. and Sharma U. D. (2005): Acute toxicity of copper sulphate to fresh water prawns. Journal of Environmental Biology, 27(3) 585-.

MacFarlane, G.R., D.J. Booth, and K.R. Brown. (2000): The Semaphore crab, *Heloecius cordifomis:* bio-indication potential for heavy metals in estuarine systems. Aquatic Toxicology 50:153-166.

Miller, T.G. and W.C. Mackay. (1982) : Relationship of secreted mucous of copper and acid toxicity in rainbow trout. Bull. Environ. Contam. Toxicol., 28, 68-74

Na, L.I., Qiang, M.A., Jian,Y., Yunlong,Z. and Jean-Claude,B.(2008):Effects of water-borne copper on the gills and hepatopancreas of *Macrobrachium rosenbergii.* Integrative Zoology, Volume 3, Number 4, (12), 299-310.

Pant, S.C., S. Kumar and S.S. Khanna. (1980) : Toxicity of copper sulphate an d zinc sulphate to fresh water teleost, Puntius conchonius. Comp. Physiol. Ecol., 5 (3), 146-149

Peebles JB (1977): A rapid technique for molt staging in live *Macrobrachium rosenbergii.* Aquaculture 12:173–180.

Shuhaimi-Othman M., Yakub N., Ramle N. and Abas A.(2011): Sensitivity of the freshwater prawn, *Macrobrachium lanchesteri* (Crustacea: Decapoda), to heavy metals. *Toxicol Ind Health vol. 27 no. 6 523-530*

Smith VJ, Johnston PA (1992): Differential haemotoxic effect of PCB congeners in the common shrimp, *Crangon crangon.* Comp. Biochem. Physiol. C 101: 641–649.

Smith VJ, Söderhäll K, Hamilton M (1984):-1, 3-glucan induced cellular defense reaction in the shore crab, *Carcinus maenas.* Comp Biochem Physiol. A. 77: 636–639.

Smith VJ, Swindlehurst RJ, Johnston PA, Vethaak AD (1995) :Distribution of host defence capability in the common shrimp, *Crangon crangon*, by exposure to harbour dredge spoils. Aquat Toxicol 32:43–58.

Söderhäll K (1983): 1,3-glucan enhancement of protease activity in crayfish hemocyte lysate. Comp Biochem Physiol B 74:221–224

Söderhäll K, Cerenius L, Johansson MW (1996): The prophenoloxidase activating system in invertebrates. In: Söderhäll K, Iwanaga SGR, Vasta GR (eds) New directions in invertebrate immunology. SOS Publications. Fair Haven NJ, p 229–253

Truscott R, White KN (1990) :The influence of metal and temperature stress on the immune system of crabs. Funct Ecol4:455–461

Tsing A, Arcier JM, Brèhèlin M (1989) :Haemocytes of penaeids and palaemonid shrimps: morphology, cytochemistry and hemograms. J Invertebr Pathol 53:64–77

Weeks-Perkins BA, Chansue N, Wong-Verelle D (1995): Assay of immune function in shrimp phagocytes: techniques used as indicators of pesticide exposure. In: Stolen J,

Weber D.N. and R.E. (1994):Spieler: Behavioral mechanisms of metal toxicity in fishes In: Aquatic toxicity, (Eds: D.C. Malin's and G.K. Ostrander). Lewis, Boca Ralon pp. 421-461

Wilson, R.W., and W.W. Taylor. (1993): The physiological responses of freshwater rainbow trout, *Onchorhynchus mykiss,* during acutely lethal copper exposure. Jour-nal of Comparative Physiology. 163B:38-47.

Ecological Services of Freshwater Biodiversity that Maintain Water Quality & Healthy Ecosystem

— Shailendra Sharma, India
— D.K. Belsare, India

ABSTRACT

Freshwater biodiversity means variety and variability of aquatic & amphibious vertebrate and invertebrate species, aquatic plants and microorganisms found in lotic and lentic aquatic ecosystems. They have specific functions and provide important ecological services like mitigation of alochthonous and autochthonous food generated in ecosystem, water temperature stability through air-water interface, transport of inorganic and organic matter to the terrestrial ecosystem, removal of particles and sediments, recharge of water table, abatement of pollution and recycling nutrients in water. Variations in their life cycle and life style depend upon the environmental conditions in which they inhabit. Therefore, their presence or absence indicates the health status of water bodies. We ignore scientific natural history of aquatic biodiversity because it is difficult and needs a more detached outlook and a more comprehensive understanding than studying mathematical branches like biotechnology. The present author's observations on the natural history of some of these aquatic species support conclusions to understand the status of water quality and health of aquatic ecosystem.

INTRODUCTION

Biodiversity of River Corridors

The river corridors are the proximate areas of river. The river ecosystems are the open systems with a strong directional headwater to the sea. However, they exhibit lateral dimension encompassing flood plains and relics channel edges delineate the river corridor system. Moreover, a vertical dimension i.e. hyporheic zone must be considered within these corridors. It is within these river corridor environments that natural retentive and transformation processes persist due to the hydrological, vegetation and sedimentary characteristics that control the movement of nutrients from the terrestrial landscapes to aquatic environment. The reactivation of these processes within riverine corridors has been suggested as one potential method to control diffuse nitrogen pollution (Haycock *et al* 1993).

The river corridors link aquatic and terrestrial ecosystems (Pinay *et al.*, 1990; Gregory *et al.*, 1991). The role of riparian forests in controlling the nutrients flowing from the upper catchment towards the river drainage system is well documented by Kaushik *et al.,* (1975). Anoxic conditions, necessary for denitrification occur where accumulations of organic material and fine-grained sediments exist (Dahm *et al.*, 1987). Floodplain geomorphology and the vegetative succession driven by the soil toposequence are the key variables influencing sediment deposition and in turn the retention of the incorporated nutrients (Peterson and Rolfe 1982, Giblin et al., 1991). Thus, geomorphic and hydraulic characteristics of stream channels condition the sorting of organic material and inorganic sediment through erosion/sedimentation during floods.

The underground fluxes of nutrients depend upon the presence of conditions conducive to high denitrification rates as well as the maintenance of stable vegetation structure. The vegetation uptake and denitrification work together to provide a buffer zone that can protect aquatic ecosystem from excessive nitrogen loadings. The primary productivity of this zone is higher than that of the terrestrial system. The water regime affects the denitrification process by saturating the flood plain soils, either by overflow or by rising water table. Moreover, sediments deposited during floods contain organic carbon, which is used by the denitrifying bacteria. Thus vegetation supplies energy (organic carbon) to bacteria through litter decay and root exudates. This carbon is in the form that is readily utilizable by the denitrifying bacteria and can sustain denitrification within the soil profile (Fail *et al* 1987).

The role of exchanges between surface and subsurface waters is important in the ecology of aquatic invertebrates (Danielopol, 1976, Gibert *et al,* 1977). Biological activity within hyporheic (between surface and subsurface area) systems may be high due to large surface area for contact between sediments and water, the slow water velocity and the buffered temperature regime. The exchanges in this zone can be a key factor in controlling stream metabolism. Underground systems are heterotrophic and water flow is controlled by pressure and hydraulic conductivity of sediments (Gibert *et al.,* 1990). In areas of hyporheic zone where the exchange with surface water is low, oxygen demand by microbial activities may be higher than oxygen supply by diffusion, enhancing microbial denitrification (Duff and Triska 1990). During lean periods, the lateral boundaries of the river channel and the hyporheic zone contract, creating gravel bars from what previously was part of the hyporheic zone. The vegetation can develop on these gravel bars. Although these bars are exposed to atmosphere enhancing oxygen diffusion to ground water, they still maintain anoxic patches by trapping sediment and organic matter (Pinney *et al.*, 1994).and can reduce nitrate concentration in the hyporheic aquifer. Thus denitrification is the most significan nitrogen transformation process within river corridors annually and as a consequence nitrogen concentration and loads are best controlled by the activation of this process.

The sludge accumulated at the bottom of river corridors undergoes active anaerobic decomposition with their end products leaching into overlying waters and thus utilizing the water's dissolved O_2. The biodegradable organic matter available at the top layers of sludge, where the anaerobic microorganisms are very active, would also affect O_2 consumption at the top layers of overlying water and at the sludge-overlying water interface. The macrobenthic organisms like trichopteran and dipteran larvae feed on organic matter and help in removing sludge slowly.

Ecological Services Provided by Invertebrate Fauna in Freshwater

The fauna of streams and rivers is represented by both invertebrate and vertebrate species diversity. The major invertebrate groups found in streams are **Porifera** (body sponge like, forming encrusting masses on submerged objects), **Coelenterata** (Sac-like animals, body small, tubular with a fringe of tentacles at the free end, radially symmetrical, attached by one end to plants etc. body contracts when disturbed), **Platyhelminthes** (flat worms, body small, dorsoventrally flattened rather leaf-like in appearance, bilaterally symmetrical and unsegmented), **Annelida** (body worm-like segmented, no obvious appendages), **Arthropoda** (joimted limb animals with a few or more segments). The arthropoda is a very large phylum which includes insects, crustaceans, isopods, amphipods, mites and arachids, **Mollusca** are soft bodied animals having no obvious segments and are partially or totally covered with a hard inflexible shell. The stream habitat is also inhabited by freshwater fishes, residential or migratory birds, amphibians, reptiles like turtle, snake, otters etc.

The macrobenthic fauna of insects is represented by either nymphs (Mayflies, Stoneflies & Dragon/damselflies) or larvae (Caddisflies, Dipteran midges, Nervewings & Beetles). Their life in water is of longer duration (1 to 4 years) as compared to their adult forms (one or a few days). The fauna also consists of pupae of holometabolous insects (Diptera & Trichoptera). The nymphs and larvae present in streams are **shreders** that eat particles > 10 μm, or **chewers**.........Caddiesflies Larvae or **Collectors** that eat particles < 10 μm...**filter feeders & sediment feeders**...............Stoneflies

& Mayflies, or **scrapers** that eat particles < 10 µm. They scrap minerals and organic matter.. Caddiesflies and Mayflies, or **predators** that eat particles > 10 µm. They either swallow (e.g. Dragon Flies, Caddiesflies, Beetles, Chironomids—Diptera) or pierce particles....True bugs & Flies

Microinvertebrates: The occurrence of planktonic population in turbulent river depends on local conditions including the season and incidence of high discharge of water when heavy precipitation occurs in catchment area. The planktonic community in river Satluj (India) and its tributaries is inherently poor and subjected to constant changes and has very little role to play in ecological niche. It is the benthic micro-flora and fauna which plays an important role in propagation of benthic fauna and fish life.

The benthic micro-flora consist of attached algae which grow as a thin film on all kinds of solid objects in the streams and even on sand and mud patches. Among the benthic micro-flora, diatoms (Bacillariophyceae) is the dominant group especially the epiphytic and epilithic genera represented by *Navicula, Gyrosigma, Nitzschia and Suriella.* During the months of February and March every stone at the bottom remains covered with dark green to blackish green patches of blue-green algae (Cyanophyceae). The density of these algae at the bottom ranges 85800-96900 units/cm^2. The predominant genera which occur during the above season include *Rivularia, Phormidium* and *Oscillatoria.* The other genera of importance recorded are *Tetraspora, Ulothrix* and *Oedogonium* amongst green algae (Chlorophyceae). The benthic micro-fauna, which occur in association with algal film, include *Arcella, Difflugia and Monostyla,* mainly as stray specimens.

Microinvertebrates of Betwa River

Mite Fauna

Hydractina,sp, Limnocharis aquatica, Elyas, sp, Prolazia, sp, *Hydroplantes* ,sp., *Sperchonopsis,* sp, *Spercon,* sp, *Lebertia porosa, Piloleberia,* sp. , *Limnesia macularis, Hydrobates,* sp, *Uniovicola intermedia, Pinopsis,* sp, *Pionam* sp & *Hydrozetes,* sp etc. The other microarthropods are also present. Some of them are lenitic, rhiobonetic-rhiophilous crenophilous-rheophilous and crenophilous-crenophilous in habit .

Spider Fauna

Most of the species are foliage weaver and predators. They are *Araneus,* sp, *Cyclosa* sp, *Cryptophora,* sp, *Larinia,* sp, *Neoscana bengalensis, Neocana mukerjjei, Zygeilla indica, Clubiona,* sp, *Drassodes,* sp, *Olios,* sp, *Labulla nepula,*

Artema, sp, *Tetragnatha,* sp, *Argyrodes,*sp, *Theridion,* sp, *Thomisus bulani, Thomisus shivajiensis* and *Uloborus krishnae* (Belsare 2006).

The distribution of stream and river biota in Indian tropical region is recently reported by Mahato *et al.,* (2001) in Subernrekha basin (extending

21º592 to 24º392 N latitude and 83º392 E to 86º542 E longitude) over a stretch of 28.5 km. All the thirty-three taxa of benthic macroinvertebrates were recorded from the lotic habitat and were assigned to seven functional feeding groups, namely shredders, collectors, filter-feeders, scrappers, predators, deposit-feeders and generalists. The shredders were represented by four taxa: namely *Amphinemura* spp, *Stenocolus* spp, *Polypedilum* spp, and *Brotia hainanensis* belonging to Plecoptera, Coleoptera, Diptera and Basommatophora respectively. They were dominant in headwaters The collectors and filter- feeders are macroconsumers, the former feed on deposited particlulate organic matter from sediments, whereas the latter filter fine organic particles from water column. The species were represented by six taxa; *Ephemera* spp, *Caenis* spp, *Baetis* spp,(Ephemeroptera), Hydrophillidae (Coleoptera) and *Chironomus* spp, *Dicrotendips* sp (Diptera)..Their percentage composition is relatively low at headwaters and attained maximum value at down streams. The scrapers are macroconsumers and are adapted for removing firmly attached algae from exposed surfaces in running waters. They feed mainly on *aufwuch* attached to rocks, stones, woody debris and vascular hydrophytes. The species were represented by four taxa; *Baetis* sp, & *Ephemerella* sp (Ephemeroptera)and *Brachyptera* sp (Basommatophora).

The scrapers do not reveal significant longitudinal variation in terms of percentage composition. In Subarnrekha River they revealed temporal change along the lower course. The predators feed on other macrobenthic invertebrates and are particle converters (particle being the prey) and the controllers of non-predator population. The species represented were *Chaetogaster* sp, *Rhycaphila* sp, *Berosus* sp, *Tanypus* sp , *Coelotanypus* sp, and *Proeladius* sp. Their density was more in clean water and in obstructed river habitat. The deposit feeders feed on silt deposited on the bottom. The organic matter present in the silt serves as source of energy for them. They were represented by four taxa; *Branchiura* sp, *Limnodrilus udekemianus*, *L. augustipenis*, and *Dero* sp (all oligochaetes). They were more predominant in the lower course of the river. The generalists are the organisms with no specific choice as regards to food particle size. They belonged to Gastropoda and were represented by five taxa; *Thiara tuberculata*, *T. scabra* and *Vivipara bengalensis*, *Indoplanorbis exutus*, *Gyraulus convexiusculus* They are pollution sensitive organisms and their reduced species composition may be attributed to organic pollution.

According to the concept of River Continnum, the shredders and collectors are co-dominant in head waters and the scrapers are primarily adapted for shearing attached algae from the surface. The dominance of scrapers follows shifts in a primary production and is maximized in mid-sized river. With increasing stream size and a general reduction in detrital particle size, the collectors (collector-gatherers and filter-feeders) should increase and dominate the macroinvertebrate assemblage in large rivers. The predator component may not change significantly.

The effect of stream regulation on stream biota is not reported in stream or rivers of Indian sub-continent. Such studies are comparatively scanty in temperate region also. Brittain *et al.*, (1983) reported the impact of water transfer scheme on the benthic macroinvertebrates of a Norwegian river. Similarly Lillehammer and Saltveit (1983) also studied the effect of the regulation on the aquatic macroinvertebrate fauna of the river Suldalslågen in western Norway. They observed that regulation in the catchment area of the river increased winter flow and reduced summer flow, together with a small increase in water temperature in the lower part of the river. The most pronounced effect of the regulation was seen in the Trichoptera, Placoptera, Ephemeroptera (nymphs) and Chironomidae fauna. Large particulate feeders (shredders) such as *Potamophylax latipennis* were reduced, while the collectors strongly increased, dominated by oligochaetes and the caddiesfly, *Polycentropus flavomaculatus*..

Stoneflies were not recorded from June to September in the upper part of the river and mayfly species composition changed from four species to a total dominance of *Baetis rhodani*. In two short- term regulated hydro-power dams, Krångede on River Indalsålven and the Byarforsen dam on the River Ljusnan in Sweden , the impact on zoobenthos favoured filterfeeders Trichoptera. The negative effects of the short term regulation were most obvious at locality with zero discharge, where the number of species was reduced. Similar situation may exist in Sutluge River in India where the streams dry up during lean period and the required water needed to run hydroelectric turbines is drawn from tunnel connected to the reservoir. The research on regulated flow on stream fauna is urgently needed to save biodiversity of this region.

Biomonitoring of Water Quality

Biological monitoring, or biomonitoring, is the use of biological responses to assess changes in the environment, generally changes due to anthropogenic causes. Biomonitoring programs may be qualitative, semi-quantitative, or quantitative. Biomonitoring is a valuable assessment tool that is receiving increased use in water quality monitoring programs of all types.

There are two types of biomonitoring. One type of biomonitoring is surveillance before and after a project is complete or before and after a toxic substance enters the water. The other type of biomonitoring is to ensure compliance with regulations or guidelines or to ensure water quality is maintained.

Biomonitoring involves the use of indicators, indicator species or indicator communities. Generally benthic macroinvertebrates, fish, and/or algae are used. Certain aquatic plants have also been used as indicator species for pollutants including nutrient enrichment (Phillips and Rainbow, 1993; Batiuk et al., 1992). There are advantages and disadvantages to each. Macroinvertebrates are most frequently used (Rosenberg and Resh, 1993). Biochemical, genetic, morphological, and physiological changes in certain organisms have been noted as being related to particular environmental stressors and can be used as indicators.

The presence or absence of the indicator or of an indicator species or indicator community reflects environmental conditions. Absence of a species is not as meaningful as it might seem as there may be reasons, other than pollution, that result in its absence (e.g., predation, competition, or geographic barriers which prevented it from ever being at the site) (Johnson et al., 1993). Absence of multiple species of different orders with similar tolerance levels that were present previously at the same site is more indicative of pollution than absence of a single species. It is clearly necessary to know which species should be found at the site or in the system.

Sentinel organisms, or indicator species that accumulate pollutants in their tissues from the surrounding environment or from food, are important biomonitoring devices (Phillips and Rainbow 1993; Kennish 1992). The Mussel Watch is one such use of a sentinel species (Phillips and Rainbow 1993; Kennish 1992). Filter feeders, such as bivalves (clams and mussels), tend to concentrate metals in their gills or other tissues

Assessment Methodology

When the pollutant type is known or well understood, certain indicators are more effectively used or are less expensive. When stressors are not known and/or less is known about species tolerance levels, multiple level assessment and more intensive and expensive studies that may include toxicity tests may be necessary (Johnson et al., 1993). Multiple level assessment involves the monitoring of indicators and behavioral changes of organisms. Indicators must display a biochemical, genetic, morphological, or physiological change. Behavioral indices are determined by particular species, populations dynamics, or community changes.

Community level biomonitoring provides information on the magnitude and ecological effects of the stressor on the system. Cause and effect relationships are difficult to establish and few definitely exist, because possible confounding factors are often present (Johnson et al., 1993). Using indicators at different organizational levels (for example, individuals, species, community, ecosystem) may be more reliable.

Biomonitoring measures may be used at the different, but related, levels of analysis:

Levels of Organization and Associated Biomonitoring Measures

Individual - Organism - genetic mutations - reproductive success - physiology - metabolism - oxygen consumption, photosynthesis rate -

enzyme/protein activation/inhibition - hormones - growth and development - disease resistance - tissue/organ damage - bioaccumulation **Population** - survival/mortality - sex ratio - abundance/biomass - behavior (migration) - predation rates - population decline/increase **Community** - Abundance ("evenness") of an organism or organisms - Biomass - Density of an organism or organisms - Richness (variety) - number of species, size classes, or other functional groups, per unit area or volume, or per number of individuals. - Diversity - the richness given the relative abundance of each species or group. **Ecosystem** - Mass balance of nutrients (from Adamus and Brandt, 1990)

Assessment Indices

There are various indices used to assess the effects of stressors on (aquatic) populations and communities:

Biotic Indices: generally specific to the type of pollution or the geographical area; they are used to classify the degree of pollution by determining the tolerance of an indicator organism to a pollutant. Indicator species are assigned scores for their tolerance level. Biotic indices assume that polluted sites or systems will contain fewer species than unimpacted sites or systems and the species that are present will reflect their particular sensitivity to a pollutant (Johnson et al., 1993). The measures are generally weighted and may include indices such as richness, pollution tolerance, trophic levels present, abundance, and deformities (Adamus and Brandt, 1990). These indices were originally devised for, and are most useful for, organic pollution (Johnson et al., 1993).

Diversity Indices: the measure of the richness, or number of distinct taxa (e.g., orders, families, species) at a site, and the evenness, the relative abundance of different taxonomic groups, determined by counts of all organisms collected.

Comparison, or Similarity Indices - the comparison of the community structure in richness and/or evenness over time or over space.

Both the diversity index and the similarity index may use the functional feeding group (e.g. herbivores, detrivores, carnivores) as a measure of the community integrity rather than taxa (i.e. species, genus, family).

On the level of the individual or species, biochemical and physiological indicators may be examined (Johnson et al., 1993). Some benthic macroinvertebrates such as stoneflies (plecoptera), caddisflies (trichoptera), mayflies (ephemeroptera), and shellfish, show increases or decreases of certain enzymes, changes in DNA, RNA, amino acids, and protein production, oxygen consumption and ion concentration, in response to environmental stressors such as temperature shifts, metals, and pesticides. Physiological indicators of contamination include deformities, sores, or lesions (Phillips and Rainbow, 1993; Kennish 1992).

The EPA Rapid Bioassessment Protocol for Use in Streams and Rivers (Plafkin et al., 1989) uses community diversity in assessing water quality. The absence of pollution sensitive benthic macroinvertebrate groups (ephemeroptera, plecoptera, and trichoptera) and dominance of pollution-tolerant groups (oligochaetes or chironomids), is indicative of pollution. Overall, low richness of benthic macroinvertebrates may indicate impairment. However, naturally low nutrient levels in pristine headwaters may be the cause of low productivity and few benthic macroinvertebrate species exist in these conditions.

Pollutant stressors tend to cause slime and filamentous algae productivity and/or fewer fish species and more tolerant species than expected (Plafkin et al., 1989). The judgment of impairment, based on these indicators should be made by an experienced biologist.

Common Organisms used for Biomonitoring

Benthic macroinvertebrates Advantages:

- Benthic macroinvertebrates are found in most aquatic habitats.
- There are a large number of species, and different stresses produce different macroinvertebrate communities.
- Small order streams often do not support fish but do support extensive macroinvertebrate communities.
- Macroinvertebrates generally have limited mobility. Thus they are indicators of localized environmental conditions.
- Since benthic macroinvertebrates retain (bioaccumulate) toxic substances, chemical analysis will allow detection in them where levels are undetectable in the water resource.
- A biologist experienced in macroinvertebrate identification will, be able to determine relatively quickly whether the environment has been degraded by identifying changes in the benthic community structure of the water resource.
- Benthic macroinvertebrates are small enough to be easily collected and identified.
- Sampling of macroinvertebrates under a rapid assessment protocol is easy, requires few people and minimal equipment, and does not adversely affect other organisms.
- Macroinvertebrates are the primary food source for recreationally and commercially important fish. An impact on macroinvertebrates impacts the food web and designated uses of the water resource.
- State water quality agencies tend to collect macroinvertebrate data.

Disadvantages:

- Benthic macroinvertebrates do not respond to all impacts.
- Seasonal variations may prevent comparisons of samples taken in different seasons.

- Drifting may bring benthic macroinvertebrates into waters in which they would not normally occur. Knowledge of drifting behavior of certain species can alleviate this disadvantage.
- Certain groups are difficult to identify to the species level.

(**Sources:** Plafkin et al.,1989; Rosenberg and Resh, 1993; Klemm et al., 1990) **Example invertebrate indicators of specific impairment types:**

The macrobenthic invertebrate fauna of a stream is shown in fig.1. The common Indian species in streams and rivers of India are observed as follows:

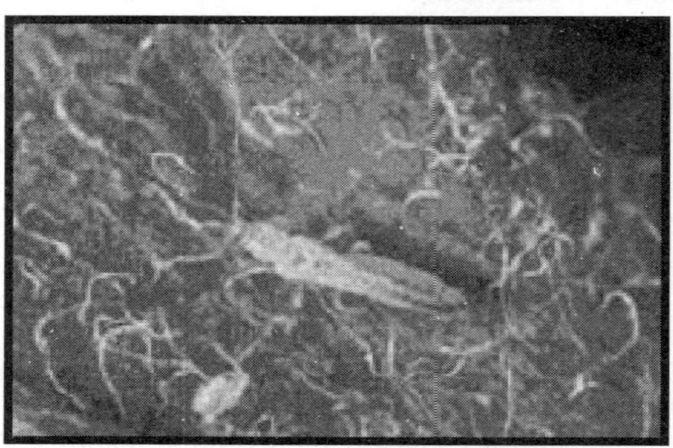

Springtail

Polychaetes & Oligochaetes

Polychaetes*:* 1. *Nephthys oligobranchia* 2.*Namalycastis indica.* **Oligochaetes:**

3. *Branchiodrilus semperi* 4. *Branchidrilus hortensi,* 5. *Chaetogaster . limnaei limnaei,* 6. *Nias communis,* 7. *Haemonias woldvogeti* 8. *Dero digitalis* 9, *Dero dorsalis,* 10. *Dero nivea* 11. *Dero sawayai* 12. *Dero pectinata* 13. *Aulophorus furcatus* 14 *Aulophorus hymanae* 15. *Aulophorus indicus,* 16. *Allonias* paragquayensis 17. Allonias inequalis, 18. Pristina acuminate, 19. Pristina *synclites* 20. *Limnodrilus hoffmeisteri,*21. *Aulodrilus pigueti,* 22. Aulodrilus pluriseta 23. Branchiura sowerbyi, 24. Glyphidrilus gangeticus 25. *Perionyx excavatus.*

Aquatic Leeches: 1. *Alboglassiphonia weberi,* 2.Alboglassiphonia heteroclitus, 3. *Placobdelloides fulvus,* 4. *Ozobranchus shipleyi* 5. *Asiaticobdella birmanica,* 6. *Barbronia weberi,* 7. *Salifa lateroculata,* 8. *Salifa biharensis.* **Higher Crustacea** : 9. *Macrobrachium* spp, 10. *Caridina* spp, **Amphipods**: 11. *Gammerus* spp, **Isopods:** 12. *Asellus* spp.

Molluscs (Gastropods)1. *Digoniostoma pulchella,*2. *Thiara scabra* 3 *Alocinma orcula,* 4. *Limnaea acuminata tipica,* 5. *Achatina fulica fulica,* 6.*Bellamya bengalensis,* 7. *Pila globosa,* 8. *Gabbia orcula producta,* 9. *Indoplanorbis exustus,* 10 *Gyraulus convexiusculus* 11. *Segmintina calatha*

12 *Ferrisiqa verruca*, (**Bivalves**):13. *Parresia caerulea* 14. ***Corbiculus striatella*** 15. *Pisidium nevillianum*, 16. *Lamellidens* ***corrianus***, 17. *Novaculina gangetica*.

Bellamya begalensis

Heridinie

Gastropda

Insects

Diptera Larvae & Pupe: Larvae 1.*Eristalis spp,* 2. *Simulium* spp, 3. *Horaia* spp, 4. *Bezzia* spp, 5. *Psychoda* spp, 6. *Chironomus* spp, 7. *Tabanus* spp, 8. *Ptychoptera* spp, 9. *Stratiomys* spp, 10. *Thaumalea* spp, 11. *Dicranota* spp, 12. *Dixia* spp, 13. *Ephydra* spp, 14. *Tipula* spp, **Pupae:** 15.Psychod*a spp, 16. Horaia spp,* 17. Syrphidae.

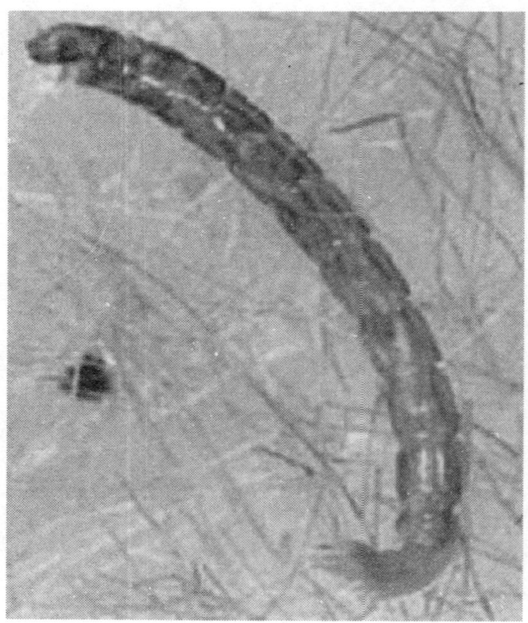

Midge pupa

Cranefly larvae

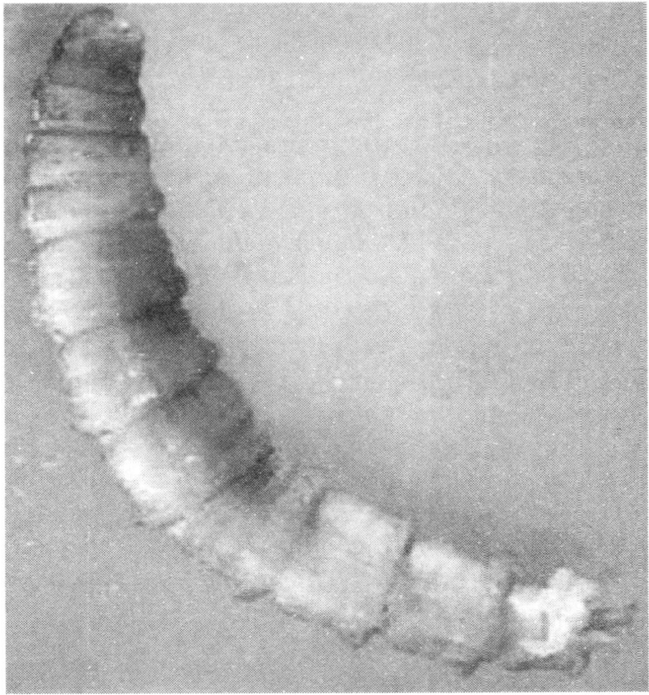

Blackfly larvae

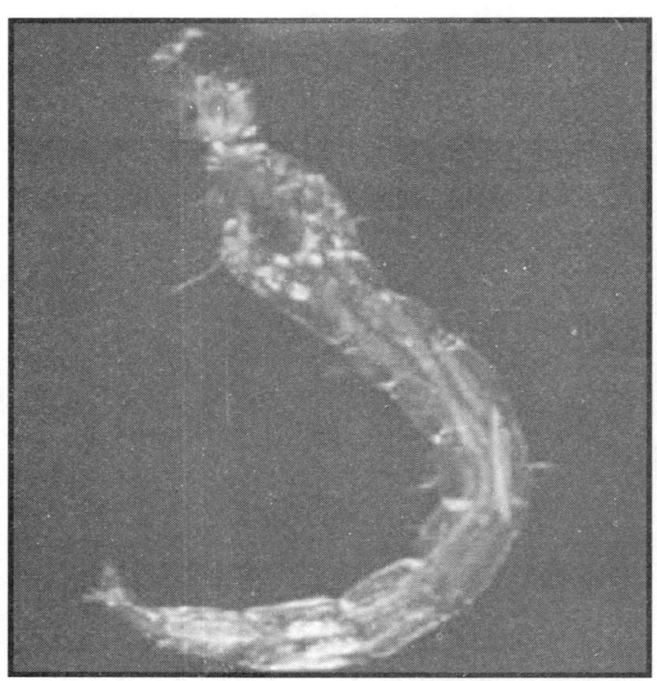

Phantom midge larvae

Mayflies Nymphs 1. *Centroptilum* spp, 2. *Campylocia* spp, 3. *Baetis* spp, 4. *Ephemera* spp, 5. *Anagenia* spp, 6.*Choroterpes* spp, 7. *Cloeon* spp, 8. *Procloeon* spp, 9. *Caenis* spp, 10. *Heptagenia* spp, 11. *Epeorus* spp, 12. *Potamanthus* spp, 13. *Ecdyonurus* spp, 14. *Rithrogena* spp, 15. *Neoephemera* spp, 16. *Siphlonurus* spp, 17. *Povilla* spp, 18. *Tricorythodes* spp, 19. *Ephemerella* spp, 20. *Oligoneureiella* spp, 21. *Nathanella* spp, 22. *Indialis* spp, 23. *Traulus* spp, 24. *Propistosoma* spp.

Stoneflies: (Fig.14.) 1. *Xanthoperla kishaganga,* 2.*Chloroperla spp,*3. *Cryptoperla* spp, 4. Neoperla spp, 5. *Brachyptera spp*

Caddisflies (Trichoptera) Larvae : *1. Molanna spp, 2. Goera spp, 3. Ganpnema spp, 4.Stenopsyche spp, 5. Phryganopsyche spp, 6. Lamnocentropus spp, 7. Micrasema spp, 8. Uenoa spp, 9. Stractobia spp, 10. Eubassilissa spp, 11. Helicopsyche spp, 12. Limnephilus spp, 13. Glossosoma spp, 14. Setodes spp, 15. Psilotreta sp, 16. Lepidostoma spp, 17.Rhyacophila spp, 18. Plectrocnemia spp, 19. Hydropsyche spp, 20. Worlmaldia spp, 21. Tinodes spp, 22. Apsilochorema spp, 23. Ecnomus spp.*

Aquatic beetle larvae: (Fig, 16). 1. *Litodactylus spp, 2. Hydroscapha spp, 3. Helichus spp, 4. Eubranax spp, 5. Gyrinus spp, 6. Heteromera spp, 7. Dytiscidae spp, 8. Stenelmis spp, 9. Scirtes spp, 10. Hydroptilus spp, 11. Heliplus spp, 12. Donacia spp.*

Coleoptera (Beetles)

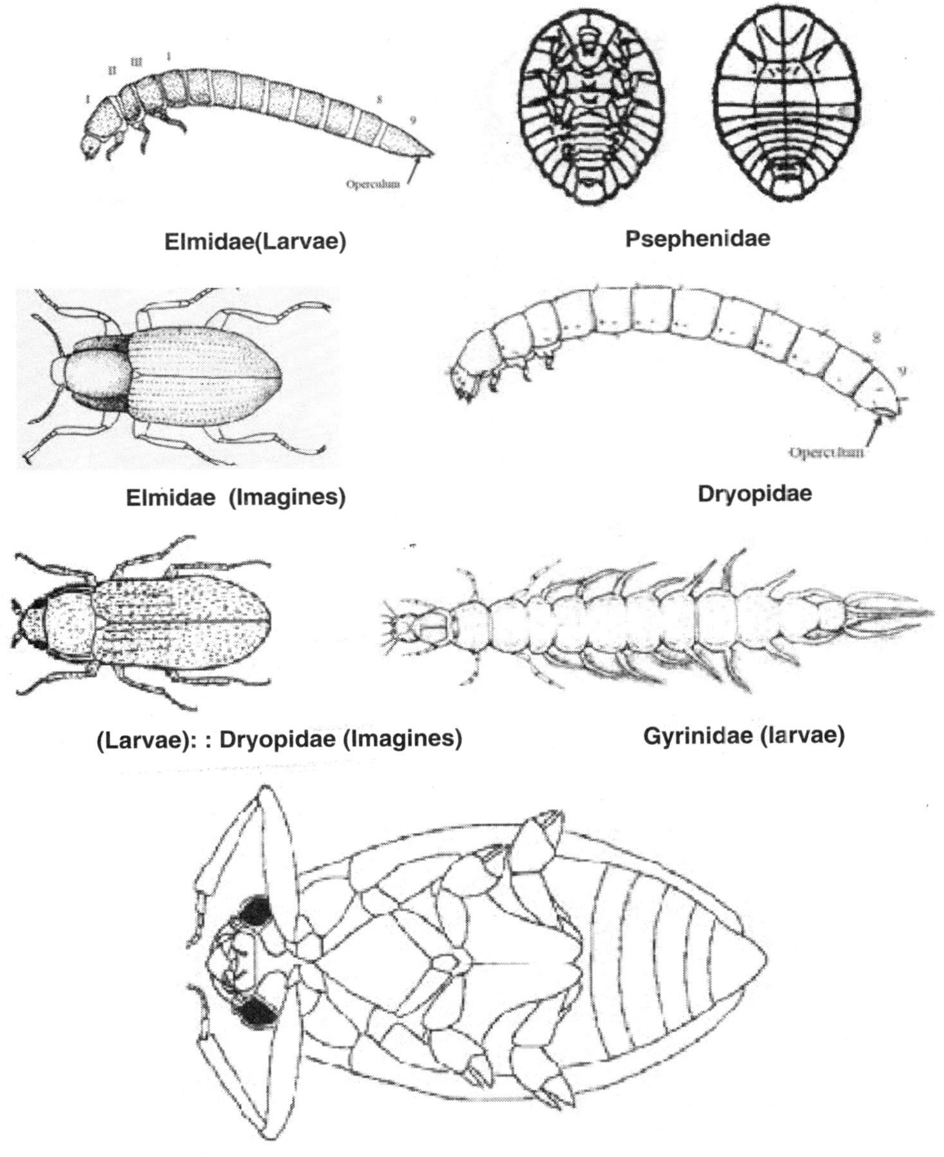

Elmidae(Larvae)

Psephenidae

Elmidae (Imagines)

Dryopidae

(Larvae): : Dryopidae (Imagines)

Gyrinidae (larvae)

Gyrinidae(Imagines)

Dragonflies/Damselflies (Odonata): Zygoptera1. *Rhinocypha spp, 2. Bayadera spp, 3. Protosticta spp, 4. Neurobasis spp, 5.Copera spp, 6. Disparoneura,* 7, Pseudagrion spp, 8. Lestes spp, **Anisoptera***: 9. Macromia spp, 10.. Anisogomphus spp, 11.. Cordulegaster spp, 12. . Anax spp, 13. . Orthretum spp, 14.. Brachythermis spp, 15. . Sympetrum spp.*

Odonata (Dragonflies & Damselflies)

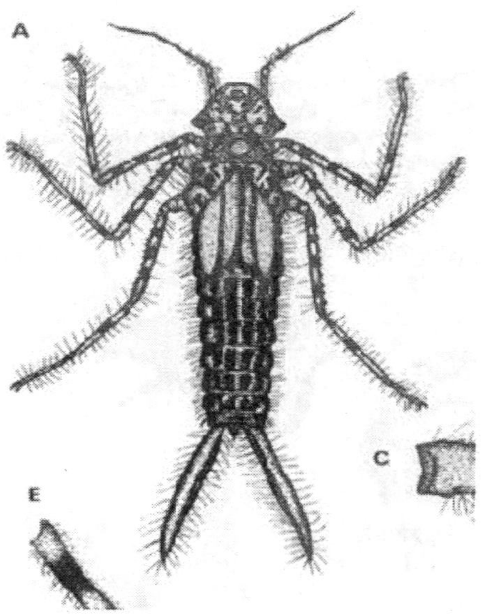

Chlorocyphidae (Rhinocypha forate)

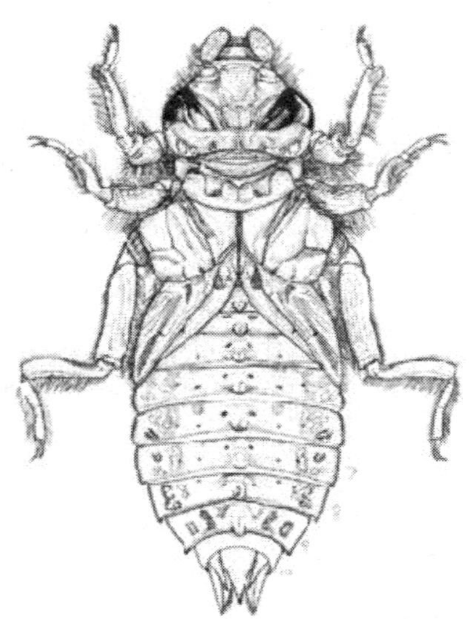

Gomphidae

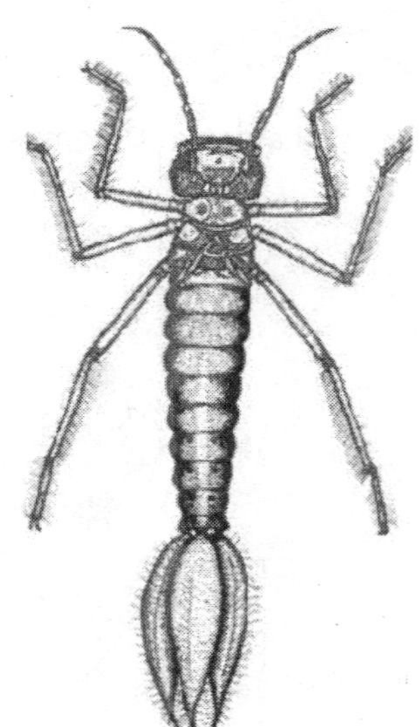

Amphipterygidae

Water Bugs (Heteroptera, Hydrocortisae) 1.*Nerthra spp, 2. Helotrephes spp, 3. Plea spp, 4. Ranatra spp, 5. Limnocoris spp, 6. Ochtherus spp, 7. Aphelocheirus spp, 8. Anisops spp, 9. Micronecta spp, 10. Laccotrephes spp. 11. Lethocerus spp,.*

HETEROPTERA (Bugs)

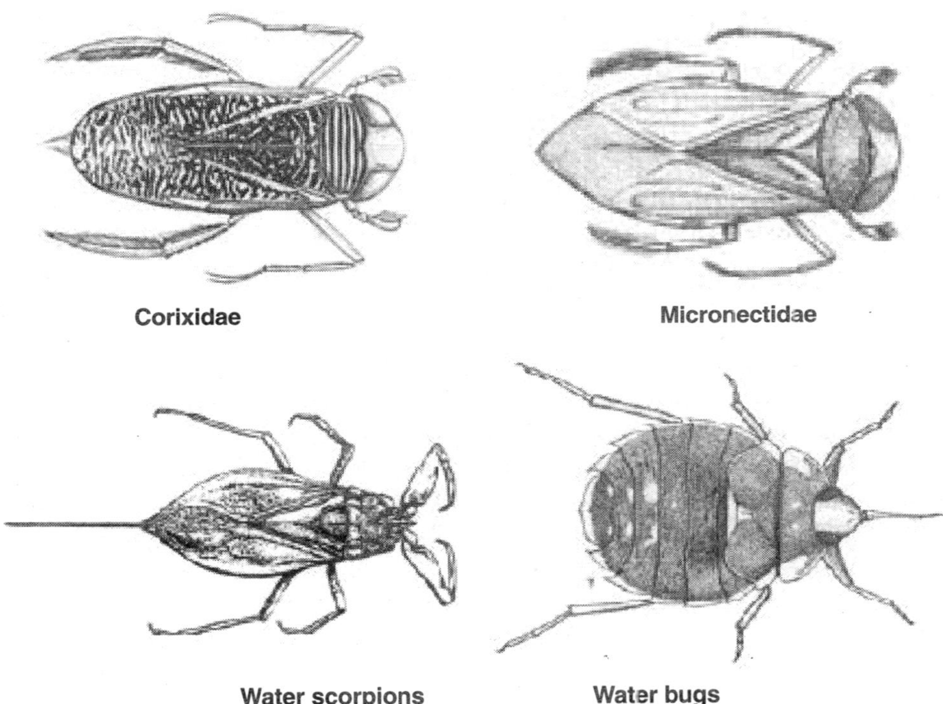

Corixidae

Micronectidae

Water scorpions

Water bugs

Flora

The floristic component of rivers and streams is dominated by algae (650 species) which are distributed in open waters, whereas the macrophytes (pteridophytes-90 species and angiosperms -700 species) are found in littoral region (Belsare 2006). There are more than 100 plant species which are endemic (Cook 1996). Some of them are : *Ammannia desertora, Aponogeton crispus, A. appendiculatus, , Cryptocoryne tortuosa, , Cyanotis cucullata, Cyathocline lutea, , Daltzellia zeylanica, Dopatrium lobelioides, Eriocaulon breviscapum, Farmeria indicalia, F. woodrowii, Fuirena capitata, Geissapsis tenelia, Helliotropium keralense, Hoppea dichomata, , Hydrobryopsis sessilis, Hydrophila balsamica, Indotristicha ramosissima, Isachne bicolor, , Lagenandra meeboldii, Limnophila polystachya, Limnopoa meeboldii, Lindernia manilaliana, Lipocarpha raynaliana, Mariscus clarkei, Murdannia pauciflora, Myriophyllum indicum, M. oliganthum.* The desert river courses have *Salix daphnoides, Myricaria elegans, Morus alba* scrubs.

There is urgent need to study the biological traits of plants on the basis of disturbed, stressed and competitive habitats defined by Grime (1979). Stressed habitat is unproductive, with a low rate of accumulation of biomass. Competitive habitats are both undisturbed and productive with the main threat to a plant's survival coming from competition for resources from other plants and are, therefore, resource-capture specialists. They tolerate stress, disturbance or competition or intermediate combinations of these strategy elements to permit growth and reproduction under prevailing conditions.

The presence or absence of the indicator or of an indicator species or indicator community reflects environmental conditions. Absence of a species is not as meaningful as it might seem as there may be reasons, other than pollution, that result in its absence (e.g., predation, competition, or geographic barriers, which prevent it from ever being at the site) Absence of multiple species of different orders with similar tolerance levels that were present previously at the same site is more indicative of pollution than absence of a single species. It is necessary to know which species should be found at the site or in the system.

Sentinel organisms, or indicator species that accumulate pollutants in their tissues from the surrounding environment or from food, are important biomonitoring devices (Phillips and Rainbow 1993; Kennish 1992). The Mussel Watch is one such use of a sentinel species (Phillips and Rainbow 1993; Kennish 1992). Filter feeders, such as bivalves (clams and mussels), tend to concentrate metals in their gills or other tissues

Assessment

When the pollutant type is known or well understood, certain indicators are more effective. When stressors are not known and/or less is known about species tolerance levels, multiple level assessment and more intensive and expensive studies that may include toxicity tests may be necessary. Multiple level assessment involves the monitoring of indicators and behavioral changes of organisms. Indicators must display a biochemical, genetic, morphological, or physiological change. Behavioral indices are determined by particular species, population dynamics, or community changes.

Community level biomonitoring provides information on the magnitude and ecological effects of the stressor on the system. Cause and effect relationships are difficult to establish and few definitely exist, because possible confounding factors are often present Using indicators at different organizational levels (for example, individuals, species, community, and ecosystem) may be more reliable. Biomonitoring measures may be used at the different, but related, levels of analysis:

Levels of Organization and Associated Biomonitoring Measures

Individual - Organism - genetic mutations - reproductive success - physiology - metabolism - oxygen consumption, photosynthesis rate - enzyme/protein activation/inhibition - hormones - growth and development - disease resistance - tissue/organ damage - bioaccumulation **Population** - survival/mortality - sex ratio - abundance/biomass - behavior (migration) -

predation rates - population decline/increase **Community** - Abundance ("evenness") of an organism or organisms - Biomass - Density of an organism or organisms - Richness (variety) - number of species, size classes, or other functional groups, per unit area or volume, or per number of individuals. - Diversity - the richness given the relative abundance of each species or group. **Ecosystem** - Mass balance of nutrients

Benthic Macroinvertebrates

Species richness, abundance, stonefly taxa, Hydropsychidae, chironomids "green", chironomids "red", air-breathing animals like rat-tail maggots,*Physella acuta*, tubificidae (mass occurance) etc.

Single approach____________Very abundant

The sensitive taxa approach: The diversity of sensitive taxa declines in response to most types of human influence such as, flow regimes are altered, physical habitat is lost, pollutants, organic degradable material or chemicals introduced disrupt energy cycles Alien taxa invade and impair the environment

Taxanomic Groups of Sensitive Taxa

(*a*) **Caddiesflies**: Generally are found in clear flowing water and are very sensitive to pollution and oxygen depletion. They occur across a range of habitats from cool streams to warm streams, lakes, marshes and ponds. In standing water they can tolerate pollution only those have been selected as 'sensitive' that are inhabiting endangered water bodies or that are tolerant to environmental degradation.

(*b*) **Stoneflies**: Stoneflies require high dissolved oxygen concentration and tend to be found in cold flowing water with a gravel or stone bottom. Some species may be found along lakeshores with wave action. The diversity of these flies declines in response to most types of human influence.

(*c*) **Mayflies**: They prefer clean water with sufficient oxygen supply. Others are typical to low land river or may be found in standing (lentic) water bodies as well. Some of mayfly species can tolerate low dissolved oxygen levels. Only those have been selected as 'sensitive' that are tolerant to any type of environmental degradation.

(*d*) **Long living (semi-voltine) taxa**: These species require more than one year to complete their life cycles. Thus they are exposed to all human activities that influence the stream throughout one or more years. If water body is flooded they disappear. Loss of long-living taxa may also indicate the ongoing problem that repeatedly interrupts their life cycle.

(*e*) **Predators**: The percentage of animals that are obligate predators provides a measure of trophic complexity supported by a site. Less disturbed sites support a greater diversity of prey species and a variety of habitats in which to find them. Predator taxa represent the peak of the food web and depend on a reliable source of other invertebrates to feed on. Thus they accumulate harmful/toxic substances.

The long-living predators are exposed to environmental stress than short living one. By this means they accumulate toxic/harmful substances. Some predators are large animals that stalk their prey; They hide between cobbles and then have a territorial behaviour that depend upon hiding places (large stones). These may be lost if fine sediments are deposited into a stream, the current is too low (residual areas). or pulse releases disturb the habitats (hydro-peaking)

***(f)* Any other taxa**: any clean water species, any species with particular environmental needs that enforce healthy ecosystems (Crayfish, crabs, large mussels)

Pollution Tolerent Benthos: Midgeflies, Worms. Leeches, Pouch Snails

Macrobenthic Invertebrates indicate pollution level of water bodies in India

Biomarkers of Oxidative Stress

Oxidative stress may ensue when the ability to buffer against ROS is exceeded either by excessive production of ROS or by depletion of antioxidant. This can alter cellular redox-poise and initiate a variety of responses via intercellular pathways (Sun & Oberley 1996, Belsare 2003).

Lipid peroxidation (LPO) leads to destruction of membrane lipids and production of lipid peroxides and their by-products such as aldehyde. Melnoaldehyde is formed from the breakdown of polyunsaturated fatty acids (PUFA) and it serves as convenient index for determining the extent of lipid peroxidation. **It is a biomarker** of effect representing the state of membrane lipid peroxidation. The LPO is induced by organics and transition metals, iron and copper (Fenton reaction), by acting as catalysts in the formation of oxygen radicals. Since the typical reaction during oxidative stress is peroxidative damage to unsaturated fatty acids, the oxidative stress response could conveniently be used as a biomarker of chemical pollutants.

CONCLUSIONS

1. Macrobenthic invertebrates indicate water quality of rivers and streams
2. They are the source of food for bottom dwelling fishes
3. LPO level in macrobenthic invertebrates serve as biomarker of stress due to organic and metal pollution
4. Animals and hydrophytes balance nutrient level in river and stream water undergoing eutrophication and pollution.
5. hyporheic zone of river corridors act as recycling system of organic and inorganic nutrient load in river water

REFERENCES

Belsare, S. D. 2003. Detoxification mechanism of corbicular honey. J. Comp.Toxicol Physiol. 1:1-8 (2003)

Belsare, D.K. 2006. Introduction to Biodiversity. APH Pub. Corp. New Delhi pp 1- 274.

Brittain, J. E., A. Lillehammer and R. Bildeng 1983. The impact of a water transfer scheme on the benthic macroinvertebrates of a Norwegian river. In Regulated Rivers. (eds A. Lillehammer and S.J.Saltveit) University Pres . Oslo. pp. 201- 210

Cook, C.D.K. 1996. Aquatic and wetland plants of India. OUP

Danielopol. D.L. 1976. The distribution of the fauna in the interstitial habitats of riverine sediments of the Danube and the Piesting (Austria) Int. J. Spéléol . 8: 23-51.

Duff, J.H. and F.J.Triska. 1990. Denitrification in sediment from hyporheic zone adjacent to a small forested stream. Can J. Fish. Aquat. Sci., 47: 1140-1147.)

Grime, J. P. 1979. Plant Strategies and Vegetation Processes. Wiley, Chichester pp.221

Fail, T.E. and R. J. Naiman 1987. Riparian forest communities and their role in nutrient conservation in agricultural watershed. Am. J. Alter. Agri. II: 114-121

Giblin, A.E. , K. J. Nadelhoffer, G.R. Shaver, J.A. Laundre and A.J. McKerrow . 1991. Biogeochemical diversity along a riverside toposequence in arctic Alaska. Ecological Monographs 61: 415-435.

Gilbert, J., R. Ginet, J. Mathieu, J.L. Raygrobellete, A. Seyed-Reihani. 1977. Structure et fonctionnement des ecosystems du Haut Rhône Français .IV. Le peuplement des eaux phréatiques . Premiers resultants. Annals. Limnol. 13: 83-97.

Gilbert , J. , M.J. Dole-Oliver, P. Marmonier and P. Vervier. 1990. Surface water – ground water ecotones. The Ecology and Management of Aquatic-Terrestrial Ecotones (eds R.J. Naiman and H. Décamps.) The Parthenon Publ. Group Publ. pp 199-227.

Gregory , S.V., F. J. Swanson, W.,A. McKee and K.W. Cummins 1991. An ecosystem perspective of riparian zones . Bioscience 41: 540-551

Helvey, and Patrick 1965.

Haycock, N.E.., G. Pinney and C. Walker. 1993. Nitrogen retention in river corridors: European perspectives. Ambio. 22; 340-346

Kennish, M.J. 1992. Ecology of Estuaries: anthropogenic effects. CRC Press: Boca Raton.

Mahoto, B., M. Kumari. And P.N. Pandey. 2001. Extrapolation and comparision of the doctrine of 'river continnum concept' in a tropical river of Chotanagpur plateau. In Current Topics in Environmental Science. (eds G. Tripathi and G.C. Pandey) ABD Publ. Jaipur India. Pp 413-465.

Peterson, D.L. and G.L.Rolfe 1982. Seasonal variation in nutrients of floodplain and upland forest soils of central Illinois. Soil SciSoc Am. J. 46: 1310-1315

Phillips, D.J.H., P.S. Rainbow. 1993. Biomonitoring of Trace Aquatic Contaminants. Elsevier Applied Science: New York, NY.

Pinney, G., N.E. Haycock, C. Ruffinoni & R.M.Holmes 1994. The role of denitrification in nitrogen removal in river corridors. In Global Wetland , Old World and New (ed W, J, Mitsch) Elsevier N.Y. pp107-116.

Sun, Y. and L. W. Oberley. 1996. Redox regulation of transcriptional activators. Free Radic. Biol. Med. 23: 335-348.

Histopathological Alterations and Bioaccumulation of Heavy Metals in *Oreochromis Niloticus* Fish

—*H.A. Kaoud, Egypt*

ABSTRACT

Copper, lead, cadmium and mercury concentrations were recorded in water and tissues of Oreochromis niloticus *from Egyptian fish farms in 2007-2009. Histopathological alterations in fish tissues were also studied. Mercury was the most accumulated metal in the muscles, while Cu was the least. The concentration of cadmium, lead and copper were highest in liver and lowest in kidney tissue, while mercury concentrations were highest in muscles, lowest in kidney tissue. Several histopathological changes were noted in muscles, liver, gills, kidney and intestine tissue attributable to heavy metal exposure.*

Keywords: *Heavy metals, Tilapia, Pollution, histopathology.*

INTRODUCTION

Heavy metals, such as copper, zinc, lead, mercury and cadmium, are among the most dangerous and abundant inorganic environmental pollutants, arising from industrial discharges and mining practices (Nriagu and Pacyna, 1988). They enter aquatic systems via natural and anthropogenic sources, including industrial, agricultural, and mining activities. The aquatic environment is more susceptible to the harmful effects of heavy metal pollution because aquatic organisms are in close and prolonged contact with the soluble metals. What's more, unlike toxic organic compounds, metals cannot be degraded but undergo bioaccumulation through the food chain (Hickey et al., 1989; Kong et al., 1995; Chang, 1996).

Heavy metals can cause dermatological diseases, skin cancer, and cancer of vital organs like the liver, kidney, lung and bladder, cardiovascular disease, diabetes, and anaemia, as well as reproductive, developmental, immunological and neurological affects in the human body (Taiz and Zeiger 1998).

When fish are exposed to elevated levels of metals in a polluted aquatic ecosystem, they tend to take these metals up from their direct environment (Seymore 1994). Heavy metal contamination may have devastating effects on the ecological balance of the recipient environment and the diversity of aquatic organisms (Farombi *et al.* 2007).

Transport of metals in fish occurs through the blood where the ions are usually bound to proteins. The metals are brought into contact with the organs and tissues of the fish and consequently accumulate to a different extent in different organs and tissues of the fish. Most heavy metals released into the environment find their way into the aquatic environment as a result of direct input, atmospheric deposition, and erosion due to rainwater. Therefore, aquatic animals may be exposed to elevated levels of heavy metals due to their wide use for anthropogenic purposes (Kalay and Canli 2000). Heavy metals are non-biodegradable and once they enter the environment, bioconcentration occurs in the fish tissue in the case of aquatic environment, by means of metabolic and biosorption processes (Wicklund-Glynn 1991).

The presence of pollutants have been associated with decreased fertility and other reproductive abnormalities in birds, fish, shellfish and mammals, as well as altered immune function (Colborn *et al.*, 1993). Heavy metals like mercury and cadmium are known to accumulate in marine organisms, and cause rapid genetic changes (Nimmo *et al.* 1978, Nevo *et al.* 1986).

It is also possible that environmental toxicants may increase the susceptibility of aquatic animals to various diseases by interfering with the normal functioning of their immune, reproductive and developmental processes (Couch 1978).

Prolonged exposure to water pollutants even in very low concentrations have been reported to induce morphological, histological and biochemical alterations in the tissues which may critically influence fish quality (Burger and Gochfeld, 2005). It was reported that aquatic organisms showed high capability to accumulate heavy metals (Bu-Olayan and Subrahmanyam, 1998) and was often regarded as an effective bioindicator of the environmental contamination.

According to EPA guidelines (2000), "the BCF (Bioconcentration Factors) is defined as the ratio of chemical concentration in the organism to that in surrounding water. Bioconcentration occurs through uptake and retention of a substance from water only, through gill membranes, or other external body surfaces. In the context of setting exposure criteria it is generally understood that the terms "BCF" and "steady-state BCF"" are synonymous. A steady-state condition occurs when the organism is exposed for a sufficient length of time that the ratio does not change. For this reason, determination of chemical quality of aquatic organisms, particularly the contents of heavy metals is extremely important for human health (Cid *et al.*, 2001; Dural *et al.*, 2007).The studied areas are polluted by different types of industrial, agricultural drainage, domestic waste waters and transfers domestic waste waters and waste from other sources of metal pollution.

The present study was carried out to investigate the accumulation of heavy metals (lead, copper, cadmium and mercury) in the tissues of *Oreochromis niloticus* and to identify any possible histopathological changes caused by the residues of these metals in the selected target organs.

MATERIALS AND METHODS

Sampling

The water samples (n = 48) were obtained from different farms that derived their water supply from some Riv-er Nile ramifications in Egyptian Governorates. One hundred adult freshwater tilapia (*Oreochromis niloticus*) ranging between 100-150 g in weight were collected from 12 Tilapia farms located in 6 Governorates (Kafer Al-Sheikh, Ismailia, Kaliobea, Damiatta, Al-Fayum and Behera) during 2007-2009.

PROCEDURES

Preparation and Analysis of Water Samples

A.P.H.A. (1992) was used for the analysis of water samples. The water samples were preserved by the addition of 1 ml of con-centrated nitric acid per liter until the time of analysis. The water samples were filtered through a 0.45μl membrane filter. The required volume (100 ml) of the filtrate was collected to measure lead, cadmium, mercury and copper levels in water samples by using Air/Acetylene Flame Atomic Absorption Spectrophotometer (UNICAM 696 AA Spectrom-eter). Flameless Atomic Absorption Spectrophotometer equipped with (MHS) mercu-ry hydride system “Cold Vapor Technique” was used for the determination of mercury levels in exam-ined water samples.

Preparation and Analysis of Fish Samples

At laboratory, the fish samples for chemical analysis were washed with deionized water and wrapped separately in acid washed polyethylene bag and stored frozen at -20°C until analysis was carried out.

Procedure (A):

Each sample was represented by one gram of tissues dissected from the gills, liver, kidney and muscles respectively, then placed in a clean screw-capped tube and digested according to the method de-scribed by Finerty *et al.* (1990). The obtained so-lutions were then analyzed by using Air/ Acetylene Flame Atomic Absorption Spectropho-tometer (UNICAM 696 AA

Spectrometer) for de-termination of copper (Cu), lead (Pb), cadmium (Cd) and mercury (Hg) levels in examined samples.

Procedure (B):

The measurement of the mercury concentration in examined fish samples was carried out at minimal temperature where 0.5 g macerated fish tissues were digested accord-ing to the technique described by Diaz *et al.* (1994). 5 ml stannous chloride solution were added to the obtained solutions to reduce mercury to elemental form and then analyzed by using Flameless Atomic Absorption Spectrophotometer equipped with "MHS" mercury hydride system "Cold Vapor Technique".

Histopathological Examination

Tissue specimens from fresh Nile tilapia were taken (gill, muscle, liver, intestine and kidney) and fixed in 10% neutrally buffered formalin. They were processed to obtain five micron thick paraffin sections and then stained with Haematoxylin and Eosin (Bancroft *et al.* 1996) and examined under a light microscope.

Characteristic gross picture of tilapia fish such as: spinal deformity and vertebral malformation (Scoliosis and Lardiosis), excessive mucus layer on the skin and gills (also showing pale, anemic congestion, hemorrhagic as well as necrotic picture) and congestion and hemorrhages in all internal organs, considered severe case. Gross picture of little changes considered moderate, while unapparent gross pictured considered mild or healthy. All samples were confirmed by histopathological examination.

Statistical Analysis

Data were analyzed using Analysis of Variance (ANOVA) and means were separated by Duncan at a probability level of < 0.05 (SAS Institute 2000).

RESULTS

Table 1 show that the mean concentration of copper in water from Tilapia cultures was 0.65 ± 0.01 ppm, while Table 2 show that the mean concentrations of copper in gills, liver, kidney and muscles of Tilapia were 4.8 ± 0.05 , 2.56 ± 0.21, 1.52 ± 0.06 and 2.54 ± 0.05, respectively.

The mean concentration of lead in water from Tilapia cultures was 0.20 ± 0.07 ppm, while the mean concentrations of lead in gills liver, kidney and muscles were 0.483 ± 0.05, 1.523 ± 0.02, 0.155 ± 0.02 and 1.521± 0.02 ppm respectively.

The mean concentration of cadmium in water from Tilapia cultures was 0.04 ± 0.009 ppm, while the mean concentrations of cadmium in gills liver, kidney and muscles were 0.891 ± 0.05 , 1.523 ± 0.02, 0.212 ± 0.02 and 1.21 ± 0.05 ppm, respectively. The mean concentration of mercury in water from Tilapia cultures was 0.07 ± 0.009 ppm, while the mean concentrations of mercury in gills liver, kidney and muscles were 0.04 ± 0.002, 0.055 ± 0.003, 0.020 ± 0.005 and.3.50 ± 0.22 ppm, respectively.

The histopathology of different Tilapia tissues revealed that there are several histopathological changes in different Tilapia organs (gills, muscles, liver, kidney and intestine) as shown in Figure $1\text{-}_{1\text{-}10}$.

Gills showed hyperplasia, proliferation of lamellar epithelium, subepithelial edema and congestion of blood spaces (Figure 1-_{1}).In some cases ,gills showed an intense lamellar epithelium lifting and epithelium interstitial edema (Figure $1\text{-}_{2\text{-}3}$). In severe cases gills showed, fusion and focal desquamation of the epithelial lining of the secondary lamellae as seen in Figures 1-_{4}.

Liver showed degeneration of the hepatocytes, haemolysis ,vaculation & necrosis and picnotic nucleus as shown in Figure $1\text{-}_{5\text{-}7}$.

Muscular tissues Several histopathological alterations were seen in the muscles of Tilapia which included degeneration of muscle bundles with aggregations of inflammatory cells between them and some focal areas of necrosis. Also, atrophy and edema of muscle bundles as well as splitting of muscle fibers were seen as in Figure 1-_{8}.

Kidney Degenerative and necrotic changes in the renal tubules with focal areas of necrosis and aggregations of inflammatory cells were seen as in Figure 1-_{9}.

Intestine The pathological findings in the intestine included atrophy in the muscularis, degenerative and necrotic changes in the intestinal mucosa and submucosa with necrotized cells aggregated in the intestinal lumen, edema and atrophy in the submucosa as shown in Figure 1-_{10}.

DISCUSSION

Mean copper concentration in water of Tilapia cultures was 0.65 ± 0.01 ppm and the maximum permis-sible limits recommended by WHO (1984) is 0.05 ppm, while in flesh was 2.54 ± 0.05. The recorded results of copper concentrations in fish were lower than the permissible limits intended by Marine Food Gov-ernment (1972) [20.0 ppm] and Boletin Official del Estado (1991) in Spain [20.0 µg/g] and Schumacher and Domingo (1996).

Table 1 show that the lead concentration in Tilapia tissues exceed the permissible limit recommended by E.Q.S.Q.C. (1993). This result was nearly higher than those reported by Seddek *et al.* (1996) and Marouf and Dawoad (2006), they recorded levels ranged from 0.42 to 0.74. This result was much higher than those recorded by Suppin *et al.,* (2005) and Celik and Oehlenschlager (2007), they recorded levels varied from 0.04 ppm to 76.1 ppb.

High levels of lead may be attributed to the presence of industrial and agricultural discharges, the use of motor boats on the river, and also from mining and smelting operations.

Lead is a non-essential element and high concentrations can occur in aquatic organisms that inhabit systems close to human activities. It is toxic even at low concentrations and has no known function in biochemical processes (Burden *et al.*, 1998). It is known to inhibit active transport mechanisms, involving ATP, to depress cellular oxidation reduction reactions and to inhibit protein synthesis (Waldorn and Stofen 1974). Lead was found to inhibit the impulse conductivity by inhibiting the activities of monoamine oxidase and acetylcholine esterase to cause pathological changes in tissue and organs (Rubio *et al.*, 1991) and to impair the embryonic and larval development of fish species (Dave and Xiu, 1991).

Mean cadmium concentration in water of *Tilapia* cultures was 0.04 ± 0.009 ppm and the maximum permis-sible limits recommended by WHO (1984) is 0.005 ppm, while in flesh was 1.21 ± 0.05. The recorded results of cadmium concentrations in fish were higher than the permissible limits intended by Boletin Official del Estado (1991) in Spain [1.0 µg/g], FAO/ WHO (1992) [0.05 ppm] and Egyptian Organization for Standardization and Quality Control "E.O.S.Q.C".[0.1 mg/ kg]. The BCF were; 38.25 and 30.25 in liver and muscles respectively. This result agree with that obtained by Daoud (1999) who reported that the cadmium concentrations in water and fish were higher than the maximum permissible limits recommended by WHO (1984). The presence of cadmium in fish in Egypt was detected by Seddek (1996) with mean levels of 0.62 ppm in Oreochromis fish and 0.39 ppm in Bagrus Byad fish. Our result was nearly parallel to those reported by Celik and Oehlenschlager (2007) who recorded Cd concentration with levels varied from 0.1 to 0.8 ppm. Cadmium is highly toxic non-essential heavy metal and it does not have a role in biological processes in living organisms. Thus even in low concentration, cadmium could be harmful to living organisms (Burden *et al.* 1998). The value of cadmium accumulation in liver of Tilapia was (1.523 ± 0.02) µg/ g dry weight. High accumulation of cadmium in liver may be due to its strong binding with cystine residues of metallothionein.

The high levels of Cd may be attributed to industrial and mining operations as well as the phosphate fertilizer which is considered the main source of Cd in the environment (Dimari *et al.* 2008).

Mean mercury concentration in water of Tilapia cultures was 0.07 ± 0.009 ppm and the maximum permis-sible limits recommended by WHO (1984) is 0.001 ppm, while in flesh was 3.50 ± 0.22. The recorded results of mercury concentrations in Tilapia tissues were higher than the permissible limits intended by Boletin Official del Estado (1991) in Spain [1.0 µg/g], FAO/WHO (1992) [0.5 p.p.m = 0.5 µg/g] and Egyptian Organization for Standardization and Quality Control (E.O.S.Q.C) (1993) [0.5 mg/ kg = 0.5 µg/g]. These findings coincide with those reported by Daoud *et al.* (1999) and Tantawy (1997).

CONAMA (2005) recommend a maximum concentration of 0.0002 mg Hg/ l in water supplies used for rearing fish species destined for human consumption in Brazil. This value is very similar to those recommended by Malaysia National Water Quality Standards (Doe-Um, 1986). Meanwhile, the most notorious mercury compounds in the environment are monomethyl and dimethyl salt of mercury which are soluble. They are produced from inorganic mercu-ry in sediment by anaerobic bacteria through the action of methyl-cobalamine and intermediate in the synthesis of methane and get into natural wa-ter (Manahan, 1989). The average (88.9%) of total mercury in fish musculature was in the form of methyl mercury (Bishop and Neary 1974) which is lipid soluble and easily absorbed and distributed through biological sys-tem.

This element is one of the most toxic metals, which are introduced into the natural environment by human interferences (Buhl, 1997). Some papers have reported situations where high mercury levels were detected in water, mainly nearby gold extraction locations (Maurice-Bourgoin *et al.* 2000; Dolbec *et al.* 2001) and industrial zones (Kime 1998, Sunderland and Chmura 2000). According to Allen (1994), the exposure of *Orechromis aureus* to 0.5 mg Hg/ l caused a raise in the number of leukocyte and erythrocyte within 24 hours. Gill and Pant (1985) also reported hematological anomalies in *Barbus conchonius* exposed to 0.18 mg Hg/ l in acute test.

It can be noticed that the highest accumulation were observed in the organs mainly implicated in metal metabolism. The concentration of cadmium, lead and copper in tissues was high in the following order; liver> muscles > gills > kidney, while mercury (Hg) concentrations were high in the muscles > liver > gills > kidney. Oladimeji, Offem (1989) noticed that the gills of *O. niloticus* consistently accumulated higher amount of lead as lead nitrate.

Mercury was the most bioaccumulated of all metals studied in the muscles of the *O. niloticus*, while Cu was the least one.

From the results of this study, the concentrations of different metals investigated in the tissues of Tilapia except copper exceed the acceptable levels proposed for human consumption (USEPA 1995).

The severe pathological changes were represented by degenerative as well as necrotic changes of the hepatocytes, beside congestion and hemorrhage. Gills also showed severe degeneration, necrosis and lifting of its epithelial cells and hyper activation of mucous or goblet cells. The kidney showed severe degenerative changes, necrosis, and leucocytic infiltration due to the possible toxic effect of metals. Damages of different organs became severe with increasing concentration of metals in these organs (Figure 4).

The histopathological alterations could have resulted from exposure to heavy metals that lead to respiratory, osmoregulatory and circulatory impairment. These findings were demonstrated by Fernandes *et al.,* (2008). Moreover, Alvarado *et al.* (2006) reported that, the dramatic increase of chloride cells in the gills that produces epithelial thickening of the filament epithelium enhances migration of chloride cells up to the edge of the secondary lamellae and provokes the hypertrophy and fusion of secondary lamellae. These could be considered as unspecific biomarker responses of heavy metals exposure and disturbed health of fish. In severe cases gills showed, fusion and focal desquamation of the epithelial lining of the secondary lamellae.

According to Mallatt (1985), the edema of the gill epithelium is one of the main structural changes caused by the exposure to heavy metals. Our results show this lesion of heavy metals exposure which may be attributed to metal exposure or are due to other causes in spite of the increasing levels of Pb, Cd and Hg in the water.

These alterations have been reported for other species exposed to heavy metals particularly Cd (Gardner and Yevich 1970; Karlsson-Norrgren *et al.* 1985; Pratap and Wendelaar Bonga 1993; Thophon *et al.* 2003) and sometimes referred as a first sign of pathology (Thophon *et al.* 2003). Cellular proliferation in the gill epithelium is also observed in fish exposed to different pollutants as described by Gardner and Yevich 1970; Arellano *et al.* 2000 and Thophon *et al.*(2003). Lifting, swelling, and hyperplasia of the gill epithelium could serve as a defense function, as these alterations increase the distance across which waterborne irritants must diffuse to reach the bloodstream. Lamellar fusion could be protective once it reduces the amount of vulnerable gill surface area (Mallatt 1985). However, branchial responses that serve to slow entry of toxicants have the undesirable side effect of impairing gas exchange. This was described by Benson *et al.,* (1987) who observed a fall in respiratory function of *Notemigonus crysoleucas* exposed to Cd.

The liver showed degeneration of the hepatocytes, , haemolysis ,vaculation & necrosis and picnotic nucleus. These findings were apparent as the liver considered the organ of detoxification, excretion and binding proteins such as metallothionein (MTs). (De Smet and Blust 2001). Similar results were observed by van Dyk (2003) and Mela *et al.* (2007). Liver of fish is sensitive to environmental contaminants because many contaminants tend to accumulate in the liver and exposing it to a much higher levels than in the environment, or in other organs (Heath 1995).

Pandey *et al.*, (1994) described the alterations in liver and intestine of *Liza parsia* exposed to Hg Cl_2 (0.2 mg Hg/l) for 15 days. Similarly, Oliveira Ribeiro *et al.* (2002) reported serious injuries in gills and olfactory epithelium of *Salvelinus alpinus* exposed to 0.15 mg Hg/l.

Similar alterations in muscles and kidney of tilapia were observed in several species of fish exposed to heavy metals and these alterations were described by Oliveira Ribeiro *et al.* (2002), Jiraungkoorskul *et al.* (2003), Thophon *et al.* (2003) and Gupta and Srivastava (2006).

The result indicates that the heavy metal contamination might be affecting the aquatic life of the fresh water fish. Hence, a scientific method of detoxification is essential to improve the health of these economic losses of fish in any stressed environmental conditions. However, the high concentrations of the analyzed metals in the whole body tissues investigated could be due to the storage role played by these tissues.

Fish contaminated by heavy metals might suffer pathological alterations, with consequent inhibition of metabolic processes, hematological changes, and decline in fertility and survival.

Table 5.1: Heavy Metal Concentrations in Water from Nile Tilapia Farms

Metal	In water samples (μg/L)			Occurrence%
	Min.	Max.	Mean ± SE	
Copper	0.044	0.887	0.65±0.01	35%
Lead	0.04	0.29	0.20±0.07	82%
Cadmium	0.001	0.082	0.04±0.009	72%
Mercury	0.01	0.11	0.07±0.009	12%

Table 5.2: Concentrations of metals in fresh Nile tilapia tissues (μg/ g dry weight mass).

Metal	Copper	Lead	Cadmium	Mercury
Tissue				
Gills				
Mean	4.8±0.005	0.483±0.05	0.891±0.05	0.04±0.002
Min	1.32	0.02	0.11	0.002
Max	6.22	1.21	1.82	0.24
Liver				
Mean	2.56±0.21	1.523±0.02	1.523±0.02	0.055±0.003
Min	1.22	0.01	0.20	0.001
Max	3.55	3.20	2.43	0.72
Kidney				
Mean	1.52±0.06	0.155±0.002	0.212±0.02	0.020±0.005
Min	0.21	0.11	0.09	0.002
Max	2.42	2.02	0.89	0.12
Muscles				
Mean	2.54±0.05	1.521±0.02	1.21±0.005	3.50±0.22
Min	0.21	0.892	0.55	1.32
Max	2.8	1.00	1.780	5.24

It could be deduced from this study that fish has the tendency to accumulate heavy metals in a polluted environment. Since virtually all metals investigated were found in higher concentration, so government should intact laws that will ensure that industries make use of standard waste treatment plants for the treatment of their wastes before they are being discharged into water bodies.

Table 5.3: Permissible Limits of Various Metals

Metal	Permissible	Country and reference
Copper	1.00 ppm 20.0 ppm 20.0 mg/g	WHO (1984) South Africa (Foodstuffs, cosmetics and disinfectants, Act. No. 54 of 1972) Spain: Boletin Official cel Estado (1991)
Lead	0.05 ppm 0.1 mg/kg 0.5 ppm 5.0 mg/g	WHO (1984) Egypt "E.O.S.Q.C. (1993) FAO/WHO (1992) Spain: Boletin Official cel Estado (1991)
Cadmium	0.005 ppm 0.05 ppm 0.1 mg/kg 1.0 pg/g	WHO (1984) FAO/WHO (1992) Egypt "E.O.S.Q.C. (1993) Spain: Boletin Official cel Estado (1991)
Mercury	0.01 ppm 0.5 mg/kg 0.5 ppm 1.0 mg/g	WHO (1984) Egypt "E.O.S.Q.C. (1993) FAO/WHo (1992) Spain: Boletin Official cel Estado (1991), Schuhmacher and Domingo (1996)

Table 5.4: Heavy Metal Concentrations in Water of Tilapia Farms in Governorates

H.metal	KAlSheikh	Ismailia		Sharkia	Kaliobea	Damiatta	Behera WHO
Cu	0.016	0.887	0.01	0.2	0.31	0.123	0.05
Pb	0.26	0.27	0.29	0.11	0.18	0.01	0.05
Cd	0.07	0.046	0.07	0.05	0.01	0.11	0.001
Hg	0.03	0.04	0.04	0.08	0.001	0.005	0.005
					Histopathological severity %:		
Severe	20	15		8	10	5	10
							Moderate &
Mild	40	35		20	20	30	20

Histopathological alterations of 70% fish samples (20%, 30% and 20%) were severe, moderate and mild lessions, respectively.

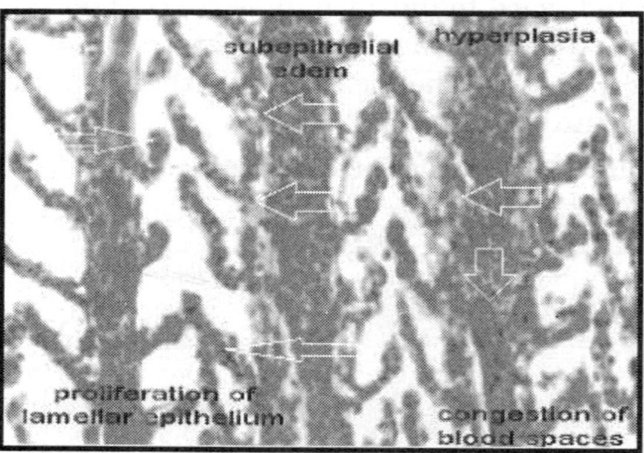

Fig. 5.1-1: Histopathlogical changes of tilapia gill: Hyperplasia, proliferation, subepithelial edema and congestion of blood spaces. (X200).

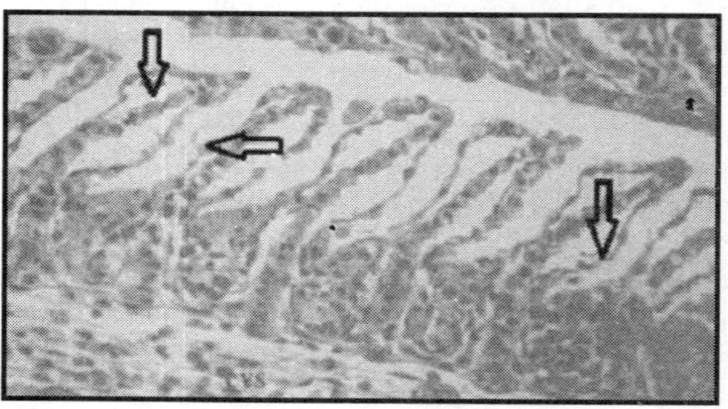

A

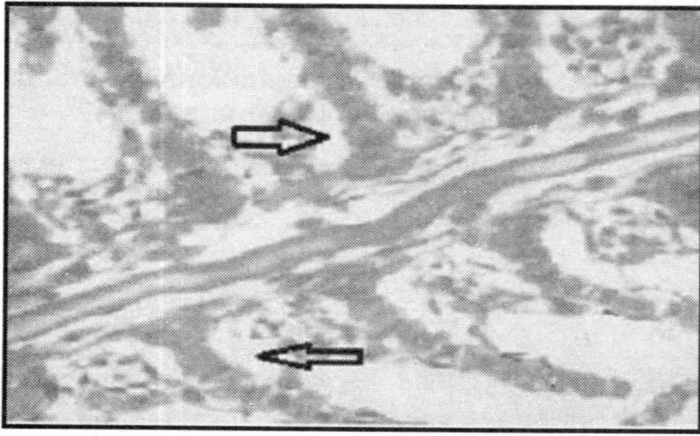

B

Fig. 5.1-2: Gills (left), showing an intense lamellar epithelium lifting and proliferation; (right), lamellar axisvasodilatation and epithelium interstitial edema (H & E 400 X).

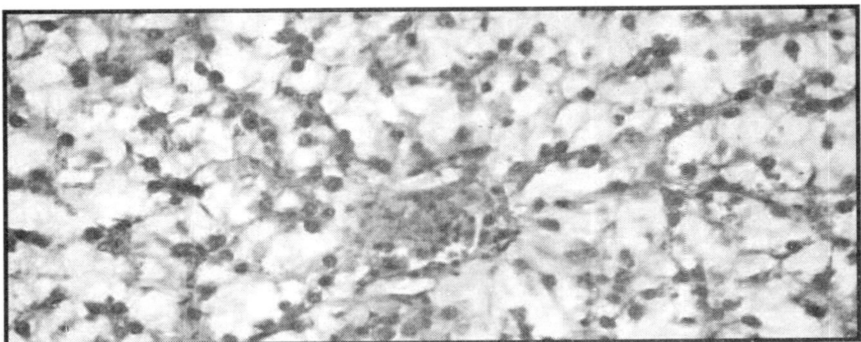

Fig. 5.1-3: Liver of Tilapia nilotica fish showed degeneration of the hepatocytes, intravascular haemolysis in blood vessels, , with diffuse hepatocellular vacuolation (H & E 200 X).

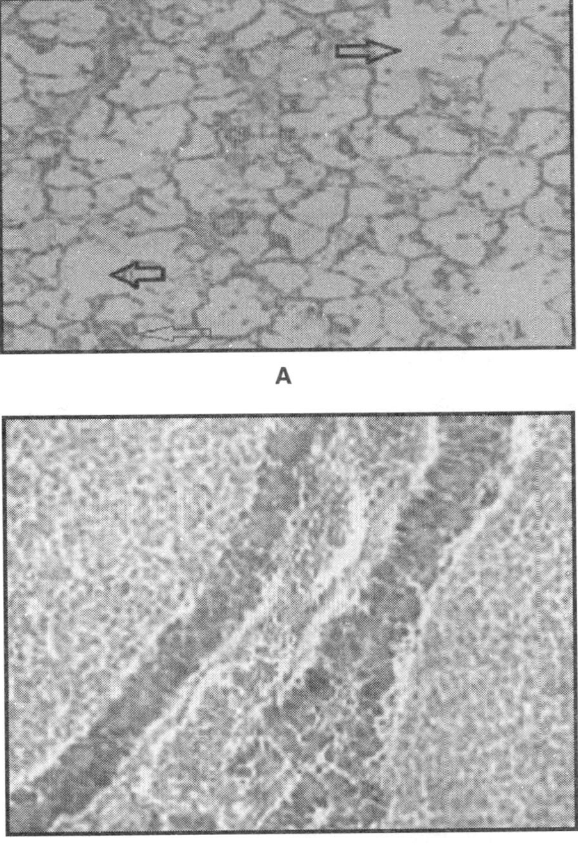

A

B

Fig. 5.1_4 (A-B): Tilapia's liver (left): showing hepatocellular vacuolation, necrosis and picnotic (arrow); (right): hemolysis (H & E 400 X).

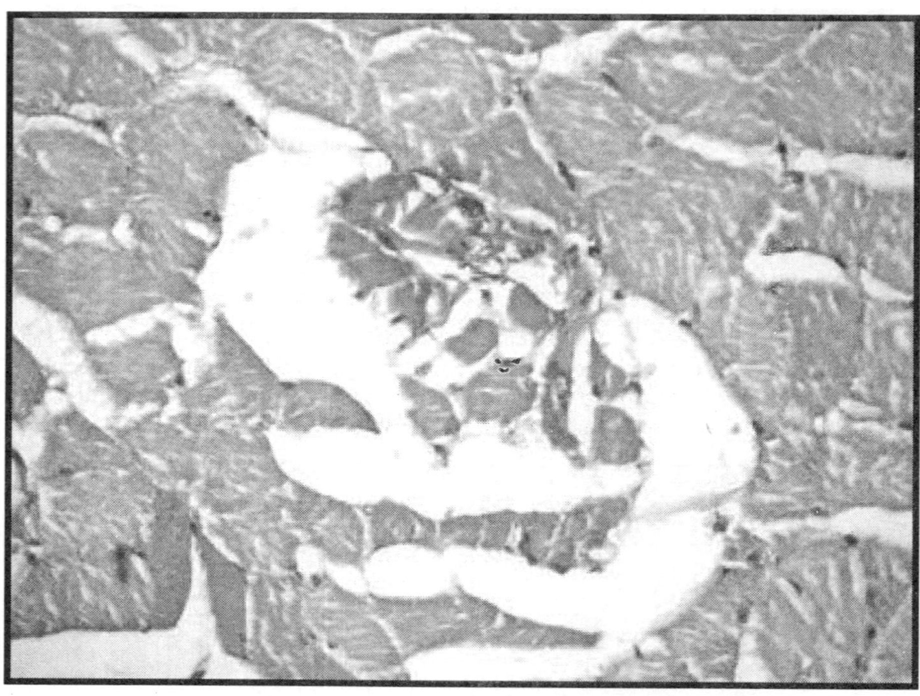

Fig. 5.1-5: Degeneration in muscle bundles with focal area of necrosis and leucocytic infiltration (X400).

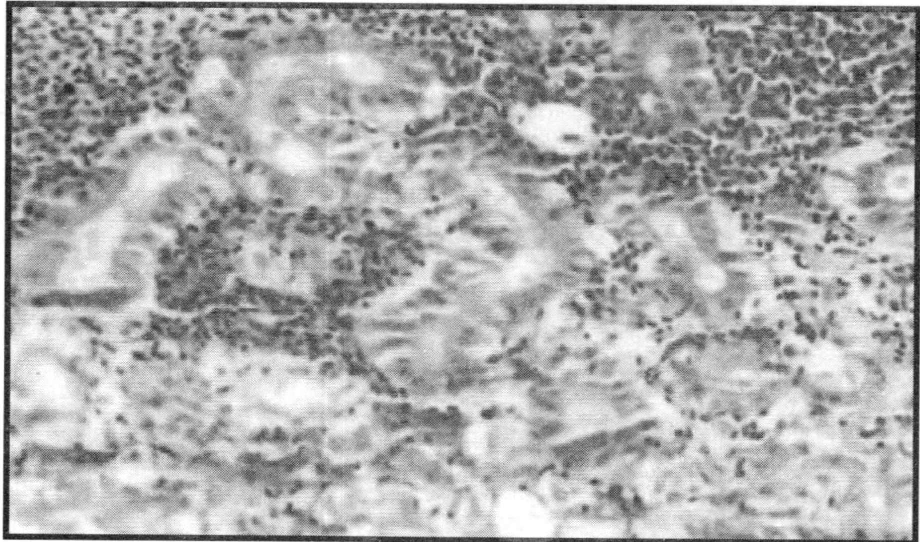

Fig. 5.1-6: Severe degenerative and necrotic changes in the renal tubules with focal areas of necrosis and infiltration & aggregations of inflammatory cells (X200).

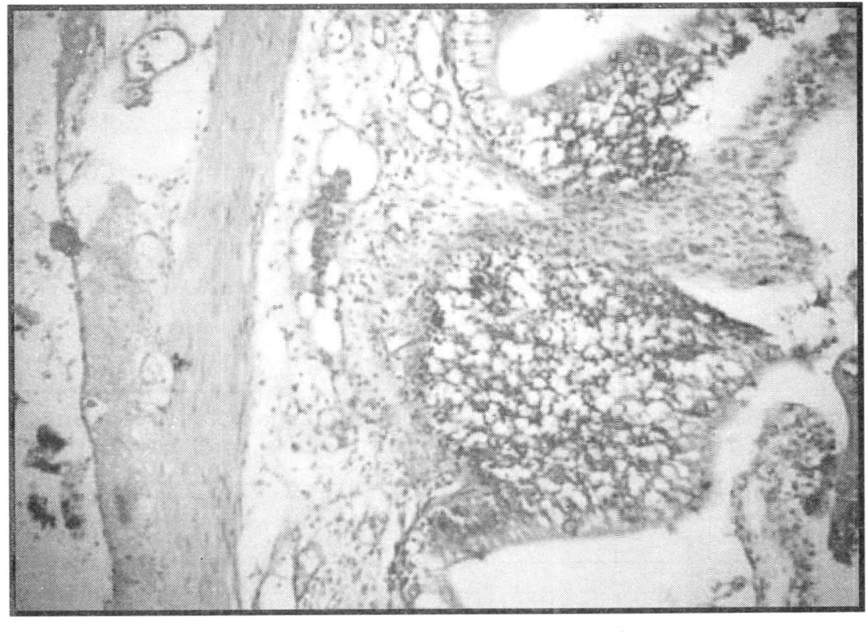

A

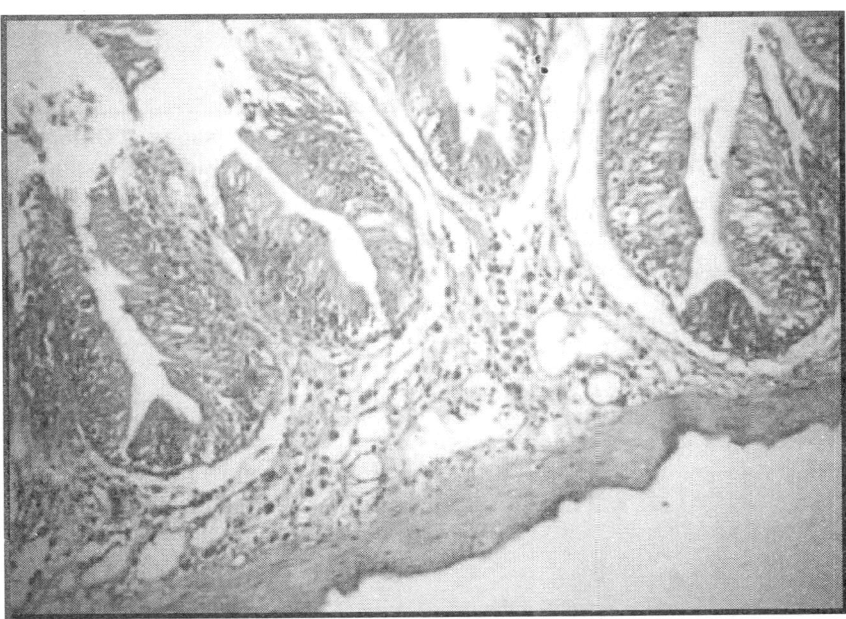

B

Fig. 5.1-7 (A-B): Degeneration, haemorrhage in the submucosa and aggregations of inflammatory cells in the mucosa and submucosa of intestine (X400).

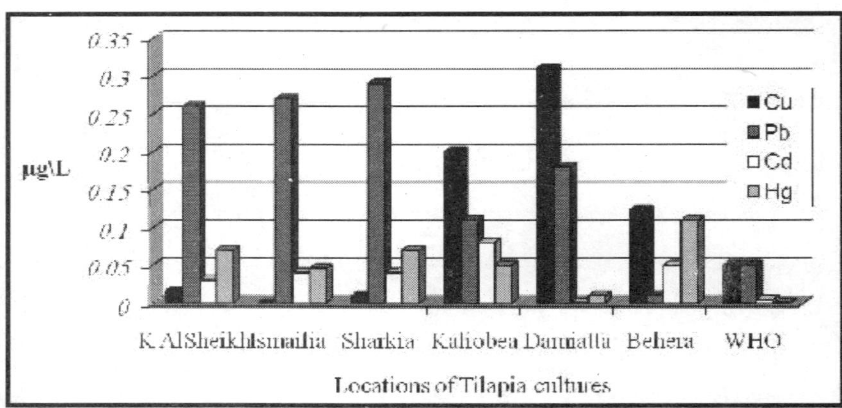

Fig. 5.2: Mean concentrations of Cu, Pb, Cd and Hg in water of fish farms in different Governorates and the permissible limits according WHO (µg/l).

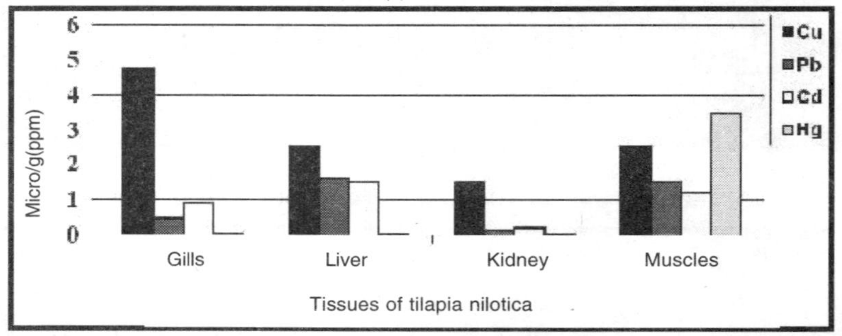

Fig. 5.3: Mean bioaccumulations of Cu, Pb, Cd and Hg in tissues of Oreochromis niloticus and the permissible limits according WHO (µg/g dry mass).

Mean residual accumulation of Cu, Pb, Cd and Hg in different organs of fresh Nile tilapia tissues showed severe histopathlogical changes (µg/g dry weight mass) in Governorates.

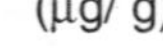

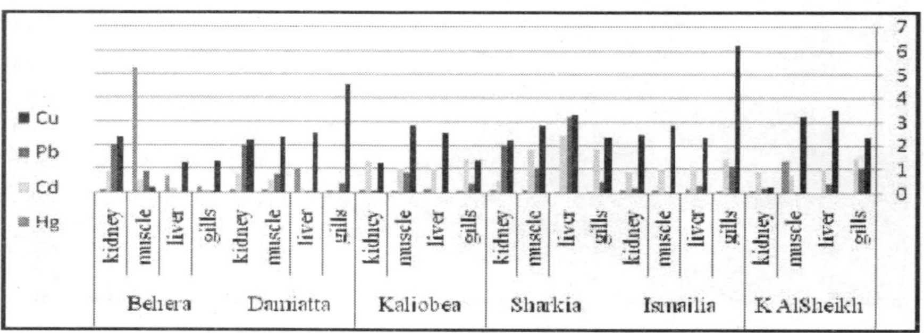

Fig. 5.4: Mean bioaccumulations of Cu, Pb, Cd and Hg in tissues showed severe histopathlogical changes.

ACKNOWLEDGEMENTS

This research was sponsored by Department of Animal Hygiene and Environmental Sanitation (Faculty of Veterinary Medicine, Cairo University). We thank Dr. Kawkb A. Ahmed, Dept. of Pathology, Faculty of Veterinary Medicine, Cairo University for technique assistance.

REFERENCE

Allen P. (1994): Changes in the haematological profile of the cichlid *Oreochromis aureus* (Steindachner) during acute inorganic mercury intoxication. *Comparative Biochemistry and Physiology* 108 C: 117-121.

Alvarado NE, Quesada K, Hylland I, Marigómez, L, Soto M. (2006): Quantitative changes in metallothionein expression in target cell-types in the gills of turbot (Scophthalmus maximus) exposed to Cd, Cu, Zn and after a depuration treatment. Aquatatic Toxicology 77: 64-77.

American Public Health Association (APHA) (1992): Standard methods for the examination of water and wastewater. 18th ed. American Public Health Association, Washington, DC.

Bancroft D, Stevens A, Turner R. 1996. Theory and practice of histological techniques. Fourth edn., Churchill Livingstone, Edinburgh, London, Melbourne.

Benson WH, Baer KN, Stackhouse RA, Watson CF (1987): Influence of cadmium exposure on selected hematological parameters in freshwater teleost, *Notemigonus crysoleucas.* Ecotoxicology and Environmental Safety 13: 92–96.

Bishop JN, Neary BP. (1974): The form of mercury in fresh water fish. Proc. Int. Conf. Transp. Persist. Chem. Aquatic Ecocyst, Ottawa, III-25-III-29.

Boletin Oficial Del Estado (1991): Separates del Boletin Oficial del Estado Espanol No. 195. Gaceta de Madrid, P: 27154. In: Schuhmacher, M. and Domingo, J. L. (1996).

Buhl KJ. (1997): Relative sensitivity of three endangered fishes, Colorado Squaw fish, Bonytail, and Razorback Sucker, to selected metal pollutants. *Ecotoxicology and Environmental Safety* 37: 186-192.

Bu-Olayan, A. H. and Subrahmanyam, M. N. V. (1998): Trace Metal Concentrations in the Crab *Macrophthalmus Depressus* and Sediments on the Kuwait Coast. *Environmental Monitoring and Assessment.* 53(2): 297-304.

Burden VM, Sandheinrich CA, Caldwell A. (1998): Effects of lead on the growth and alpha amino levulinic acid dehydrates activity of juvenile rainbow trout, *Oncorhynchus mykiss.* Environmental Pollution 101: 285-289.

Burger, J. and Gochfeld, M. (2005): Heavy metals in commercial fish in New Jersey. Environ. Res., 99:403–413.Celik U, Oehlenschlager D. 2007. High contents of Cd, Pb, Zn and Cu in popular fishery products sold in Turkish Supermarkets. Food Control 18: 258-261.

Celik U, Oehlenschlager J .2007. High contents of Cd, Pb, Zn and Cu n popular Control, 18(3): 258-261.

Chang L. W. (1996): Toxicology of metals. CRC/ Lewis Publishers, Boca Raton, 253-284.

Cid, B. P.; Boia, C.; Pombo, L. and Rebelo, E. (2001): Determination of trace metals in fish species of the Ria de Aveiro (Portugal) by electrothermal atomic absorption spectrometry. Food Chemistry, 75:93–100.

Colborn, T., F.S. vom Saal, and A.M. Soto. (1993): Developmental effects of endocrine -disrupting chemicals in wildlife and humans. Env. Hlth. Persp. 101(5):378-384.

CONAMA (Technical Assistance on the Development of a Regulatory Framework for Environmental Remediation Projects in Chile) 2005 Resolução no 357, de 17 de março de 2005. Brasília: Ministério do Meio Ambiente. Conselho Nacional do Meio Ambiente. Publicação D.O.U. 18/03/2005. Disponível em: http://www.mma.gov.br/port/conama/res/res05/ res35705.pdf Acesso em: 18/abril/2006.

Couch C, John A. (1978): Diseases, parasites, and toxic responses of commercial penaeid shrimps of the Gulf of Mexico and South Atlantic soasts of North America.

Daoud JR, Amin AM, Abd El-Khalek MM. (1999): Residual analysis of some heavy metals in water and *Oreochromis niloticus* fish from polluted areas. Veterinary Medical Journal (2) 47: 351-365.

Dave G, Xiu R. (1991): Toxicity of mercury, copper, nickel, lead and cobalt to embryos and larval of Zebra fish *Brachydanio rerio*. Archive of Environmental Contamination and Toxicology 21: 126-134.

De Smet H, Blust R. (2001): Stress responses and changes in protein metabolism in carp (*Cyprinus carpio L.*) during cadmium exposure. Ecotoxicology and Environmental Safety 48: 255-62.

Diaz-Ravina M, Baath E, Frostegard A. (1994): Multiple heavy metal tolerance of soil bacterial communities and its measurement by a thymidine incorporation technique. Applied Environmental Microbiology 60: 2238–2247.

Dimari GA, Abdulrahman JC, Garba ST. (2008): Metals concentrations in tissues of *Tilapia gallier, Clarias lazera* and Osteoglossidae caught from Alau Dam, Maiduguri, Borno State, Nigeria. American Journal of Environmental Sciences 4: 373-379.

Doe-um M. (1986): Water quality criteria and standards for Malaysia. Executive Summary. Final Report. Department of Environment, Ministry of Science, Technology and Environment, Malaysia/ Consultant group of water quality, Institute of Advanced Studies, Univ. of Malaya, Kuala Lumpur, Malaysia, 1, V-XII.

Dolbec J, Mergler D, Larribe F, Roulet M, Lebel J, Lucotte M. (2001): Sequential analysis of mercury levels in relation to fish diet of an Amazonian population, Brazil. Science of the Total Environment 271: 87-97.

Dural, M.; Ziya Lugal Göksu, M. and Özak, A.A. (2007): Investigation of heavy metal levels in economically important fish species captured from the Tuzla lagoon. Food Chemistry, 102: 415–421.

Egyptian Organization for Standardization and Quality Control (EOSQC). (1993): Maximum residue lim-its for heavy metals in food. Ministry of Industry. No. 2360/ 1993. PP. 5.

EPA-600/J-78-072. U.S. Fish and Wildlife Service.2000. Fishery Bulletin 76: 1-44. (ERL, GB 283).

FAO/WHO. (1992): Food Monitoring and Assessment Programme, (Assessment of dietary intake of chemical contaminants), WHO, Geneva 5, UNEP, Nairobi. 52. Report of the Third Meeting of the GEMS/Food

Farombi EO, Adelowo OA, Ajimoko YR.(2007): Biomarkers of oxidative stress and heavy metal levels as indicator of environmental pollution in African Catfish (*Clarias gariepinus*) from Nigeria Ogun River. International Journal of Environmental Research and Public Health 4: 158-165.

Fernandes C, Fernandes AF, Ferreira M, Salgado M. (2008): Oxidative stress response in gill and liver of *Liza saliens*, from the Esmoriz-Paramos coastal lagoon, Portugal. Archives of Environmental Contamination and Toxicology 55: 691-700.

Finerty MW, Madden JD, Feagly SE, Grodner RM. (1990): Effect of environs and seasonality on met-al residues in tissues of wild and pond-raised Crayfish in southern Louisiana. Archives of Environmental Contamination and Toxicology 19: 49-55.

Gardner GR, Yevich PP. (1970): Histological and hematological responses of an estuarine teleost to cadmium. Canadian Journal of Fish Research 27: 2185–2196.

Gill TS, Pant JC. (1985): Mercury-induced blood anomalies in the freshwater teleost (*Anguilla rostrata*). Water, Air and Soil Pollution 24: 165-171.

Gupta P, Srivastava N. (2006): Effects of sublethal concentrations of zinc on histological changes and bioaccumulation of zinc by kidney of fish *Channa punctatus* (Bloch). Journal of Environmental Biology 27: 211-215.

Heath AC. (1995): Water pollution and fish physiology. 2nd ed., Lewis Publishers, Boca Raton. pp. 125-140.

Hickey, R. F., Vanderwielen, J., and Switzenbaum, M. S. (1989): The effect of heavy metals on methane production and hydrogen and carbon monoxide levels during bath anaerobic sludge digestion. Water Res. 23, 267-273.

Jiraungkoorskul W, Uptham ES, Kruatrachue M, Sahaphong S, Vichasri-Grams S, Pokethitiyook P. (2003): Biochemical and histopathological effects of glyphosate herbicide on Nile tilapia (*Oreochromis niloticus*). Environmental Toxicology. 18 (4) :260-267.

Kalay, M and Canil, M. (2000): Elimination of essential (Cu, Zn) and non-essential (Cd, Pb) metals from tissues of a freshwater fish *Tilapia zilii*. Turkish J. Zoology. 24, 429-436.

Karlsson-Norrgren L, Runn P, Haux C, Förlin L. (1985): Cadmium-induced changes in gill morphology of zebra fish *Brachydanio rerio* (Hamilton-Buchanan) and rainbow trout *Salmo gairdneri* Richardson. Journal of Fish Biology 27: 81–95.

Kime J. (1998): Endocrine Disruption in Fish. Kluwer, Dordrecht,Academic Publisher,101Plip Drive, Assinippi Park,Norwell,US.

Kong, I. C., Bitton, G., Koopman B., and Jung, K. H., (1995): Heavy metal toxicity testing in environmental samples, *Rev Environ Contam Toxicol*. 142, 119-147.

Manahan SE. 1989. Toxicological chemistry; a guide to toxic substances in chemistry. pp. 256-257. Brooks/Cole Publishing, C.A.

Mallatt J. (1985): Fish gill structural changes induced by toxicants and other irritants: a statistical review. Canadian Journal of Fisheries and Aquatic Sciences 42: 630–648.

Marine Food Gov-ernment Gazette. (1972): (Foodstuffs, Cosmetics, Disinfectants). Regulation No. R 2064. Government Printer, Pretoria. Act. No. 54 of 1972.

Marouf HA, Dawoud AS. (2006): Evaluation of heavy metals content in freshwater Crayfish in Damietta. Journal of Veterinary Medical Association. Egypt. 66(3): 217-225.

Mela MR, Ventura F, Carvalho DF, Pelletier CE, Ribeiro CA. (2007): Effects of dietary methylmercury on liver and kidney histology in the neotropical fish *Hoplias malabaricus*. Ecotoxicology and Environmental Safety 68: 426 - 35.

Maurice-Bourgoin L, Quiroga I, Chincheros J, Courau P.(2000):Mercury distribution in waters of the upper Madeira Rivers and mercury exposure in Riparian Amazonian populations. Science of the Total Environment 260: 73-86.

Nriagu, J. O. and Pacyna, J. M. (1988): Quantitative assessment of worldwide contamination of air, water and soils by trace metals. Nature. **333**, 134-139.

Nevo E, Noy R, Lavie B, Beiles A, Muchtar S. (1986): Genetic diversity and resistance to marine pollution. Biological Journal of the Linnean Society 29: 139-144.

Nimmo DR, Rigby RA, Bahner LH, Sheppard JM. (1978): The acute and chronic effects of cadmium on the estuarine mysid *Mysidopsis bahia*. Bulletin of Environmental Contamination and Toxicology 19: 80–85.

Oladimeji AA, Offem BO. (1989): Toxicity of lead to *Clarias lazera, O. niloticus, Chironomus tantans* and *Benacus* sp. Water, Air and Soil Pollution 44: 191-201.

Oliveira-Ribeiro CA, Belger L, Pelletiter E, Rouleau C. (2002): Histopathological evidence of inorganic mercury and methylmercury toxicity in the arctic charr (*Salvelinus alpinus*). Environmental Research 90: 217-225.

Pandey AK, Mohamed MP, George KC. (1994): Histopathological alterations in liver and intestine of *Liza parsia* (Hamilton-Buchanan) in response to mercury toxicity. Journal of Advanced Zoology 15(1): 18-24.

Pratap HB, Wendelaar Bonga SE. (1993): Effect of ambient and dietary cadmium on pavement cells, chloride cells, and sodium, potassium-ATPase activity in the gills of the freshwater teleost *Oreochromis mossambicus* at normal and high calcium levels in the ambient water. Aquatic Toxicology 26: 133–150.

Rubio R, Tineo P, Torreblance A, Del-Romo J, Mayans JD. (1991): Histological and electron microscopical observations on the effects of lead on gills and midget gland of *Procamarus clarkii.* Toxicology and Environmental Chemistry 31: 347-352.

SAS Institute. (2000):SAS User's Guide: statistics, SAS Institute, Cary, NC.

Schumacher M, Domingo JL. 1996. Concentra-tions of selected elements in oysters (*Crassostrea angulata*) from the Spanish coast. Bulletin of Environmetal Contamination and Toxicology 56: 106-113.

Seddek AS, Salem DA, El-Sawi NM, Zaky ZM. (1996): Cadmium, lead, nickel, copper, manga-nese and flourine levels in River Nile fish. Assiut Veterinary Medical Journal35(68): 95-102.

Seymore T. (1994): Bioaccumulation of metals in *Barbus marequensis* from the Olifants River, Kruger National Park, and lethal levels of Mn to juvenile *Oreochromis mossambicus.* MSc thesis, Rand Afrikaans University, South Africa.

Sunderland EM, Chmura GL. (2000):An inventory of historical mercury emissions in maritime Canada: implications for present and future contamination. *Science of the Total Environment* 256: 39-57.

Suppin D, Zahlbruckner R, Krapfenbauer CC, Hassan I, Hauser C, Smulders F. (2005): Mercury, lead and cadmium content of fresh and canned fish collected from Austrian retail operations. Ernahrung Nutrition 29: 456-460.

Taiz L, Zeiger E. (1998): Plant defenses: surface protectants and secondary metabolites. In: Taiz L and Zeiger E (eds). Plant physiology. Sinauer Associates, Massachusetts. pp. 347-377.

Tantawy EA. (1997): Safety and quality of fishes infested with parasites. PhD thesis (Meat Hygiene), Faculty of Veterinary Medicine, Cairo University, Egypt.

Thophon S, Kruatrachue M, Upatham ES, Pokethitiyook P, Sahaphong S, Jaritkhuan, S. (2003): Histopathological alterations of white seabass, *Lates calcarifer*, in acute and subchronic cadmium exposure. Environmental Pollution 121: 307–320.

U.S. Environmental Protection Agency (USEPA). (1995): National Water Quality Inventory: 1994 Report to Congress. EPA 841-R-95-005. U.S. Environmental Protection Agency, Office of Water, Washington, DC.

van Dyk JC. (2003):Histological changes in the liver of *Oreochromis mossambicus* (Cichlidae) after exposure to cadmium and zinc. MSc thesis, Rand Afrikaans University, South Africa.

Waldorn HA, Stofen S. 1974. Sub-clinical lead poisoning. Academic Press, New York, pp: 1-224.

World Health Organisation (WHO). (1984): Guidelines for drinking water quality. WHO, Geneva, No.111.

Wicklund-Glynn A. (1991): Cd and Zn kinetics fish: studies on water-borne Cd and Zn turnover and intracellular distribution in minnows, *Phoxinus phoxinus*. Pharmacology and Toxicology 69: 485-491.

Zooplankton Composition in Fresh Water Bodies of Aligarh, India

—*Habeeba Ahmad Kabir, India*
—*Saltanat Parveen, India*

INTRODUCTION

Water is the basic and primary need of all vital life processes of animal and plants and it is now well established fact that life first arose in aquatic environment. The fresh water being indispensible and essential element for all living beings, the best known and easily available universal solvent which provides significant transport system, as it carries the various unchanged and essential elements from external medium to living cells. The term '*Plankton*' was given by Victor Hensen in 1887 to designate the heterogeneous assemblage of very minute organisms and finely divided non living matter, which we now call as seston. The term plankton is now restricted to minute organisms including both plants and animals. These organisms have very little power of locomotion and, therefore, they move in the water-body at the mercy of water movements. The individual organism in the plankton community is called a *plankter* or *planktont.*

Plant organisms compose phytoplankton and animal organisms compose zooplankton. Zooplankton are microscopic organisms and many of them feed on algae and bacteria and, in turn, are fed by numerous invertebrates and vertebrates. Zooplankton mediates the transfer of energy from lower to higher trophic levels (Waters, 1977). Thus, zooplankton represent an important link in aquatic food chain and contribute significantly to secondary production in freshwater ecosystem (Sharma, 1998). These animals, found in all kind of waterbodies, are extremely diverse and are represented by nearly all invertebrate phyla. Zooplankton communities respond to a wide variety of disturbances including nutrient loading (Mc.Cauley and Kalff, 1981; Pace, 1986; Dodson, 1992), acidification (Brett, 1989) and sediment input (Cucker, 1997). Zooplankton organisms, therefore, in the field of fisheries have an immense place and significance (Jhingran, 1991). Zooplankton also play an important role as indicator of trophic conditions in both cold temperate and warm tropical waters (Gannon and Stemberger, 1978; Sharma, 1998).Truly planktonic animals are dominated by three major groups, the *Rotifers* and two subclasses of the class Crustacea, the *Cladocera* and *Copepoda. Ostracoda* forms a minor group.

Evaluation of their functional roles within aquatic ecosystem requires a balanced understanding between the mode and timing of growth and utilization of food. Zooplankton communities respond to a wide variety of disturbances including nutrient loading (Mc.Cauley and Kalff, 1981; Pace, 1986; Dodson, 1992), acidification (Brett, 1989) and sediment input (Cucker, 1997). Zooplankton organisms, therefore, in the field of fisheries have an immense place and significance (Jhingran, 1991). Zooplankton also play an important role as indicator of trophic conditions in both cold temperate and warm tropical waters (Gannon and Stemberger, 1978; Sharma, 1998).Truly planktonic animals are dominated by three major groups, the *Rotifers* and two subclasses of the class Crustacea, the *Cladocera* and *Copepoda. Ostracoda* forms a minor group.

Zooplankton also include protozoans and larval forms of many animals. Among protozoans, a number of ciliates and flagellates are common to the zooplankton. Ciliates dominate in very shallow waterbodies in the deeper strata of nearly or completely anaereobic hypolimnion. They can move much more rapidly than other protozoans and contribute significantly to their greater feeding rates. Most of the ciliates are holozoic and feed on bacteria, algae, detritus and other protozoans. A few are carnivore and feed on small metazoans. These protozoans can serve as functional link in freshwater planktonic food chains. They utilize bacteria and very small particulate detritus.

Important contributions on zooplankton studies are those of Khan et al (1966a), Khan et al (1974), Pennak (1978), Khan et al (1978), Ali et al., (1979), Stenson (1982), Dumont and Pensart (1983), Greshon (1983), Gunter (1983), Malone and Mc Queen (1983), Pejler (1983), Shiel and Koste (1983), Sladecek (1983), Evans (1984), Fernando and Kanduru (1984), Stevenson (1984), Khan et al (1985), Murtaugh (1985), Khan et al (1986), Outridge (1987), Sharma and Micheal (1987), Berzins and Pejler (1989), Sharma and Pudani (1992), Kellar *et al.* (1993), Sharma (1978, 1981, 1983, 1991, 1998, 2001, 2001 a & 2001 b), Sharma and Wanswett (1999), Gaur et. al (1999), Sharma and Sharma (1999), Khan et al (1999), Khan and Alam (1999), Gaur et al (2001), Alam et. al (2002), Alam et. al (2002a), Khan et al (2002), Hosmani (2002), Sharma and Lyngdoh (2003), Sharma and Lyngskor (2003), Sharma (2003), Francis *et al.* (2003), Parveen (2003), Pluiraite (2003), Murugesan *et al.* (2003), Singh and Das (2003 a), Jeelani *et al.* (2004), Mishra (2004), Saranan (2005), Brucet *et al.* (2006), Rao *et al.*(2006), Mukhopadhyay *et al.* (2007), Ansari *et al.* (2007) and Pradhan *et al.* (2007).

Table 6.1 : Zooplankton population observed in Derelict Water Body of Aligarh

Cladocera	Copepoda	Rotifera	Ostracoda
Daphnia pulex	Cyclops viridis	Brachionus calyciflorus	
D. carinata	Mesocyclops hyalinus	B. bidentata	Cypridopsis
D. similis	M. leuckarti	B. havanaensis	
D. rosea	Diaptomus sp.	B. quadridentata	
D. galeata D. lumholtzi	Cletocamptus sp.	B. angularis	
Diaphanosoma sp.		B. urceolaris	
Ceriodaphnia reticulata		B. plicatilis	
Simocephalus sp.		Keratella tropica	
Bosmina sp.		K. quadrata	
Moina micrura		K. serrulata	
Leptodora sp.		K. procurva	
		Asplanchna priodonta	
		Filinia longiseta	
		F. terminalis	
		Notholca sp.	
		Lecane sp.	
		Epiphanes senta	
		Monostyla	
		Rotaria	
		Conochilus unicornis	
		Hexarthra sp.	
		Polyarthra sp.	
		Testudinella sp.	

Zooplankton composition identified in derelict water body is constituted by cladocera, copepoda, ostracoda and rotifera (Table-1). In total 41 species of zooplankton were recorded from two ponds. Of these 23 species to rotifer, 12 species of cladocera, 5 species of copepod and 1 species of ostracoda (table-1).

They form the most important animal group of aquatic environment constituting a major portion of the diet of fish and other aquatic organisms.

Rotifera is one of the most dominating groups among all other group followed by cladocera, copepoda and ostracoda respectively in the water bodies of Aligarh region. Maximum cladoceran density during winter was reported by Khan and Siddiqui (1974), whereas Khan *et al.* (1986) have reported higher numerical strength of cladocera during summer. Their occurrence in these ponds have showed wide fluctuations in their existence providing evidences of favourable and unfavourable conditions due to incoming sewage effluents and other surface run off from the catchment areas during the period of investigation. Besides, various species of this group are regarded as useful indicators of water quality. Further, the members of this group are also increasingly employed in environmental toxicological endeavors and bio-assay experiments.

Cladocera

Cladocera comprise a group of primitive and usually microscopic crustaceans to which the general name of Entomostraca was formerly applied (Sharma, 2001). The members of the group are also commonly termed as "water fleas" because of their characteristic jerky swimming action during locomotion. Cladocerans inhabit almost all sorts of freshwater biotopes and frequently occur in the littoral, limnetic, benthic, interstitial and ground water environs. All have a distinct head and the body is covered by a bivalve cuticular carapace. The apparent body segmentation is lost. Cladocerans are important components of microfaunal food web and an integral link in aquatic food chains in freshwater. Gulati (1978) stated that if the food supply is high or increasingly up for stretch of time, cladocera build up in high number and biomass to dominate lake zooplankton. Till now, over 10,000 species of copepods are known. A vast majority of copepods are separable into three groups, the Calanoids, Cyclopoids and Harpacticoids. Accurate identification is based largely on the morphological details of appendages. The body consists of the anterior metasome, representing antennal and mouth parts, and the thorax with six pair of swimming legs. As to their importance, copepods are significant primary and secondary consumers in aquatic food chains. Their grazing contributes to the transfer of algal primary production to higher trophic levels. The calanoid copepods are almost exclusively planktonic and cyclopoid copepods are primary littoral benthic species (Sharma, 2001). The harpacticoid copepods are almost exclusively littoral inhabiting macrovegetation, mosses in particular, and the littoral sediments (Sharma, 2001).

Significant work has been done on these organisms in the past by Smirnov (1976), Pennak (1978), Chiang and Du (1979), Wetzel (1983), Fernando and Kanduru (1984), Sharma and Michael (1987), Michael and Sharma (1988), Sharma and Sharma (1990), Sharma (1991 & 2001), Dumont (1994), Shiel (1995), Ingram *et al.* (1997), Olesan (1998), Sinha and Khan (1998) and Negra *et al.* (1999). Individual species density revealed significant differences among different ponds.

Cladocera is represented by species of *Daphnia, Diaphanosoma, Ceriodaphnia, Simocephalus, leptodora sp., Bosmina* and *Moina.*

***Daphnia pulex*:**

Anterior margin of head is broadly rounded, sometimes almost a straight line, normal to body axis, in lateral view (Edmondson, 1959).

Daphnia similis :

It has a long shell spine (Edmondson, 1959).

***Daphnia carinata* :**

Daphnia carinata is a species of remarkable variations having eight different morphological varieties (Sars, 1914).

***Daphnia lumholtzi*:**

Spinulation extends over slightly more than ½ ventral margin of valve (Edmondson, 1959).

***Daphnia rosea*:**

Its shell spine is slender and weak. This species frequently bears a low rounded crest on the dorsal margin of the head but never produced into helmet (Edmondson, 1959).

***Daphnia galeata*:**

It's head is produced anteriorly into a broad helmet. It may be sharply or bluntly pointed, of various shapes (Edmondson, 1959).

***Diaphanosoma sp.*:**

Ocellus is absent (Edmondson, 1959).

***Ceriodaphina reticulata*:**

Body is rounded to oval. It is usually terminating posteriorly into a sharp dorsal angle or short spine. Head is small and depressed. It is limnetic in nature (Sharma, 2001).

***Simocephalous sp.*:**

Body is large and quadrate. Head and rostrum are small. Ocellus rhomboidal, rounded or elongated. Postabdomen is large and broad (Sharma, 2001).

***Bosmina sp.*:**

Antennules are almost parallel to each other, curving backward. Post abdomen is almost quadrate, anus is terminal, oral denticles small and inconspicuous (Sharma, 2001).

***Moina micrura*:**

Body is thick and heavy. Antennules large, movable and arising from flat ventral surface of head. It is commonly found in muddy pools and eutrophic ponds (Sharma, 2001).

Leptodora sp.:

This remarkable, transparent form is the largest cladocera, female reaching a lenth of 18 mm (Edmondson, 1959).

Copepoda

Copepods are very ancient arthropods and the diminutive relatives of crabs and shrimps. In terms of their size diversity and abundance they are often called "water fleas" (Reddy, 2001). Some species disappeared under unfavorable conditions and reappeared when the conditions became favorable. Copepods have been reported to be good indicators of water quality (Khan and Rao, 1981). Vast literature exists on the diversity of copepods like those of Ansari *et al.* (2007 a) etc. Vast literature exists on the diversity of copepods like those of Rajendran (1973), Mamaril and Fernando (1978), Fernando (1980), Swar and Fernando (1980), Dussert and Fernando (1985), Hazarika and Dutta (1988), Reddy (1994 & 2001), Nayer *et al.* (1999), Pathak and Mudgal (2002), Prakash *et al.* (2002), Sharma and Lynghdoh (2003), Sharma and Lyngoskar (2003), Jeelani *et al.* (2004), Surkad (2004), Menzar *et al.* (2005), Rao *et al.* (2006) and Ansari *et al.* (2007 a) etc.

Copepods were represented by *Cyclops viridis, Mesocyclops hyalinus, Mesocyclops leuckarti, Diaptomus sp.* and *Cletocamptus sp.*

Cyclops viridis :

Caudal setae are four in number and unequal in length. Innermost terminal caudal setae much longer than ramus. (Edmondson, 1959).

Mesocyclops hyalinus :

Inner terminal spine of endopod of leg 4 shorter than terminal segment of endopod (Edmondson, 1959).

Mesocylops leuckarti :

Inner spine of second segment of leg 5 shorter than terminal seta (Edmondson, 1959).

Diaptomus sp. :

Terminal caudal setae are four in number and more or less equal in length (Edmondson, 1959).

Cletocamptus sp. :

Exopod of fifth leg is separated from base by only a notch or gap (Edmondson, 1959).

Rotifera

Rotifera is one of the oldest groups and a minor phylum of invertebrates, include animals commonly termed as "Wheel Animalcules" because of their characteristic "wheel organ" or "corona" (Sharma, 2001). They depict cyclomorphosis and exhibit different ecotypes (Khan and Alam, 1999). Rotifera is a minor phylum but form a major group of zooplankton. They are commonly called as "wheel animalcules" because of their characteristics wheel organ or corona that bear close resemblance to a pair of revolving wheels (Edmondson, 1959). About three quarter of the rotifers are sessile and associated with littoral substrates. The rotifers exhibit a very wide range of morphological variations and adaptations. The body shape tends to be elongated and regions of head, trunk and foot usually are distinguishable. The cuticle is thin and flexible but in some rotifers it is thickened and more rigid and is termed as **Lorica**. The anterior end or corona of rotifers is ciliated. In some species, the periphery is also ciliated as well. The movement of the cilia functions both in locomotion, especially among planktonic forms, and in movement of food particles towards the mouth. Mouth is variously located but, generally, anterior. Most rotifers, both sessile and planktonic, are herbivorous. Some are carnivorous too. They form essential food source for vertebrate and invertebrate predators. They also serve as valuable indicators of trophic conditions of water (Sladecek, 1983). Rotifers play an important role as grazers, suspension feeders and predators in the zooplankton community. Important publications relating to rotifers are those of Donner (1965), Ruttner-Kolisko (1974), Pontin (1978), Pennak (1978), Sladecek (1983), Wallace and Snell (1991), Sharma (1991, 1995, 1996, 1998, 2000 & 2001), Shiel (1995), De Smet (1995 and 1996), De Smet and Purriot (1996) and Melone *et al.* (1998).

Rotifers are represented by species of *Brachionus, Keratella, Notholca, Filinia, Testudinella, lecane sp., Monostyla, Rotaria, Polyarthra, Conochilus, Hexarthra, Epiphanes* and *Asplanchna.*

Brachionus calyciflorus:

Anterior occipital margin with four broad based spines, median occipital spines distinctly longer than laterals. (Sharma, 1998 a).

Brachionus bidentata :

Anterior margin with occipital spines, lateral and medians longer than intermediate occipital spines (Sharma, 1998 a).

Brachionus havanaensis:

Foot annulated, retractile with in body (Edmondson, 1959).

Brachionus quadridentata :

Anterior margin is with six occipital spines, median spines longest and ventrally curved, laterals are longer than intermediates. Postero – lateral spines well developed (Sharma, 1998 a).

Brachionus angularis :

Anterior margin is with two median occipital spines. Posterior spines lacking (Sharma, 1998 a).

Brachionus urceolaris :

Anterior margin is with six occipital spines, median longest and laterals and intermediates are of almost equal length (Sharma, 1998 a).

***Brachionus plicatilis* :**

Anterior margin with six occipital spines, almost equal in length and broad based (Sharma, 1998 a).

***Keratella tropica* :**

Six anterior occipital spines are present, median occipital spines are longest, pointed and out curved. Posterior spines unequal and variable in length, the right spine generally longer than the left, the left posterior spine much reduced in some specimen (Sharma, 1998 a).

***Keratella quadrata* :**

Six anterior occipital spines are present, median spines longest and curved (Sharma, 1998 a).

***Keratella serrulata* :**

Lorica is divided in dorsal and ventral plate. Occipital margin is with 4 spines. The median ones are curved. Posterior spines absent sometimes present (Sharma, 1998 a).

***Keratella procurva* :**

Six anterior occipital spines, median spines longest and curved outwards (Sharma, 1998 a).

***Asplanchna priodonta* :**

Body is illoricate, transparent, polymorphic and with thin cuticle, body shape sacciform, bell shaped or with humps or projections. Foot absent. Corona comprised of a broken single ring of cilia (Sharma, 1998 a).

***Polyarthra sp.*:**

Body is illoricate and slightly flattened dorsoventrally. Corona is with a circumapical band of cilia and two cylindrical ciliated antennae (Sharma, 1998 a).

***Filinia longiseta* :**

Body is thin, barrel shaped and with two long movable antero lateral setae and one long immovable posterior seta usually folded ventrally (Sharma, 1998 a).

***Filinia terminalis* :**

Body is thin, cylindrical and with two movable antero – lateral setae and one immovable posterior seta (Sharma, 1998 a).

***Notholca sp.*:**

Its lorica is oval to elongate and spindle shaped, with six occipital spines. Dorsal plate is with longitudinal striations. Foot is absent. It is planktonic or semi - planktonic in nature (Sharma, 2001).

***Epiphanes senta* :**

Foot is with short toes. Corona with groups of large cilia. Body is pyriform. This species is planktonic or semi planktonic in nature (Sharma, 2001).

***Conochilus unicornis* :**

These forms are colonial, with 5 – 25 individuals in each colony bounded by a gelatinous case. Body is vase shaped, foot contractile and almost as long as the body in extended form (Sharma, 1998 a).

***Hexarthra sp.* :**

Body is conical with six arm like appendages and pinnate bristles at their tips. Corona wavy, with double band of cilia and with or without ventral lip (Sharma, 1998 a).

***Testudinella sp.* :**

Body is loricate and circular, elliptical, oval or vase shaped and is more or less compressed. Foot opening is ventral, located near middle or in the posterior half or posterior end of lorica. Foot is annulated and terminates with a band of cilia. Corona is with a circumapical band of cilia (Sharma, 1998 a).

Lecane sp.:

Foot projects through hole in ventral plate near posterior end (Edmondson, 1959).

Monostyla sp.:

With 1 toe which may be split toward distal end (Edmondson, 1959).

Rotaria:

Eyes if present, in rostrum; may be absent, viviparous (Edmondson, 1959).

Ostracoda

They inhabit all types of substrates, both in standing and running waters, including rooted vegetation, algal mats, debris, mud, sand and rubble. Superficially, the members of the subclass Ostracoda resemble miniature mussels and, therefore, "*mussel shrimps*" is an old European vernacular name (Edmondson, 1959). Most of the fresh water ostracods are bottom dwellers, although some appear occasionally in plankton samples. One truly planktonic species is *Cypris sp.* (Cole, 1983). Ostracods are small bivalve crustaceans which are found in both freshwater and marine environments. They are all free living with the exception of some commensal forms. They have received much less attention than the cladocerans and copepods (Pennak, 1978). They inhabit a wide variety of environments and found almost every where in all types of freshwaters, like lakes, ponds, swamps, cave water and even heavily polluted areas etc. Ostracoda is represented by only *cypris* sp.

Cypris sp.:

Second antenna with penultunate segment individual (Edmondson, 1959).

REFERENCES

Alam, A. Khan, A. A., Parveen, S. and Untoo, S. A. (2002) - Morphological variations in a Branchionid Rotifier, *Brachionus bidentatus* (Anderson). In: *Wetlands Conservation and Management* (Ed. B.B. Hosetti). Pointer Publishers Jaipur, (Raj.). India, 142-150.

Alam, A. Khan, A. A., Parveen, S. and Untoo, S.A (2002a) - *Asplanchna* Induced Phenotypic plasticity in *Brachionus calyciflorus* and its adaptive significance: A laboratory approach. *In: Ecology and Ethology of aquatic Biota* (Ed. A. Kumar). Daya Publishing House, Delhi, India, 294-298.

Ali, M. and Khan, A.A. (1979) - Limnological studies on sewage fed pond of Aligarh. *Science & Environment,* **10** (2): 1985-1991.

Ansari, S., Raja, W. and Khan, A. A. (2007) – Phytoplankton population and it Relation with Physicochemical Parameters of two fresh water Bodies of Aligarh Region. *National symposium on Ecosystem health and Fish for tomorrow.* Inland Fish Soc. India and Cent. Inland Fish Res. Inst., Barrackpore, 14th – 16th December, 2007.

Ansari, S., Raja, W. and Khan, A. A. (2007 a) – Zooplankton diversity in Freshwater Bodies of Aligarh Region. *Proceedings of DAE – BARNS. National Symposium on Limnology. NSL – 07.* February 19 – 21, Udaipur (Raj.) pp – 170 – 175.

Berzins, Brno and Pejler, Birger (1989) - Rotifer occurrence in relation to temperature. *Hydrobiologia,* **176** (1-3): 223-231.

Brett, M.T. (1989) - Zooplankton communities and acidification process: A review. *Water, Air and Soil Pollution,* **44**: 387 414.

Brucet, Sandra., Boix-Dani, Lopez – flora, Rocie., Badosa, Anna and Quitana, Xavier D. (2006) – Size and species diversity of Zooplankton communities in fluctuating Mediterranean salt marshes. *Estuarine, Coastal and Shelf Science.* Vol. **67**, Issue 3, April 2006, Pages 424-432.

Chiang, S.C. and Du, N.S. (1979) - Freshwater Cladocera: Fauna Sinica, 6, *Crustacea.* Academia sinica, science press, Peking. 297pp.

Cole, G.A. (1983) - *Textbook of Limnology.* (3rd ed.). The C.V. Mosby Company, London, 401 pp.

Cuker, B.E. (1997) - Field experiment on the influence of suspended clay and P on the plankton of a small lake. *Limnol. Oceanogr.,* **32** : 840-847.

De Smet, W.H. (1995) - Rotifera. 3- The Notommatidae and Scaridiidae. In: *Guide to the Identification of Micro-invertebrates of Continental Waters of the World.* Vol. **8** (Eds. H.J. Dumont and T. Nogrady). SPB Academic Publishers, Amsterdam, The Netherlands.

De Smet, W.H. (1996) - Rotifera. 4- The Proalidae (Monogononta). In: *Guide to the Identification of Micro-invertebrates of Continental Waters of the World.* Vol. **9** (Eds. H.J. Dumont and T. Nogrady). SPB Academic Publishers, Amsterdam, The Netherlands.

Dodson, S.I. (1992) - Predicting crustacean zooplankton species richness. *Limnol. Oceanogr.,* **37**: 848-856.

Donner, J. (1965) - Ordnung Belloidea (Rotatoria Radertiere). *Best Bucher Z. Bodenfauna Europas,* Berlin **6**: 1-297.

Dumont, H.J. (1994) - On the diversity of the cladocera in the tropics. *Hydrobiologia,* **272**: 27-38.

Dumont, H.J. and Pensaert, J. (1983) - A revision of the Scapholeberinae (Crustacea, Cladocera). *Hydrobiologia,* **100** : 3-45.

Dussart, B.H. and Fernando, C.H. (1985) - Les Copepodes en Sri Lanka (Calanoides et Cyclopoides). *Hydrobiologia,* **127**: 229-252.

Edmondson, W. T. (1959) - *Ward and Whipple's Freshwater Biology.* 2nd Ed. John Wiley & Sons Inc., New York, 1248pp.

Evans, Wayne, A. (1984) - Seasonal abundance of the Psammic rotifers of a physically controlled stream. *Hydrobiologia,* **108** (1-2): 105-114.

Fernando, C.H. (1980) - The freshwater zooplankton of Sri Lanka with a discussion of triopical zooplankton composition. *Int. Rev. ges. Hydrobiol.*, **65** : 85-125.

Fernando, C.H. and Kanduru, A. (1984) - Some remarks on the latitudinal distribution of Cladocera in the Indian subcontinent. *Hydrobiologia,* **113** : 69-76.

Francis, T., Ramanathan, N., Athithan, S., Daisy Rani, R.P., Padmavathy, P. (2003) - Rotifer diversity of fish ponds manured with livestock waste. *Indian J. Fish.,* **50** (2): 203-209.

Gannon, J. E. and Stemberger, R. S. (1978) - Zooplankton, especially crustaceans and rotifers as indicators of water quality. *Trans. Amer. Micros. Soc.,* **97** (1): 16-35.

Gaur, R.K. Khan, A.A., Afaq M. and Alam, A. (1999) - Pollution status of a leachate resevoir receiving effluents from a thermal power plant within reference to plankton population. In: *Freshwater ecosystem of India* (ed. K. Vjaykumar) Daya Publishing House, Delhi, 226-236.

Gaur, R.K., Khan, A.A., Parveen, S. and Untoo, S.A. (2001) - Sediment quality characteristics of a leachate reservoir receiving effluents from a thermal power plant. *J. Ecophysiol. Occup. Hlth.*, **1** (1& 2): 161-178.

Greshon, (1983) - Distribution patterns and habitat characteristics of Amphipoda (Crustacea) in the inland waters of Israel and Sinai. *Hydrobiologia,* **98** (1-3): 17-24.

Gulati, R.D. (1978) - The ecology of common planktonic crustacea of fresh water in the Netherlands. *Hydrobiologia,* **59**: 101-112.

Gunter, T. zschaschel (1983) - Seasonal abundance of psammon rotifers. *Hydrobiologia,* **104** (1-3): 275-278.

Hazarika, A.K. and Dutta, A. (1988) – Limnological studies of two fresh water ponds of Guwahati, Assam. *Environment & Ecology,* **12**: 26-29.

Hosmani, S. (2002) - Ecological diversity of algae in freshwaters. In: *Wetlands Conservation and Management.* (Ed. B.B. Hosetti). Pointer Publisher, Jaipur, India, 65-84.

Ingram, B.A., Hawkings, J.H. and Shiel, J. (1997) - Aquatic life in freshwater ponds. In: A guide to the identification and ecology of life in aquaculture ponds and farm in South Eastern Australia. Identification guide no. 9. Co-operative research Center for Freshwater Ecology, Albury, NSW, Australia, -105.

Jeelani, M., Kaur, H. and Sarwar, S. G., (2004) – Population dynamics of rotifers in the Anchar lake, Kahmir (India). *Indian J. Environ. & Ecoplan.,* **8** : 315-318.

Jhingran, V.G. (1991) - *Fish and Fisheries of India.* Hindustan Publishing Corporation, India, Delhi, 954 pp.

Keller, W., Yan, N.D., Howel, T., Molat, L.A. and Taylor, W.D. (1993) - Changes in zooplankton during the experimental nutrilization and early reacidification of Bowland lake, near Sudbury, Ontario. *Canadian J. Fish. Aquat. Sci.*, **49**: 52-62.

Khan, A.A. and Alam, A. (1999) - Cyclomorphosis, the morphological responses in Cladocera (Water fleas) to certain environmental factors: A review. In: *Freshwater Ecosystem of India.* (Ed. K. Vijaykumar). Daya Publishing House, N. Delhi, 193-207.

Khan, A.A. and Siddiqui, A.Q. (1974) - Seasonal changes in limnology of a perennial fish pond at Aligarh. *Indian J. Fish.*, **21**: 463-478.

Khan, A.A., Alam, A. and Gaur, R.K. (1999) - A comprehensive study of water quality parameters in the river Ganga between Narora and Kannauj : primary production. In: *Freshwater ecosystem of India* (ed. K. Vijaykumar) Daya Publishing House, N. Delhi, 287-294.

Khan, A.A., Ali, M. and Haque, N. (1986) - Population ecology of zooplankton in a polluted pond at Aligarh. *Proc. Nat. Symp. Environ. Biol., Coastal Ecosystem. Manglore Univ. Mangalore,* 75-62pp.

Khan, A.A., Untoo, S.A. and Parveen, S. (2002) - Limnology of a reservoir receiving effluents from a thermal power plant. In: *Ecology of Polluted Waters.* (Ed. A. Kumar), A.P.H. Publishing Corporatiopn Delhi, 1109-1117.

Khan, I.A. and Khan, A.A. (1985) - Physico-chemical conditions in Seikha Jheel at Aligarh. *Environment and Ecology,* **3**: 269-274.

Khan, J.A. and Qayyum, A. (1966 a) - On the ionic composition of five tropical fish ponds of Aligarh, U.P., India. *Hydrobiologia,* **28** (2): 195-201.

Khan, M.A. and Rao, I.S. (1981) - Zooplankton in the evaluation of pollution. *Cent. Bd. Prev. Cont. Poll. Osm. Univ. Hyderabad, India,* 121-133.

Malone, B.J. and Mc Queen, D.J. (1983) - Horizontal patchiness in zooplankton population in two Ontario kettle lakes. *Hydrobiologia,* **99** (2-3): 101-124.

Mamaril, A.C. and Fernando, C.H. (1978) - Freshwater zooplankton of the Philippines (Rotifera, Cladocera and Copepoda). *Univ. Philipp. Nat. Appl. Sci. Bull.* **30**:109-221.

Mc Cauley, E. and Kalff, J. (1981) - Emperical relationship between phytoplankton and zooplankton biomass in lakes. *Can. J. Fish. Aquat. Sci.,* **38**: 458-463.

Melone, G., Ricci, C., and Segers, H., (1998) - The trophy of Bdelloidea (Rotifera): a comparative study across the class. *Can J. Zool,* **76**: 1755-1765.

Menzer, M.B.H., Nehal, M., Kahmatullah., and Bazmi, S.H. (2005) – A comparative study of population kinetics and seasonal fluctuation of zooplankton in two diverse ponds of North Bihar. *Nature Environment & Pollution Technology,* **4:** 23-26.

Michael R. G. and Sharma, B. K. (1988) – Fauna of India and adjacent countries. *India Cladocera (Crustaceae; Branchiopoda; Cladocera). Zool. Sur. India.,* pp. 216.

Mishra, S. (2004) - Significance of plankton in aquaculture with reference to its trophic potentials. *Fishing Chimes,* **23** (10 & 11): 53-59.

Mukhopadhyay, Subhra Kumar., Chattopadhyay, Buddhadeb., Goswami, Abhisek Roy and Chatterjee, Asitava. (2007)- Spatial variations in zooplankton diversity in waters contaminated with composite effluents. *J. Limnol.,* **66** (2): 97-106.

Murtaugh, A. Paul (1985) - Vertical distribution of zooplankton and population dynamics of Daphnia in a meromectic lake. *Hydrobiologia,* **123** (1-3): 47-57.

Murugesan, V.K., Palaniswamy, R. and Manoharan, S. (2003) - Productivity of reservoir in Tamil Nadu with reference to their plankton population. *J. Inland Fish. Soc. India,* **35** (2): 50-56.

Nayer, S., Gupta, T.R.C. and Gowda, G. (1999) - Secondary production and zooplankton biomass in a tropical coastal lagoon near Mangalore, Southwest coast of India. *India J. Fish.,* **46** (3): 281-288.

Negra, S., Botnariuc, N. and Dumont, H.J. (1999) - Phylogeny, evolution and classification of the Branchiopoda (Crustacea). *Hydrobiologia,* **412**: 191-212.

Olesen, J. (1998) - A phylogenetic analysis of the Conchostraca and Cladocera (Crustacea, Diplostraca). *Zool. J. Linn. Soc.,* **122**: 491-536.

Outridge, D.M. (1987) - Possible causes of high species diversity in tropical Australian freshwater macrobenthic communities. *Hydrobiologia,* **150** (1-3): 59-107.

Pace, M.L. (1986) - An empirical analysis of zooplankton size structure across lake trophic gradients. *Limnol. Oceanogr.,* **31** : 45-55.

Parveen, S. (2003) - *Studies on the Limnology of some Derelict Waterbodies and their Utilization for Fish Culture,* Ph.D. Thesis, Aligarh Muslim University, Aligarh. 186 pp.

Pathak, S.K. and Mudgal, L.K. (2002) – A prerliminary survey of zooplankton of Virla Reservoir of Khargone (Madhya Pradesh), India. *Indian J. Environ. & Ecoplan.,* **6** : 267-300.

Pejler, B. (1983) - Zooplankton indicators of trophy and their food. *Hydrobiologia,* **101**: 111-114.

Pennak, R.W. (1978) - *Freshwater Invertebrates of United States.* (2nd Ed). John Wiley & Sons Inc., New York, 803pp.

Pluiraite, V. (2003) - Species Diversity of Zooplankton in the Curomian Lagoon in 2001. *Acta Zoologica Lituanica,* Vol.**13** (2): 106-112.

Pontin, R.M. (1978) - A key to freshwater planktonic and semi-planktonic Rotifera of British Isles. *Freshwat. Biol. Assoc. Sci. Publ.,* **38**: 1-178.

Pradhan, Prasjit, Giri, Sunirmal and Chakraborty, Susanta Kumar (2007) - Zooplanktonic rotifers in River Tanuma. *J. Inland Fish Soc. India,* **39** (2), 43-47.

Prakash, S., Ansari, K.K. and Sinha, M. (2002) – Seasonal dynamics of zooplankton in a freshwater pond developed from the wasteland of Brick - kiln. *Poll Res.,* **21**: 81-83.

Rajendran, M. (1973) - Copepoda. In: A Guide to the Freshwater Organisms. (Ed. R.G. Michael). *J. Madurai Univ. Suppl.,* **1**: 103-151.

Rao, N. Durve, V. S. and Srikhande, V. J. (2006)- Concept of planktonic species diversity in small water bodies – a case study of lake Rangasagar (Udaipur : Rajasthan). *Acta Hydrochimica et Hydrobiologica,* Vol. **16** (Issue 5): 517-524.

Reddy, Y.R. (1994) - Copepoda: Diaptomidae. In: *Guides to the Identification of the micro-invertebrates of the Continental Waters of the world.* (Eds. H.J. Dumont and T. Nogrady). Vol. **5**, SPB Academic Publishers, Amsterdem, Netherlands, 221 pp.

Reddy, Y.R. (2001) - Zooplankton diversity: Freshwater planktonic copepoda with key to common calanoid and cyclopoid genera in India. In: *Water Quality Assessment Biomonitoring and Zooplankton Diversity.* (Ed. B.K. Sharma). Ministry of Environment and Forests, Government of India, New Delhi, 174 189.

Ruttner-Kolisco, A. (1974) - Plankton rotifers: Biology and taxonomy. *Die Binnengewasser, Suppl.*, **26**: 1-146.

Saranan, S.P. (2005) - Role of zooplankton in the prevention of loose shell in *P. monodon. Aqua International,* 28-31.

Sars, G. O. (1914) – *Daphnia carinata* King and its remarkable varieties. *Arch. Math. Naturvid.*, **34**:1-14.

Sharma, B.K. (1983) - The rotifer community of Mondsee, an alpine lake in Austria. I. Species Diversity and Commmunity Structure. II. Ecology of Planktonic Rotifera. Inst. of Limnology, Austria, Academy of Science, Mondsee, Austria, 80pp.

Sharma, B.K. (1987) - Indian Brachionidae (Eurotatoria: Monogononta) and their distribution. *Hydrobiologia,* **144**: 269-275

Sharma, B.K. (1991) - Rotifera. In: *Animal Resources of India: Protozoa to Mammalia.* State of Art. Zool. Surv. India, 69-88.

Sharma, B.K. (1995) - Freshwater Rotifers (Rotifera: Eurotatoria): Fauna of West Bengal: State Faunal Series, Zool. Surv. India, **3** (13): 1-121.

Sharma, B.K. (1996) - Biodiversity of freshwater rotifers in India: A status report. *Proc. Zool. Soc. India,* **49**: 73-85.

Sharma, B.K. (1998) - Faunal Diversity in India: Rotifera. In: Faunal Diversity of India. (Eds. J.R.B. Alferd, A.K. Das and A.K. Sanyal). Zool. Surv. India, Envis Centre, 57-70.

Sharma, B. K. (1998 a) – State Fauna Series 3: Fauna of West Bengal, ZSI. Part **11**: 341 – 361.

Sharma, B.K. (2000) - Synecology of rotifers in a tropical flood plain lake of upper Assam. *Indian J. Anim. Sci.,* **70**: 880-885.

Sharma, B.K. (2001) - Biological monitoring of freshwaters with reference to role of freshwater Rotifera as biomonitors. In: *Water Quality Assessment, Biomonitoring and Zooplankton Diversity* (Ed. B.K. Sharma). Ministry of Environment and Forests, Government of India, New Delhi, 83-97.

Sharma, B.K. (2001 a) - Zooplankton Diversity: Freshwater Planktonic and Semi-Planktonic Rotifera. In: *Water Quality Assessment, Biomonitoring and Zooplankton Diversity* (Ed. Prof. B.K. Sharma), Department of Zoology, North Eastern Hill University, Shillong, Meghalaya, 190-210pp.

Sharma, B.K. (2001 b) - Zooplankton Diversity: Freshwater Planktonic Cladocera (Crustacea : Branchiopoda). In: *Water Quality Assessment, Biomonitoring and Zooplankton Diversity* (Ed. Prof. B.K. Sharma), Department of Zoology, North Eastern Hill University, Shillong, Meghalaya, 215-235pp.

Sharma, B.K. and Lyngdoh, R.M. (2003) - Abundance and ecology of net plankton and phytoplankton of sub-tropical reservoir of Meghalaya (N.E. India). *Eco. Env. & Cons.,* **9** (4): 485-491.

Sharma, B.K. and Lyngskor, C. (2003) - Planktonic communities of a sub-tropical reservoir of Meghalaya (N.E. India). *Indian J. Animal Science,* **73** (2): 88-95.

Sharma, B.K. and Michael, R.G. (1987) - Review of taxonomic studies on freshwater Cladocera from India with remark on biogeography. *Hydrobiologia,* **145**: 29 33.

Sharma, B. K. and Pudani, V. K. (1992) – Rotifer from some tropical ponds in Bihar (species composition, similarities and trophic indicators). *Jr. India Inst. Sci.,* **72**,121-130.

Sharma, B.K. and Sharma, S. (1990) - On the taxonomic status of some Chadoceran taxa (Custacea: Cladocera) from Central India. *Rev. Hydrobiol, Trop,* **23**:105-133.

Sharma, B.K. and Sharma, S. (1997) - Lecanid rotifers (Rotifera: Monogononta: Lecanidae) of North-Eastern India. *Hydrobiologia,* **356**: 159-163.

Sharma, B.K. and Sharma, S. (1999) - Freshwater Rotifera (Rotifera: Eurotatoria). In: *Fauna of Meghalaya.* State Fauna Series. Zool. Surv. India., **4** (9): 11-161

Sharma, B.K. and Wanswett, D. (1999) - Abiotic environment of a lentic ecosystem of Cherrapunjee (East Khasi Hill District), Meghalaya. *Proc. Nat. Conf. Pollution Man & Environment, Shillong* : 7-11.

Sharma, K.P., Goel, P.K. and Gopal, B. (1978) - Limnological studies of pollued freshwater I. Physico-chemical characteristics. *Int. J. Ecol. Environ. Sci.,* **4**: 89-105.

Sharma, O.P. (2003) - Zooplankton production using *Eichhornia cressipes* as Biofertilizer. *Fishing Chimes,* **23** (7): 42-45.

Shiel, R.J. (1995) - *A guide to identification of rotifers, cladocerans and copepods from Australian inland waters.* Identification Guide No. 3. Co-operative Research Centre for Freshwater Ecology, Albury, NSW, Australia, 1-144.

Shiel, R.J. and Koste, W. (1983) - Rotifer communities of Billabongs in northern and south eastern Australia. *Hydrobiologia,* **104** (1-3): 41-47.

Singh, P. and Kumar, C.H. (1997) - Plant production of Rott river, Bhittha-More. Sitamarhi, Bihar. *Environment and Ecology,* **15** (34): 396-698.

Sinha, C. and Khan, R.A. (1998) - Ecology and diversity of cladocerans in some Calcutta wetlands. *Proc. Nat. Seminar on Envir. Biol. on Biodiversity and Environment,* 154-164.

Sladecek, V. (1983) - Rotifers as indicator of water quality. *Hydrobiologia,* **100**: 169-201.

Smirnov, N.N. (1976) - World Macrothricidae and Oinidae (in Russian). Fauna USSR. *ZooL. Inst. Acad. Nauk. USSR, New Ser.*, **112**: 1-237.

Stenson, J.A.F. (1982) - Fish impact on rotifer community structure. *J. Hydrobiol.*, **87** (1-3): 57-64.

Stevenson, R. Jan (1984) - Epilithic and epiphilic diatoms in the Sandowsky River with emphasis on species diversity and water pollution. *Hydrobiologia,* **114** (2-3): 161-175.

Surkad, B.N. (2004) – Diversity of zooplankton in Rakasakoppa resorvoir of Belgaun of North Karnataka, India. *Indian J. Environ. & Ecoplan.,* **8**: 399- 404.

Swar, K. and Fernando, C.H. (1980) - Effect of environmental factors on zooplankton. *Arch. Hydrobiol.,* **26**: 310-321.

Wallace, R.L. and Snell, T.W. (1991) - Rotifera. In: *Ecology and Classification of North American Freshwater Invertebrates* (Eds. S.H. Thorpe and A.P. Covch). American Press, New York, 187-248.

Waters, T.F. (1977) - Secondary production in inland waters. *Adv. Ecol. Res.,* **10**: 11-164.

Wetzel, R.G. (1983) - *Limnology.* 2nd ed. Saunders College Publishing Co., New York, 767pp.

Effect of Exposure to Mercury on Health in Tropical Macrobrachium Rosenbergii

—*Hussein A. Kaoud, Egypt*

ABSTRACT

The effects of Hg on mortality, resistance and bioconcentration in the tropical giant freshwater Macrobrachium rosenbergii were studied. Mortalities of prawns exposed to mercury doses below 100 µg L–1 were sig¬nificantly lower than those exposed to higher doses. After 96 hours prawns ex¬posed to >400 µg L–1of mercury had a greater reduction in total haemocyte count and phagocytic activity than those exposed to lower concentrations. Bioconcentration of mercury (Hg) in the gills, hepatopancreas and muscles was variable. Mercury accumulated in gills and hepatopancreas but Hg accumulation in the muscles only increased marginally. Macrobrachium rosenbergii manifested histopathological alterations in gills, hepatopancreas and muscles when exposed to different concentrations of mercury.

Keywords: Macrobrachium rosenbergii, *mercury, total haemocyte count, phagocytic activity*

INTRODUCTION

The contamination of fresh water with a wide range of pollutants has become a matter of concern over the last few decades (Voegborlo *et al.*, 1999; Dirilgen, 2001; Vutukuru, 2005). The natural aquatic systems may extensively be contaminated with heavy metals released from domestic, industrial and other man-made activities (Conacher, *et al.*, 1993; Velez and Montoro, 1998). Heavy metal contaminations may have devastating effects on the ecological balance of the recipient environment and a diversity of aquatic organisms (Ashraj, 2005; Vosyliene and Jankaite, 2006; Farombi, et al., 2007).

The toxic effects of heavy metals have been reviewed, including bioaccumulations (Adami *et al.*, 2002; Waqar, 2006). Heavy metals are surrounded with great care and special importance due to their highly toxic effects on fish as they affect survivability, growth and reproduction. The immune system in all living creatures and the immune response come about as protective mechanism to protect the fish from attack by various microorganisms and parasites (Vorkamp et al., 2004; Andreji et al., 2005). Suppression of immune system and immune response may result from action of several pollutants including heavy metals which provide opportunities for the entering of many pathogens.

Mercury (Hg) is one of the most toxic heavy metals in our environment including the lithosphere, hydrosphere, atmosphere and biosphere (Barbosa *et al.*, 2001). So, Hg was the most toxic of all metals in *Penaeus monodon*, followed by Cu, Cd and Zn and that Cd toxicity was the most rapid (Chen, 1979).

In freshwater prawn, *Macrobrachium malcolmsonii*, both Hg and Cu had inhibitory effects on the functions of the hemocytes but, the difference between the two metals is the time and concentration at which the effects become apparent (Alcivar-Warren *et al.,* 2006). In decapod crustaceans, 3 types of circulating hemocytes are recognized: hyaline, semi-granular and large granular cells (Tsing *et al.*, 1989). They are involved in cellular immune responses that include phagocytosis and constitute the primary method of eliminating microorganisms or foreign particles (Bayne, 1990). In addition to phagocytosis, hemocytes are involved in the process of coagulation and production of melanin via the prophenoloxidase system (Johansson & Söderhäll 1989, Söderhäll *et al.*, 1996). Enzymes for the prophenoloxidase system are present in the granular hemocytes and released as proenzymes upon stimulation by microbial cell components such as 1, 3-glucan or lipopolysaccharide from fungal cell walls, and activated by a serine protease (Söderhäll 1983, Smith *et al.*, 1984, Söderhäll *et al.*, 1996). Several physico-chemical parameters and environmental contaminants have adverse effect on the immune response of crustaceans (Le Moullac & Haffner, 2000). Environmental toxicants have been reported to cause a reduction in hemocyte count in the common shrimp *Crangon crangon* (Smith & Johnston 1992).Moreover , Heavy metals like mercury and cadmium are known to be accumulated in marine organisms, and cause rapid genetic changes (Nimmo *et al.,* 1978, Nevo *et al.*, 1986).

Histopathological examination has been increasingly recognized as a valuable tool for ûeld assessment of the impact of environmental pollutants on ûsh (Heath, 1995; Teh et al., 1997). Speciûc lesions occurring in organs of ûsh exposed to toxic substances under laboratory conditions help to identify biomarkers of exposure. Many authors have studied the histopathological effects of mercury on ûsh exposed to water-borne inorganic mercury (inorganic Hg) on liver, kidneys, gills, olfactory epithelium, and spleen (Oliveira-Ribeiro et al., 2002; Samson and Shenker, 2000).

Knowledge of the toxicity of mercury will be helpful to water quality management in fish farms so; this study evaluates the impact of the short-term mercury exposure on survival, resistance, tissue bioconcentration and histopathological alterations in gills, hepatopancreas and muscles in tropical freshwater prawn (*Macrobrachium rosenbergii*).

Materials and Methods

Experimental design

Experiments were carried out in Department of Veterinary Hygiene and Management, Faculty of Veterinary Medicine, Cairo University. Fresh water was adjusted with the desired parameters as follow: temperature of 20-28°C, pH 7-7.8, dissolved oxygen 5-8 mgL^{-1}, salinity 2 ppt, hardness 100-150 ppm Ca(CO)3, total ammonia less than10 ppm, nitrate 20 ppm and nitrite1 ppm) according to, New (1995).

A stock mercury solution was prepared as follow: 135.3 mg Hg Cl2 salt dissolved in a solution composed of 700 mL water plus 1.5 mL concentrated nitric acid and then diluted up to 1000 mL with water (1.00 mL = 100 µg Hg). Seven different concentrations of Hg were then prepared from the stock solutions (10, 50, 100, 200, 300, 400, 500 $\mu gL^{-1)}$.

Macrobrachium rosenbergii were obtained from commercial farms in Alexandria and Al-Kalubia, Egypt, and acclimated in the laboratory for two days before the experiment was done.

The toxicity tests were conducted according to the standard procedures of FAO (1985). Seven concentrations of Hg (10, 50, 100, 200, 300, 400 and 500 μgL^{-1}) and a negative control were set up. Ten shrimps each of 13.2 to 16.5 g body weight with an average of 14.85±0.15 g were transferred from the holding tanks into the control and experimental tanks. Three trials were carried out for each concentration. The aquaria were aerated continuously, while the test solution in each tank was changed with the appropriate fresh solution every 24 hrs to maintain the definite concentration of Hg for 96 hrs. Observations for mortality were made twice (10.0 am and 6.0 pm) daily.

Analysis

The 96 hrs LC50 values were calculated using probit analysis according to Finney (1971).

Cell Counts

Hemolymph (100 µl) was sampled individually at the beginning of each test and at 96 h post exposure to Hg. It was withdrawn from the ventral sinus of each prawn into a 1 mL sterile syringe containing 0.9 mL anticoagulant solution (trisodium citrate 0.114 M, sodium chloride 0.1 M, pH 7.45, osmolality 490 mOsm kg^{-1}). A drop of the anticoagulant-hemolymph mixture was placed on a hemocytometer to measure total hemocyte count (THC) using an inverted-phase contrast microscope.

Culture of *Lactococcus garvieae*

The bacterial strain *L. garvieae* isolated from diseased *Macrobrachium rosenbergii* after artificial infection was used in this study. The bacterium was cultured on tryptic soya agar (TSA) for 24 h at 28 °C before being transferred to 10 mL of tryptic soya broth (TSB) for 24 h at 28 °C as a stock culture. The stock cultures were centrifuged at 7155 x g for 15 min at 14 °C and then the supernatant fluid removed and the sediment resuspended in a saline solution (0.85 NaCL) and adjusted at 10^{10} cfu mL^{-1} as stock bacterial suspensions for testing.

Phagocytic activity of *M. rosenbergii* to *L. garvieae*

After 96 hrs of Hg exposure in each treatment, prawns were injected in the cephalothorax with 20 µl of the bacteria suspension (10^{10} cfu mL^{-1} in 0.85% NaCI) resulting in 2 x 10^8 cfu prawn l^{-1}. After injection, the prawns were held in their respective solutions for 3 hours. Hemolymph (200 µl) was collected from the ventral sinus and mixed with 200 µl of sterile anticoagulant containing sodium citrate (0.8 g), EDTA (0.34 g), Tween 80 (10 µl) and distilled water (100 mL with pH of 7.45).

Phagocytic activity was measured using the method described by Weeks-Perkins et al., (1995) where 200 µl of diluted hemolymph sample was mixed with 0.2 mL of 0.1% paraformaldehyde for 30 min at 4 °C to fix the hemocytes. They were then centrifuged at 800x g at 4 °C, washed and resuspended in 0.4 ml of sterile phosphate buffer solution. The suspension (50 µl) was spread onto a slide glass and air-dried and stained with Diff-Quick stain according to Skipper R and DeStephano (1989). 200 hemocytes were counted using light microscope and the phagocytic rate was estimated as follows:

PR = [(phagocytic hemocytes) /(total hemocytes)] x 100.

Preparation and Analysis of Tissue Samples

Were carried out in two procedures. Procedure A: Each sample was represented by 0.5 gram of tissues dissected from the gills, hepatopancreas, and muscles, then placed in a clean screw-capped tube and digested according to the method de-scribed by Finerty *et al.,* (1990).

Procedure B: The measurement of the mercury concentration in examined tissue samples was carried out at minimal temperature for all samples where 0.5 gram macerated tissues was digested accord-ing to the technique described by Diaz *et al.,* (1995). 5 ml stannous chloride solution were added to the obtained solutions to reduce mercury to elemental form and then analyzed by using Atomic Absorption Spectrophotometer equipped with mercury hydride system "MHS" "Cold Vapour Technique".

Histopathological Examination

Tissue specimens from gills, hepatopancreas and muscles of experimental *M rosenbergii* were taken and fixed in 15 % buffered neutral formalin. Tissues were processed to obtain five micron thick paraffin sections then stained with hematoxylin and eosin, (H&E) according to the methods described by Bancroft *et al.*, (1996) and examined under light microscope.

Bioconcentration factor (BCF) is the concentration of a particular chemical in a biological tissue per concentration of that chemical in water surrounding that tissue. That is, a dimensionless number representing how much of a chemical is in a tissue relative to how much of that chemical exists in the environment (Chiou, 2002).

$$BCF = \frac{\text{Concentration}_{\text{Organism}}}{\text{Concentration}_{\text{Environment}}}$$

Tissues with BCF greater than 1,000 are considered high, and less than 250 low, with those between classified as moderate.

Statistical Analysis

Data were analyzed using Analysis of Variance (ANOVA) and means were separated by the Duncan post-hoc test at a probability level of < 0.05 (SAS, 2000).

RESULTS

Mortality

Tropical *Macrobrachium rosenbergii* exposed to Hg had significantly lower THC and Phagocytic activity than the control ones. After 96 hours, mean (±SD) mortality of prawns in control tanks (0 Hg) was 4±2.20 % and significantly lowers *(P < 0.05)* than that of prawns in all other treatments as shown in Table 1 and Figure 1-a. 96 h(s) post-exposure, mortality rates of prawns ex-posed to 10-50 μgL^{-1} concentrations of mercury were significantly lower *(P < 0.05)* than those exposed to higher concentrations (100 μgL^{-1} or greater), but were not significantly different from each other *(P < 0.05)*. In Table 1 and Figure 1-a,mortality rates of prawns exposed to 100, 200, 300, 400 and 500 μgL^{-1} of mercury were sig-nificantly higher *(P < 0.05)*, with means of (±SD) 23 ± 0.70%, 40 ± 0.70%, 43 ±0.70%, 60 ± 0.20% and 70 ± 0.21%, respectively.

Resistance

Table 1 and Figure1-b,show the significant reduction (P < 0.05), in THC and Phagocytic activity for prawns exposed to 100, 200, 300, 400 and 500

μgL^{-1} of mercury with means of (±SD) 170±19 , 70±7.00 ; 160±28 , 62±7.00; 145±21, 50±2.70; 138±19, 40±0.70 and 132±16 , 0 respectively.

Bioconcentration and residues of mercury (Hg) in different tissues of tropical *M. rosenbergii*

Table 2 and Figure 2, show the residues of mercury (Hg) in gills, hepatopancreas and muscle tissues of tropical *M. rosenbergii* which were higher in the hepatopancreas> gills > muscles. The BCF for 96 h(s)-exposure were less than 250 in hepatopancreas, gills and muscles respectively.

Hepatopancreas

The rate of accumulation of mercury was maximum in hepatopancreas of exposed prawns and no detectable amount of mercury was observed in the hepatopancreas of control prawns as well as in exposed prawns to very low concentration of mercury (10-50 μgL^{-1}). The rate of accumulation increased along with the increasing of mercury concentration reaching 11.12± 0.032 at 400 μgL^{-1}.

Gills

As with the case of hepatopancreas, mercury could not be traced in the gills of the control prawn as well as in exposed prawns to very low concentration 10 μgL^{-1}, even though the quantity of accumulated mercury was relatively less in the case of gills (9.14± 0.042 at 400 μgL^{-1}) when compared to hepatopancreas, the pattern of accumulation showed a more or less continuous increasing trend.

Muscles

The rate of accumulation of mercury in muscle increased along with exposure to increased mercury concentration. The mean quantity of mercury residue at 400 $\mu gL^{-1}$was 1.025± 0.002. The rate of accumulation was less as compared with other tissues.

The LC50 of Hg in Tropical *M. Rosenbergii*

The 96-hour LC50 values of mercury in tropical *M. rosenbergii* were calculated using probit analysis, to be 430 $\mu g\ L^{-1}$ (Fig.3).

Histopathological Alterations in different tissues of Tropical *M. Rosenbergii*

Results of the present study revealed that, tropical M. rosenbergii manifested histopathological changes in gills, hepatopancreas and muscles.

Exposure to concentration 0.4 mg L^{-1} for 96 hours resulted in profound structural changes as shown in Figures 4, 5 and 6.

Gills showed mild congestion, swelling and edema at low doses of Hg exposure. Severe edema, hyperplasia, at highest doses of intoxication was observed. Moreover, accumulation of hemocytes in the hemocoelic space;

swelling of the lamellae; abnormal gill tips; and hyperplastic, necrotic, and clavate–globate lamellae in the gills (Fig.4).

Hepatopancreas showed hemocytic infiltration in the interstitial sinuses, an increased number of hemocytes, thickening and ruptures of the basal laminae, and necrosis of the tubules were observed in the hepatopancreas (Fig.5 a&b).

Muscular tissues showed several histopathological alterations. The pathological findings included degeneration in muscles with infiltration and aggregations of hemocytes between them and focal areas of necrosis. Also, atrophy of muscle bundles, edema, hyaline degeneration and splitting of muscle fibers were seen (Fig. 6 a & b).

Table 7.1: Effect of mercury 96 hrs-exposure on mortality, total hemocyte count (THC) and phagocytosis in tropical freshwater prawns, *Macrobrachium rosenbergii*

Hg[1] Conc.	Mortality%	Immune response	
		THC[2]	Phagocytic%
0	4±2.20	186±60	91±7.50
0.01	14±1.70	185±36	90±.9.78
0.05	14±1.60	179±22*	88±6.00
0.10	23 ± 0.70*	170±19*	70±7.00*
0.2	40 ± 0.70*	160±28 *	62±7.00*
0.3	43 ±0.70*	145±21*	50±2.70*
0.4	60 ± 0.20*	138±19*	40±0.70*
0.5	70 ± 0.21*	132±16 *	0

[1]: Hg^{2+} mg L^{-1}, [2]: x $10^5 mL^{-1}$, *Significant ($P < 0.05$). Values are means± SD (n = 4 prawns in each case).

Table 7.2: Bioaccumulation of mercury in tissues of tropical freshwater prawns, *Macrobrachium rosenbergii*, exposed to mercury for 96 hours

Conc. of Hg[1]	Bioaccumulation in tissues[2]		
	Gills	Hepatopancreas	Muscles
0	0	0	0
0.01	0.005 ±0.00	0.002±0.006	0
0.05	0.01 ±0.009	0.025±0.008	0.001±0.0001
0.10	2.15 ±0.018	5.03±0.012	C.42±0.013
0.2	5.066 ±0.021	7.14±0.098	0.52±0.005
0.3	7.28± 0.032	10.06±0.011	0.83±0.31
0.4	9.14± 0.042	11.12± 0.032	1.025± 0.002
0.5	9.00 ±0.011	11.12 ±0.022	1.015±0.021

Hg^{2+} μg gm^{-1} = mg kg^{-1} = ppm. Values are means± SD.: [2] [1]: Hg^{2-} mg L^{-1}.

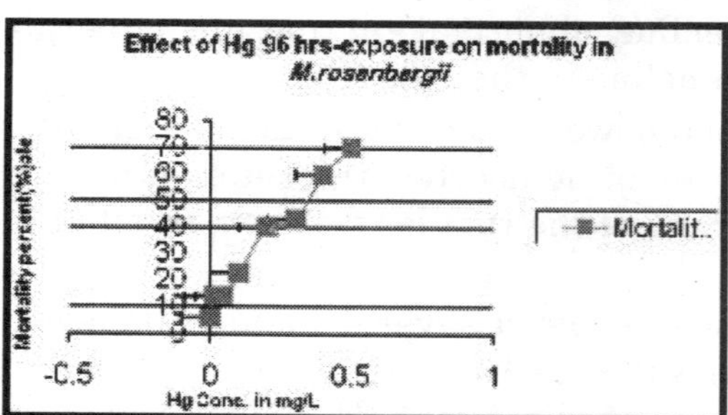

Fig. 7.1(a): mortality rates of prawns exposed to 100, 200, 300, 400 and 500 μg L^{-1} of mercury were sig-nificantly higher ($P < 0.05$), with means of (±SD) 23 ± 0.70%, 40 ± 0.70%, 43 ±0.70%, 60 ± 0.20% and 70 ± 0.21%, respectively

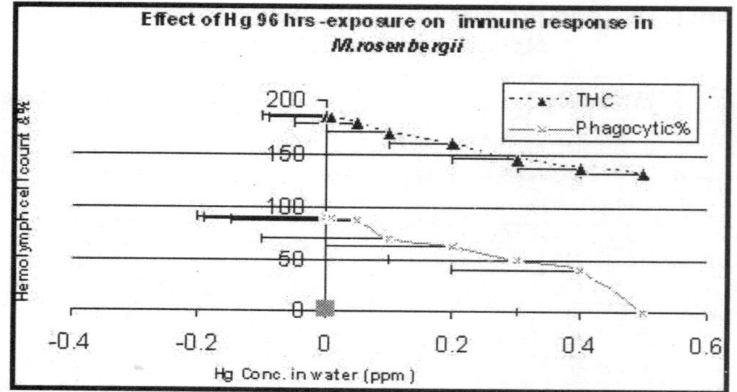

Fig. 7.1(b): the significant reduction ($P < 0.05$), in THC and Phagocytic activity for prawns exposed to 100, 200, 300, 400 and 500 μg L^{-1} of mercury with means of (±SD) 170±19, 70±7.00 ; 160±28 , 62±7.00; 145±21, 50±2.70; 138±19, 40±0.70 and 132±16 , 0 respectively

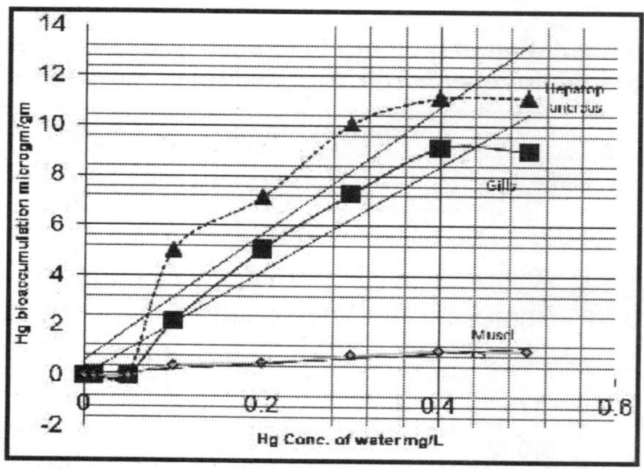

Fig. 7.2: The residues of mercury (Hg) in gills, hepatopancreas and muscle tissues of tropical *M. rosenbergii* which were higher in the hepatopancreas> gills > muscles. The BCF for 96 h(s)-exposure were less than 250 in hepatopancreas, gills and muscles respectively

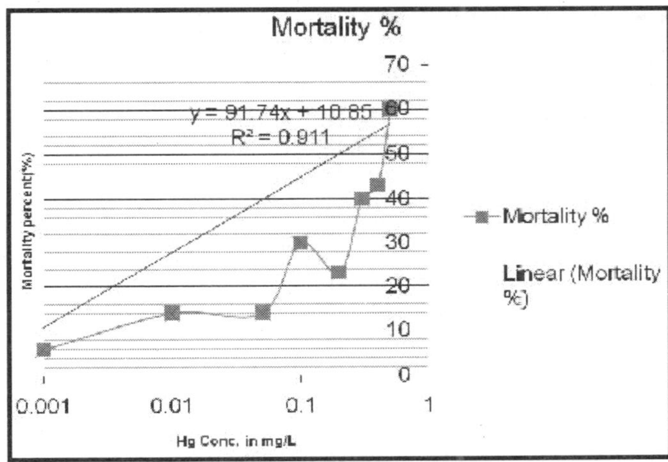

Fig. 7.3: The 96-hour LC50 values of mercury in tropical *M. rosenbergii* were calculated using probit analysis, to be 430 µg L^{-1}

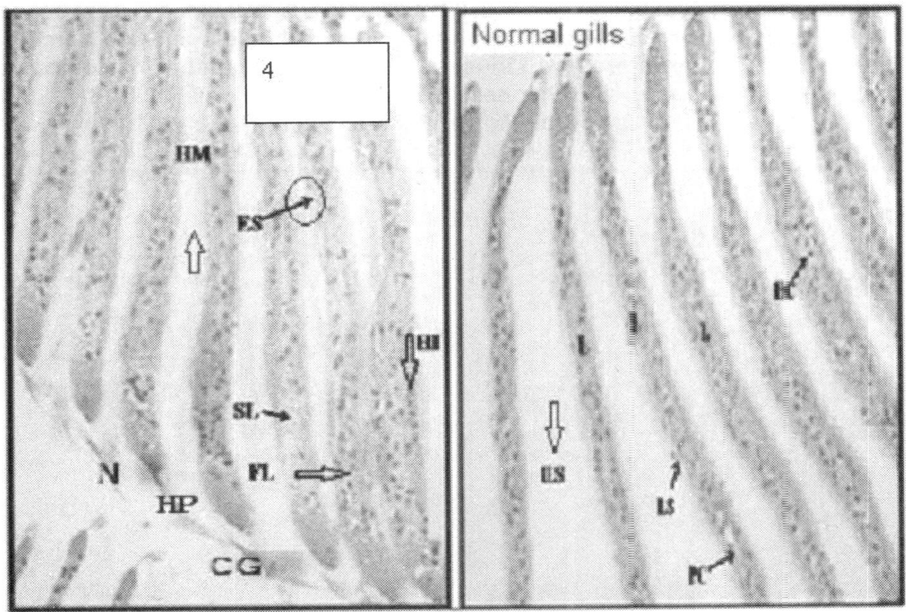

Fig. 7.4 :Cross-sections of gill lamellae of M. rosenbergii after 96 h of exposure to a control solution and Hg . Control prawn showing normal lamellae (L) with uniform interlamellar spaces (ILS), the lamellar sinus (LS), and pillar cell (PC) and hemocyte (HC) in the lamella. Mercury exposed prawn showing hemocytic infiltration (HI), swollen (SL) and fused (FL) lamellae, enlargement of the lamellar sinuses (ES) and hyper-mucus (HM) in the interlamellar spaces, necrosis (N) and hyperplasia (HP) tip of lamellae. H&E stain, (x200)

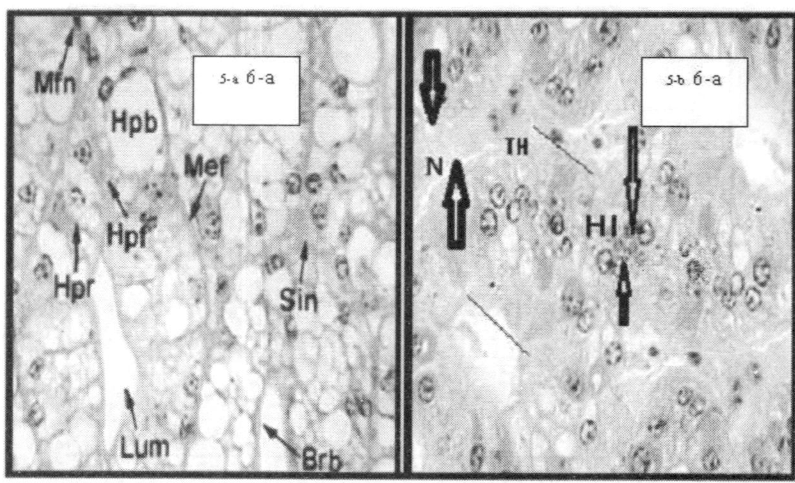

Fig. 7.5 : Cross sections of hepatopancreatic tubules: normal lumens (Lum), tubule tissues (Hpf: F-cell; Hpb: B-cell; Hpr: R-cell; Mfn: myoepithelial cell nuclei; Mef: myoepithelial layer; Brb: microvillus brush borders) and hemal sinuses (Sin) between tubules. Fig.5-b: Cross sections of hepatopancreatic tubules: showed hemocytic infiltration (HI) in the interstitial sinuses, an increased number of hemocytes, thickening (TH) and ruptures of the basal laminae, and necrosis (N) of the tubules (arrowheads). H&E stain, (x200)

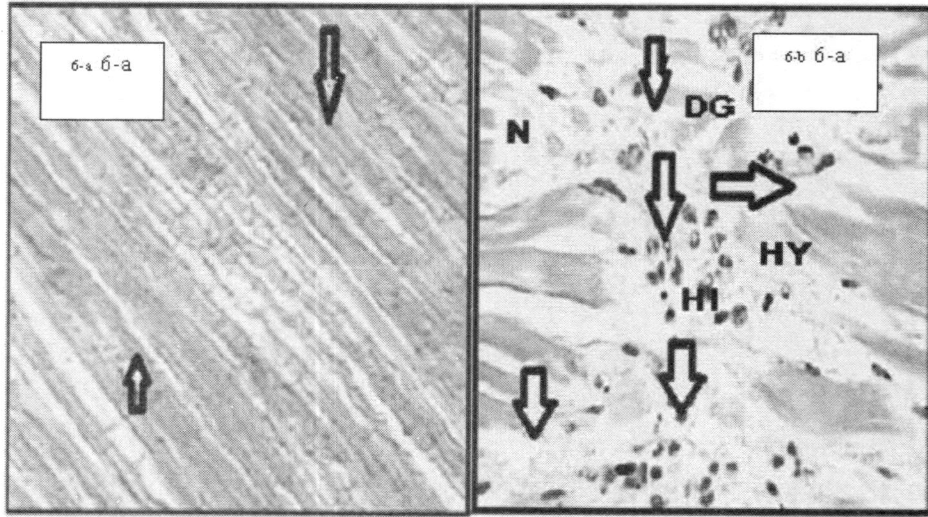

Fig. 7.6(a): Longitudinal sections of muscle tissue Healthy prawn tissue showing normal muscle fibres. Fig.6-b: Cross section showing degeneration (DG), focal areas of necrotic musculature (N) infiltrated by hemocytes (HI) (arrowheads). Also, atrophy of muscle bundles, edema, hyaline degeneration (HY) and splitting of muscle fibers were seen. H&E stain, (x200)

DISCUSSION

After 96 h(s) post-exposure, the survival of tropical *M. rosenbergii* ex-posed to 10-50 μgL^{-1}concentrations of mercury were significantly greater *(P < 0.05)* than those exposed to higher concentrations (100 μgL^{-1} or greater).

Cheng (1979) tested Hg, Cu, Cd and Zn in *Penaeus monodon* and found that, Hg was the most toxic of all metals, followed by Cu, Cd and Zn. In our study in which prawns exposed to 100, 200, 300, 400 and 500 μgL^{-1} of mercury concentrations had significantly greater reduction in THC and phagocytic activity than prawns exposed to lower concentrations (10 – 50 μgL^{-1}), ($P < 0.05$). Our findings may confirm the results reported by Cheng (1979).

Several scientists have investigated the effects of environmental contaminants on crustacean defense mechanisms. Carolina (2009) studied the effect of Mn on the immune system of marine invertebrates and found that Mn severely suppresses the number of circulating hemocytes in *Nephrops norvegicus* by inducing apoptosis. However, Mn increased the number of circulating hemocytes in *Asterias rubens* and at the same time affected their ability to phagocyte. Circulating hemocytes can be affected by extrinsic factors in several species of decapods crustaceans (Truscott & White 1990, Le Moullac et al. 1998, Le Moullac & Haffner 2000, Cheng & Chen2001).

In freshwater prawn, *Macrobrachium malcolmsonii* , Alcivar-Warren, (2006) reported that both Hg and Cu had inhibitory effects on the functions of the hemocytes, the difference between the two metals being the time and the concentration at which the effects become apparent and suppression of total counts of hemocytes (hemopoeisis) appears to involve metal transport (96 h LC50 for Hg = 0.145 mgL^{-1} when 0.024 mgL^{-1} Hg (1/6th of LC50) was used, the total hemocyte count, percentile phagocitosis and superoxide anion production was significantly lower than the controls.

The immune system in all living creatures and the immune response come about as protective mechanism to react and protect the fish from attack by various microorganisms and parasites (Vorkamp et al., 2004; Andreji et al., 2005). Suppression of immune system and immune response may results from action of several pollutants including heavy metals which provide opportunities for entering of many pathogens.

In the present study the highest bioaccumulation of mercury was observed in the organs mainly implicated in metal intoxication (hepatopancreas). Mercury (Hg) in tissues was high in the hepatopancreas> gills > muscles.

Tropical M. rosenbergii manifested histopathological changes in gills, hepatopancreas and muscles. Exposure to concentration 400 $\mu gL^{-1}$for 96 hours resulted in profound structural changes as shown in Figures 4, 5 and 6.

Victor et al., (1990) studied the effect of HgCl2 on Macrobrachium idae exposed to 1 × 10^{-3}mg/L of HgCl2 and found that there were hyperplastic gill lamellae engorged with hemocytes as a specific toxic reaction in these prawns, then hemocytes were released into the interlamellar spaces through necrotic regions and blanketed the entire gill lamellae.Also, Piyan et al (1985) revealed that stage 1 larvae had the lowest threshold lethal concentration (TLC) of mercury, 0.041 ppm Hg, while the post-larvae had a TLC of 0.325 ppm Hg.

Similar results were observed by Mela et al. (2007) and Frías-Espericueta et al., (2008) who studied the effect of three concentrations of Cu (3.512, 1.756 and 0.877 mg L^{-1}) on juvenile Litopenaeus vannamei and found that there were severe time- and dose-dependent structural damages, such as necrosis, loss of regular structure and infiltration of hemocytes in the gill tissues, as well as atrophy, necrosis and irregular tubular structure in the hepatopancreas, similar to that reported by Li et al., (2009).

The higher Hg concentration in the hepatopancreas suggested that this organ plays a role in metal storage and/ or in detoxification process by a metal binding component (White and Rainbow 1986). In crustacean, the hepatopancreas is the primary organ responsible of absorption and storage of ingested materials (Vogt et al., 1989; Johnston et al., 1998). Also, this organ is involved in the synthesis of digestive enzymes and the detoxification of xenobiotics (Barker and Gibson, 1979; Icely and Nott, 1992) were apparent as the hepatospleen consider the organ of detoxification, excretion and binding proteins such as metallothionein (MTs). The metal-binding proteins that present in the nuclei of hepatocytes suggested an increase in cell damage (De Smet and Blust, 2001).

Liver of fish is sensitive to environmental contaminants because many contaminants tend to accumulate in the liver and exposing it to a much higher levels than in the environment, or in other organs (Heath 1995). Pandey et al., (1994) described the alterations in liver and intestine of Liza parsia exposed to Hg Cl_2 (0.2 mg Hg L^{-1}) for 15 days. Similarly, Oliveira Ribeiro et al. (2002) reported serious injuries in gills and olfactory epithelium of Salvelinus alpinus exposed to 0.15 mg Hg L^{-1}.

M. rosenbergii are able to tolerate low levels of mercury pollution but, high levels lead to cellular injury and tissue damage in hepatopancreas. Hg^{2+} disrupted the histostructures of the hepatopancreas, causing decreases in activities of pepsin, tryptase, amylase, and cellulose, which are synthesized in the hepatopancreas, and worst survival rate of the crabs in 0.30 mgL^{-1} (Zhao et al., 2010).

Mean mercury accumulation in muscles of M. rosenbergii at 400 μg L^{-1} was 1.025 μg $g^{-1}$and the maximum permis-sible limits recommended by WHO, (1984) is 1μg g^{-1}. The recorded results of mercury concentrations in muscles of M. rosenbrgii were higher than the permissible limits intended by Spain: Boletin Official del Estado (1991), Schumacher and Domingo (1996) in Spain [1 µg g^{-1}], FAO/WHO (1992) [0.5 µg g^{-1}] and Quality Control (E.O.S.Q.C) (1993) [0.1 µg g^{-1}].

Frías-Espericueta et al. (2009) found that the mean contents of Cd, Cu, Pb and Zn of the white shrimp (Litopenaeus vannamei) were lower in the muscle than in the corresponding hepatopancreas samples, which is in agreement with most literature on the metal contents in the tissues of different aquatic organisms because the hepatopancreas is the main organ for metal accumulation (Roesijadi and Robinson 1994, Yang et al. 2007).

Conclusion

This study reveals an important precaution for prawn cultivation. Knowledge of the toxicity of mercury will be helpful to water quality management in fish farms with reference to prawn culture since it affected the immune response and cause a reduction in hemocyte count in Macrobrachium rosenbergii. Mercury (Hg) caused a decrease in hemocyte-related functions of tropical freshwater shrimp, including hemocyte count and percentile phagocitosis. Caution should be exercised against water source contamination and exposure to industrial pollution. For this reason, the assessment of risk and the safe levels of toxic substances added to any natural environment through human or natural sources, should not neglect the effects on biological systems caused by exposure to minute amounts of toxicants.

Acknowledgements

The authors are grateful to Dr. Sherin Saeid, assistant professor in the Department of Pathology, Faculty of Veterinary Medicine, Cairo University and Dr. Sahar Tawfik, Researcher in the Institute of Animal Health Research, Agricultural Research Centre, Dokki, Giza, for their valuable input and good collaboration during planning and writing of this review.

REFERENCES

1. Adami G. M., Barbieri P., Fabiani M., Piselli S., Predonzani, S., Reisenhofer E., (2002): Levels of cadmium and zinc in hepatopancreas of reared *Mytilus galloprovincialis* from the Gulf of Trieste (Italy). Chemosphere, 48 (7), 671 – 677.
2. 2.Alcivar-Warren A., Primavera J. H., Leobert D. de la Pena L D., Pettit P. , Xu Z.(2006): Heavy Metals, Pcbs And Pahs In *Penaeus Monodon* Shrimp From The Philippines: Indicators Of Environmental Contaminants Exposure
3. Andreji J., Stranai I., Massanyi P., Valent M., (2005): Concentration of selected metals in muscle of various fish species. J Environ Sci Health. 40A:899–912.
4. Ashraj, W., (2005): Accumulation of heavy metals in kidney and heart tissues of *Epinephelus microdon* fish from the Arabian Gulf. Environ. Monit. Assess., 101 (1-3), 311-316.
5. Bancroft J.D, Stevens A., Turner D.R. .(1996): Theory and Practice of Histological Techniques. 4th Ed. New York, Churchill, Livingstone.

6. Barbosa A.C., Jardim W., Dorea J.G., Fosberg B., Souza J., (2001): Hair mercury speciation as a function of gender, age and body mass index in inhabitants of the Negro River basin, Amazon, Brazil. Arch Environ Contam Toxicol 2001; 40: 439–44.
7. Bayne, C. J., (1990): Phagocytosis and non-self recognition in invertebrates. Phagocytosis appears to be an ancient line of defense. Bioscience 40:723–731
8. Boletín Oficial del Estado (1991): Además, las distintas editoriales jurídicas (el BOE, Cívitas, Aranzadi o Tecnos, por ejemplo) suelen hacer ediciones reducidas de las principales leyes agrupadas por bloques temáticos, ediciones que resultan muy asequibles y son de fácil manejo.
9. Chen, C.A., (1979): Preliminary report on the Gonadal Development and Induced Breeding of *Penaeus monodon Fabricius.* M.S. Thesis. Institute of Oceanography, National University Taipei, Taiwan
10. Chiou, C.T.,(2002): Bioconcentration of Organic Contaminants, *in* Partition and Adsorption of Organic Contaminants in Environmental Systems: Hoboken, NJ, John Wiley & Sons, Inc., p. 257
11. Conacher, H. B., Page, B. D., Ryan, J. J., (1993): Industrial chemical contamination of foods [Review]. Food Addit. Contam., 10 (1), 129-143.
12. DeSmet H,, Blust R., (**2001):** Stress responses and changes in protein metabolism in carp (*Cyprinus carpic*) during cadmium exposure. Ecotoxicology and Environmental Safety 48: 255-62.
13. 13.Diaz, V.R., (1995): Preliminary results of acute toxicity tests for mercury and cadmium on Milkfish (*Chanos chanos Forsskal*) juveniles. In: Watson D, Ong KS, Vigers G. (eds). ASEAN Criteria and Monitoring: Advances in Marine Environmental Management and Human Health Protection. Proceedings of the ASEAN-Canada Midterm Technical Review Conference on Marine Science (24-28 October 1994), Singapore. EVS Environment Consultants, Vancouver, and National Science and Technology Board, Singapore.
14. Dirilgen, N., (2001): Accumulation of heavy metals in freshwater organisms: Assessment of toxic interactions. Turk. J. Chem., 25 (3), 173-179.
15. Carolina O., (2009): Immunotoxicology in marine invertebrates: effects of Mn on the immune responses. MD thesis, School of Life Sciences, Heriot-Waff University, Edinburgh, UK.
16. Cheng W,, Chen J .C., (2001): Effect of intrinsic and extrinsic factors on the haemocyte profile of the prawn, *Macrobrachium rosenbergii.* Fish Shell fish Immunol 11:53–63.
17. Cheng, H.C., (1979): Acute toxicity of heavy metals to some marine prawns. China Fish. Mon. 316:3-10. In Chinese with English abstract.
18. Egyptian organization for standardization and quality control (E.O.S.q.c.) (1993): Maximum residue limits for heavy metals in food. Ministry of Industry.No.2360/1993. pp.5, Cairo, Egypt.
19. FAO, (1985): Manual of methods in aquatic environment research. Part 4. Bases for selecting biological tests to evaluate marine pollution: FAO fish tech paper 164.
20. FAO/WHO,(1992): Joint Expert Committee on food Additives, WHO Technical Reportseries No. 505(1972); No.555(1974c); No.683(1982); No751(1987) and No. 776(1989) Evaluation of certain food additives and contaminants, Geneva.

21. Farombi, E. O., Adelowo, O. A., Ajimoko. Y. R., (2007): Biomarkers of oxidative stress and heavy metal levels as indicators of environmental pollution in African Cat fish (*Clarias gariepinus*) from Nigeria ogun river. Int. J. Environ. Res. Public Health., 4 (2), 158-165.

22. Frías-Espericueta, M.G., J.I. Osuna-López, D. Voltolina, G. López-López, G. Izaguirre-Fi-erro & M.D. Muy-Rangel. (2008): The metal content of bivalve molluscs of a coastal la-goon of NW Mexico. Bull. Environ. Contam. Toxicol., 80: 90-92.

23. Frías-Espericueta, M.G., J.I. Osuna-López, D. Voltolina, M.A. Beltrán-Velarde, G. Iza-guirre-Fierro, G. López-López, M.D. Muy-Rangel & W. Rubio-Carrasco. (2009): The content of Cd, Cu, Pb and Zn of the white shrimp *Litopenaeus vannamei* of six coastal lagoons of Sinaloa, NW Mexico. Rev. Biol.Mar. Oceanogr., 44: 197-201.

24. Finerty M.W., Madden J.D., Feagly S.E., Grodner R.M., (1990): Effect of environs and seasonality on met-al residues in tissues of wild and pond raised Cray fish in Southern Louisiana. Archives of Environmental Contamination and Toxicology 19: 49-55.

25. Finney D.J., (1971): Probit Analysis. Cambridge University Press 1971.

26. Gibson R. , Barker P. (1979).The decapod heptopancreas. Oceanoger. Mar. Biol. Ann. Rev. 17, 285-346.

27. Heath A.C., (1995): Water pollution and fish physiology. 2nd edn., Lewis Publishers, Boca Raton. pp. 125-140.

28. Icely JD, Nott JA (1992): Digestion and absorption: digestive system and associated organs. In: Microscopic anatomy of invertebrates: Decapod, Crustacea. Vol. 10. F.W. Harrison and A.G. Humes, Eds. Wily-Liss Inc., N.Y., pp 147-201.

29. Johansson M.W, Söderhäll K., (1989): Cellular immunity in crustaceans and the proPO system. Parasitol. Today. 5:171–176.

30. Johnston, J. A., Ward, C. L., Kopito, R. R., (1998): Aggresomes: A cellular response to misfolded proteins. The Journal of Cell Biology, 143, 1883–1898.

31. Le Moullac G., Haffner P., (2000): Environmental factors affecting immune response in Crustacea. Aquaculture 191: 121–131

32. Le Moullac G., Soyez C., Saulnier D., Ansquer D., Avarre J.C., Levy P., (1998): Effect of hypoxia stress on the immune response and the resistance to vibriosis of the shrimp *Penaeus stylirostris.* Fish Shell fish Immunol 8:621–629

33. Li , X., Cai, W., An, J., Kim, S., Nah, J., Yang, D., Piner, R., Velamakanni A., Jung I., Tutuc, E., Sanjay, K., Banerjee, K., Colombo, L and Ruoff, R. S. (2009): Large-Area Synthesis of High-Quality and Uniform Graphene Films on Copper Foils. Science, 324(5932): 1312-1314.

34. Mela M.R., Ventura .F, Carvalho D.F, Pelletier C.E, Ribeiro C.A., (2007): Effects of dietary methyl mercury on liver and kidney histology in the neotropical fish *Hoplias malabaricus.* Ecotoxicology and Environmental Safety 68: 426 - 35.

35. Nevo E., Noy R., Lavie B., Beiles A., Muchtar S., (1986): Genetic diversity and resistance to marine pollution. Biological Journal of the Linnean Society 29: 139-144.

36. New, M.B., (1995). Status of freshwater prawn farming: a review. Aquatic Research 26: I-54.

37. Nimmo D.R., Rigby R.A., Bahner L.H., Sheppard J.M., (1978): The acute and chronic effects of cadmium on the estuarine mysid, *Mysidopsis bahia*. Bulletin of environmental Contamination and Toxicology 19: 80–85.
38. Oliveira-Ribeiro .CA., Belger L., Pelletiter E., Rouleau C., (2002): Histopathological evidence of inorganic mercury and methyl mercury toxicity in the arctic charr (*Salvelinus alpinus*). Environmental Research 90: 217-225.
39. Pandey A,K,, Mohamed M.P., George K.C., (1994): Histopathological alterations in liver and intestine of *Liza parsia* (Hamilton-Buchanan) in response to mercury toxicity. Journal of Advanced Zoology 15: 18-24.
40. Piyan
41. This article is not included in your organization's subscription. However, you may be able to access this article under your organization's agreement with Elsevier.
42. B. T., Law A. T. , Cheah S. H.,(1985): Toxic levels of mercury for sequential larval stages of *Macrobrachium rosenbergii* (de Man). Aquaculture Volume 46, Issue 4, 15 . 353-359
43. Roesijadi G., Robinson W.E., (1994): Metal regulation in aquatic animals: mechanisms of uptake, accumulation, and release. In: Malins DC, Ostrander GK (eds). Aquatic toxicology: molecular, biochemical and cellular perspectives; pp. 387-420. Lewis Publishers, Boca Raton.
44. SAS Institute, (2000): SAS User's Guide: statistics, SAS Institute, Cary, NC.
45. Schuhmacher M., Domingo J.L., (1996): Concentrations of selected elements in oysters (*Crassostrea angulata*) from the Spanish Coast. Bulletin of Environmental Contamination and Toxicology, 56, 106–113.
46. Skipper R, , DeStephano D,, (1989): Diff-Quik stain set. J.Histotechnol., 12 (4), 303.
47. Smith V.J., Johnston P.A., (1992): Differential haemotoxic effect of PCB congeners in the common shrimp, *Crangon crangon*. Comp. Biochem. Physiol. C 101: 641–649.
48. Smith V.J., Söderhäll K., Hamilton M., (1984): 1, 3-glucan induced cellular defense reaction in the shore crab, *Carcinus maenas*. Comp Biochem Physiol. A. 77: 636–639.
49. Söderhäll K., (1983): 1, 3-glucan enhancement of protease activity in crayfish hemocyte lysate. Comp Biochem Physiol B 74:221–224
50. Söderhäll K., Cerenius L., Johansson M.W., (1996): The prophenoloxidase activating system in invertebrates. In: Söderhäll K, Iwanaga SGR, Vasta GR (eds) New directions in invertebrate immunology. SOS Publications. Fair Haven NJ, pp. 229–253.
51. Truscott R., White K.N., (1990): the influence of metal and temperature stress on the immune system of crabs. Funct Ecol4:455–461.
52. Tsing A., Arcier J.M., Brèhèlin M., (1989): Haemocytes of penaeids and palaemonid shrimps: morphology, cytochemistry and hemograms. J Invertebr Pathol 53: 64–77.
53. Velez D., Montoro R., (1998): Arsenic speciation in manufactured seafood products: a review. J. food. Protect, 61 (9), 1240-1245.

54. Victor B., Narayanan M., Nelson D. Jones., (1990): Gill pathology and hemocyte response in mercury exposed *Macrobrachium idae* (Heller) Journal of Environmental Biology 11(1), 61-5

55. Voegborlo R. B., Methnani A. M. E., Abedin M. Z., (1999): Mercury, cadmium and lead content of canned Tuna fish. Food Chem., 67 (4), 341 – 345.

56. Vogt G., (1994). Life cycle and functional cytology of the hepatopancreatic cells of *Astacus astacus.* Zoomorphology 114, 83-101.

57. Vorkamp K., Christensen J.H, Riget F., (2004): Polybrominated diphenyl ethers and organochlorine compounds in biota from the marine environment of East Greenland. Sci Total Environ. 331:143–55.

58. Vosyliene M. Z., Jankaite A., (2006): Effect of heavy metal model mixture on rainbow trout biological parameters. Ekologija., 4, 12-17.

59. Vutukuru S. S., (2005): Acute effects of Hexavalent chromium on survival, oxygen consumption, hematological parameters and some biochemical profiles of the Indian Major carp, *Labeo rohita.* Int. J. Environ. Res. Public Health., 2 (3), 456-462.

60. Waqar A., (2006): Levels of selected heavy metals in Tuna fish. Arab. J. Sci. Eng., 31 (1A), 89–92.

61. Weeks-Perkins, B.A., Chansue, N., Wong-Verelle, D. (1995): Assay of immune function in shrimp phagocytes: techniques used as indicators or pesticide exposure. In: Stolen, J.S., Fletcher, T.C., Smith, S.A., Zelikoff, J.T., Kaattari, S.L., Anderson, R.S., So¨derha¨ll, K., Weeks-Perkins, B.A. (Eds.), Techniques in Fish Immunology-4. SOS Publications, Fair Haven, USA, pp. 223– 231.

62. White S.L., Rainbow P.S., (1986):Accumulation of cadmium by *Palaemon elegans* (Crustacea: Decapoda). Marine Ecology Progress Series 32: 17-25.

63. World Health Organisation (WHO), (1984). Guidelines for drinking water quality. WHO, Geneva, No.111.

64. Yang Z.B., Zhao Y.L., Li N., Yang J., (2007): Effect of waterborne copper on the microstructure of gill and hepatopancreas in *Eriocheir sinensis* and its induction of metallothionein synthesis. Archives of Environmental Contamination and Toxicology 52: 222-228.

65. Zhao Y., Wang X., Qin Y. , Zheng B., (2010): Mercury (Hg^{2+}) effect on enzyme activities and hepatopancreas histostructures of juvenile Chinese mitten crab *Eriocheir sinensis* . Chinese Journal of Oceanology and Limnology Volume 28, (3): 427-434.

Structure and Functions of Aquatic Ecosystem and its Biodiversity

—*Fouzia Ishaq, India*
—*Amir Khan, India*

ABSTRACT

The ecosystem concept is fundamental to examination of human impacts on life on earth. It provides a way of looking at the functional interactions between life and environment which helps us to understand the behaviour of ecological systems, and predict their response to human or natural environmental changes. Ecosystems are found throughout the biosphere. The ecosystem concept provides a convenient means of structuring and understanding the highly complex system which is our world. Plants and animals live where they have water, food, and shelter. An ecosystem contains all the plants, animals, and nonliving things in an environment. The different parts of an ecosystem work together. Change to ecosystems may be caused by human actions. One of the issues that give rise to the greatest concern among scientists concerned with the environment, and among the public at large, is the effects that humans are having upon ecosystems and their functioning.

***Keywords**: Ecosystem, Ecosystem functioning, Human Impacts, Environment.*

INTRODUCTION

An ecosystem has been defined in two ways; 1) It is an energy-driven complex of a community of organisms and its controlling environment. 2) An ecosystem is a community of living organisms together with the physical processes that occur within an environment.

These two definitions, nearly 25 years apart, provide consistent statements on the key attributes of ecosystems. These key attributes are directly related to the concepts of functional ecology. In particular, interactions between the physical environment and organisms and between organisms and other organisms direct the evolutionary trends of competition, tolerance of stress, and tolerance of disturbance. These interactions are central to the functional processes specified in the definitions of ecosystems. (Pullin, 2002).

Energy Flow in Ecosystems

All organisms need energy to grow, move, repair, and reproduce. Most organisms get their energy from sunlight. This can happen either directly or indirectly. Lettuce and most other plants, get energy directly from sunlight through photosynthesis. During photosynthesis, plant leaves produce glucose. The plants use the chemical energy in glucose to carry out life functions (DeAngelis, 1980). In an ecosystem, plants are called producers because they use energy from sunlight to make, or produce, their own food. A rabbit, however, cannot get energy directly from sunlight. But as the rabbit eats the lettuce, it indirectly gets energy from the Sun that is stored in the leaves. Organisms that get energy by eating other organisms are called consumers. The fungus cannot make its own food from sunlight, but it doesn't eat other organisms either. It gets it by breaking down the remains of organisms that were once alive, such as trees that have fallen down. Organisms such as the fungus are called decomposers. They release materials from dead plants and animals back into the environment, where other consumers can use them. Without decomposers, nothing would decay. Most living things on Earth depend on the Sun's energy either directly or indirectly. The leaves of a berry bush use energy from the Sun to make food known as glucose. Plants use the chemical energy in glucose as energy for their life functions. Plants are producers; organisms that can make their own food (Ulanowicz, and Kay, 1991). Animals cannot use sunlight to make their own food. Animals are consumers; organisms that get energy by eating other organisms. When a bear eats berries, it gets the energy stored in them. The bear uses energy from the Sun indirectly. Toadstools cannot make their own food. But they cannot eat other organisms either. When organisms die and fall to the ground, their bodies decay. A decomposer is an organism that gets energy by breaking down the remains of dead organisms. Toadstools are decomposers. Decomposers return the materials from the dead organism's body back into the environment. Decomposers help provide materials that other organisms can use. Without decomposers, nothing would ever decay. Dead organisms would just pile up forever (Jonsson, and Malmqvist, 2000).

Food Chains

As you know, organisms either use energy from sunlight to produce their own food or they eat other organisms that have energy. A food chain shows one possible path of how organisms within an ecosystem get their food. Because the original source of energy is sunlight, a food chain begins with plant life and ends with an animal. Notice that the arrows in a food chain always point toward the organism that receives the energy (Post, *et al.*, 2000). *E.g.*, in the food chain, the food chain that connects the path of energy from wheat, to the mouse, to the snake, and on to the owl. In an ecosystem, some organisms produce food, while others consume food. This is how energy travels in an ecosystem. A food chain shows a path of energy through an ecosystem. Follow the food chain from the microscopic organisms to the common mussel, then to the herring gull (Krause, *et al.*, 2002).

Food Web

Every chain has a producer that makes its own food and consumers that eat other organisms. Most organisms are part of more than one food chain and eat more than one kind of food (Dunne, *et al.*, 2002). Because organisms in an ecosystem often belong to more than one food chain, the food chains become interconnected, or mixed. These interconnected food chains form a food web. Study the food web is given here. Wheat, clover, and dandelions are the producers at the bottom of this food web. The owl and the hawk are the consumers at the top because no animals in this ecosystem eat them (Berryman, 1993). Many different food chains exist in an ecosystem. Food chains have producers and consumers. Consumers often eat other consumers. Organisms may be part of several food chains. A food web is made up of several food chains that are interconnected.

Energy Pyramids

A food chain shows the path that energy takes from producers to consumers. However, it does not give any information about how much energy moves from organism to organism. Not all of the energy that plants receive from sunlight is available to be passed on to animals that eat the plant. This is because the plant uses some energy to stay alive. The same is true for animals. They use energy to grow, move, and reproduce (Polis, and Strong, 1996). They pass on only the energy that is left over.

An energy pyramid shows how energy moves through an ecosystem. In an energy pyramid, the greatest amount of energy is available from the trees and bushes on the bottom level. Giraffes eat these plants then use most of the energy they get to carry out life processes. When a lion eats a giraffe, there is little energy stored in the giraffe's body to pass on to the lion. Because of this, an ecosystem needs many giraffes to support a small number of lions. A food chain shows how energy travels from producers to the top consumer. But a food chain does not show how much energy moves from one organism to another. Not all of the energy that a green plant takes in from the Sun moves to other organisms. The plant uses some of the energy for its own life processes. Some energy is lost as heat. This repeats throughout a food chain. A snake uses energy to slide along the ground. A wood mouse uses energy to dig itself a hole. Organisms must use energy to grow, move, and reproduce. So, only part of the energy can move to the next level of the food chain. An energy pyramid is a model that shows how energy moves through an ecosystem. The pyramid gets smaller as it nears the top. There is more energy at lower the levels (Levine, 1980). There is less energy towards the top of the pyramid because most of it has been used by organisms for life processes or has been given off as heat. Only energy stored in the tissues of an organism can pass from one level to the next.

Competition between Organisms for Resources

All plants and animals need food, water, and space. Within an ecosystem, these resources are limited, so there is always a competition for them. Animals with different needs can live side by side with little competition. This is because the birds eat different foods. These birds do not need to compete for food in this ecosystem. Competition occurs only when organisms of an ecosystem have the same needs. Sometimes competition is between members of the same species, such as two herons. If there is a drought and the marsh becomes dry, the herons that can survive with less food and water have a better chance of survival than those who need more. Sometimes competition is between different species. Suppose a stork came to this marsh to find food. Since storks and herons eat the same kind of fish and frogs, the two species would compete for the same resources (Downing, and Leibold, 2002).

Ecosystems Change

All ecosystems sustain natural changes over time. People also cause changes to ecosystems. Sometimes ecosystems change. First, one part of the ecosystem changes. Then the other parts change too. Long ago, many wolves lived in Yellowstone National Park. The wolves ate elk and other animals. People wanted to get rid of the wolves. They killed many of them. When the wolves were gone, there were not enough animals to eat the elk. Yellowstone's elk population grew out of control. There were too many elk and not enough food. Many of the elk died. Finally, people divided to bring wolves back to the park (Knops, *et al.*, 2002)

Natural Changes

In the summer of 1988, raging forest fires burned throughout Yellowstone National Park. The fires, which were started by lightning, charred one-third of this national park. The park follows a "natural burn" rule. This means that fires started accidentally by humans are put out, but fires started by a natural event, such as lightning, are allowed to burn unless they threaten people's lives and property. Park managers know that natural disasters, such as forest fires, volcanic eruptions, and floods, are an important part of ecology. They change ecosystems by killing old plants and allowing new ones to grow. Succession is a series of changes that occur in an ecosystem (Jørgensen, *et al.*, 2000). This is how succession worked in Yellowstone after the fires. Plants called pioneer species began to grow on the damaged land.

Pioneer plants can grow under difficult conditions. The following spring, about two dozen different kinds of plants began to grow out of the ashes. Many of these plants had existed before the fires, but only as roots. The forest floor had been so thick that they could not compete for the resources necessary to grow stems and leaves. As the pioneer plants died each season, their bodies decomposed and built up the soil. After enough soil formed, other organisms were able to live in the ecosystem. Seeds took root and formed new plants in the rich soil. Some of these seeds may have survived the fire because they were buried deep in the ground. Others blew in from unburned areas. For the most part, park rangers did not replant Yellowstone. Yellowstone's forests replanted themselves.

Competition

Competition is the struggle between organisms to survive when resources are limited. Like all organisms, the animals on the African savannah need food, water, and shelter. The animals that survive get these resources. Organisms that have different needs can live together without competing. Zebras eat the tall, coarse grass. After the zebras eat, the wildebeests eat the shorter grass left behind. Competition takes place between organisms that have similar needs. Resource, such as food, water, and shelter are limited in an ecosystem (Dierssen, 2000). Organisms can survive when their adaptations are best suited to their conditions. Organisms with adaptations not well suited to their conditions will not survive. Some competition takes place between members of the same species. For instance, lack of rainfall can make water scarce. Only some zebras that compete for water will survive. The successful ones will be those who can live on less water. Competition also occurs between different species. Wildebeests and gazelles both eat short, tender grass. If drought kills many grass plants, gazelles and wildebeests must compete for what is left. All organisms, not just animals, compete for resources. Plants compete for water, space to grow, minerals, and sunlight. Some plants even have ways to reduce competition. They release chemicals into the soil that kill other species around them (Fath, *et al.*, 2004).

Human Impact on Ecosystems

People have an enormous impact on the ecosystems we live in. Our daily activities change ecosystems in ways that make it difficult, and sometimes even impossible, for other animals and plants to survive. Landfills that we build to hold our trash change ecosystems. Each person in the United States creates about four pounds of trash every day. Together, we create about 600,000 tons per day. Some is recycled, some is burned, but most is taken to landfills. An advantage of landfills is that they reduce health hazards created by open-air dumps. However, hazardous materials, such as paint, acid from batteries, and chemicals, can leak out of landfills and harm ecosystems.

People often harm the environment without even realizing it (Marques, *et al.*, 2003). When fossil fuels are burned, they create air pollution. Many of our everyday activities, such as driving cars and using electricity, depend on the use of fossil fuels. Think about how many times you rode in a car or a bus this week, and how many times you used electricity. Another way people harm the environment without realizing it is by using too much water. Water is an important resource in every ecosystem. People in the United States use more water every year than people in any other country. Humans are part of the ecosystem where they live. Human activity can change the environment. Some organisms cannot survive these changes. Think of the trash you threw away so far today. In 2001 each American produced about four pounds of trash a day. Much of it ends up in landfills. The advantage of using landfills is that they reduce odor. They are safer than open dumps. But they can cause problems too. Unsafe waste, such as paint and batteries, can leak and harm ecosystems. Building landfills can cause some organisms to lose their habitats and die. Over time, landfill space gets used up, and new areas must be found for the waste. People may cause harm without even knowing it (Hall, and Raffaelli, 1993). Pollution enters the air when people drive their cars. Power plants cause pollution too. Even ranching and farming can have harmful results. When livestock overgraze, plants die. The soil erodes. Fertilizers can enter the water cycle and pollute lakes and rivers.

Saving Ecosystems

During a winter storm in 1996, an oil barge ran aground off the coast of Rhode Island. About 828,000 gallons of oil spilled into the ocean. The oil spill killed more than nine million lobsters, two thousand marine birds, and about one million pounds of clams, oysters, and scallops in the ecosystem. The oil also damaged the habitat of a bird called the piping plover, which was already on the list of endangered species (Ho, and Ulanowicz, 2005). Crews of workers tried to soak up the oil from the water's surface and the beaches. Ninety-seven volunteers spent hundreds of hours in an effort to seed new scallop beds. They carefully placed about eight thousand healthy scallops in the area to try to grow a new scallop population. Similar projects are underway to replace the oyster population. Unfortunately, even with the efforts of scientists and volunteers, much of the damage done to the animals and the ecosystem they live in cannot be undone. In 1989 an oil spill damaged the coast of Prince William Sound in Alaska. Millions of gallons of oil leaked from an ocean oil tanker. It polluted the land and water and put a great strain on the ecosystem. Thousands of workers helped to clean up the mess. Many washed oily animals, such as otters, with soap and water. They scrubbed oil from the rocks. But even with all the work and money spent, much of the damage could not be undone. Billions of animals died, including 22 orca whales and 250,000 sea birds. The area still has not fully recovered (Herendeen, 1981).

Preventing Problems

Crews of workers tried to soak up the oil from the water's surface and the beaches. Ninety-seven volunteers spent hundreds of hours in an effort to seed new scallop beds. They carefully placed about eight thousand healthy scallops in the area to try to grow a new scallop population. Similar projects are underway to replace the oyster population (Hannon, 1973). Unfortunately, even with the efforts of scientists and volunteers, much of the damage done to the animals and the ecosystem they live in cannot be undone, environment healthy for all its organisms. Become a recycling "watchdog" at home and at school. More than four billion individual drink boxes are thrown away each year in the United States. These can sit in a landfill for more than three hundred years before they decompose. Setting up a program to recycle just these small items is a good way to begin. It's better to prevent problems before they happen in the first place. Here are ways you can help:

- Understand how you affect your ecosystem.
- Learn how to reduce the harm you cause.
- Reuse, recycle, or reduce your use of natural resources.
- Know how ecosystems work.
- Get involved. Join environmental groups to help.

As an adult, you will make decisions that affect yourself and your community. And what your community does will affect other regions in your state and country. These choices may even affect the world at large. Learn to be an informed citizen now. It will make it easier for you to become a responsible adult (Gunderson, *et al.*, 2000).

Saltwater Ecosystems

Earth's oceans contain almost all of its salt water. They cover most of the planet. Near the land, the ocean is not very deep. Clams, crabs, and some kinds of fish live there. Far from land, the ocean water is deep. Large fish, sharks, and whales can live in deep water. The deepest parts of the oceans are dark and cold. Very few plants can grow there because there is little sunlight (Shugart, 1998). Rivers flow into oceans. The fresh water from rivers mixes with salt water from the ocean. When this happens, salt marshes are formed. A salt marsh is a type of wetland. Most of the salt marsh is covered with water. Many grasses grow in the salt marsh. These grasses can live in water and soil that is salty. Some of the animals in the salt marsh are so small that you can't see them. Many sea animals start their life in salt marshes before moving out to the ocean (Engelhardt, and Ritchie, 2002).

Freshwater Ecosystems

Some aquatic ecosystems have fresh water. Other ecosystems have salt water. In some places fresh water and salt water come together. Lakes, ponds, rivers, and streams are all freshwater ecosystems. Lakes and ponds have land all around them (Reynolds, 1984). In rivers and streams, the water moves from one place to another. The water in some lakes and rivers comes from under the ground. The water in others comes from rain or melting snow. A wetland is land that is covered by water most of the time. Trees, grasses, and plants grow in a wetland. Many animals live there too. Some wetland birds have long legs that help them walk in the water. They have beaks for catching fish to eat. Wetland frogs and toads can live in the water and on the land. The largest freshwater wetland is in Brazil. Many large rivers run through Brazil. When it rains, these rivers can overflow, flooding the surrounding land. The flooded land becomes a wetland habitat for many plants and animals. Many birds stay in the wetlands of Brazil for a short time while they are traveling to other places. Many fish live there too. The wetlands of Brazil are also home to capybaras. They have webbed feet, like a duck. Their webbed feet help them swim (Simon, and Townsend, 2003).

Freshwater ecosystems may well be the most endangered ecosystems in the world. Declines in biodiversity are far greater in fresh waters than in the most affected terrestrial ecosystems (Sala et al., 2000). What makes freshwater habitats and the biodiversity that they support especially vulnerable to human activities and environmental change? The main reason is the disproportionate richness of inland waters as a habitat for plants and animals. Over 10,000 fish species live in fresh water (Lundberg et al., 2000); approximately 40% of global fish diversity and one quarter of global vertebrate diversity. When amphibians, aquatic reptiles (crocodiles, turtles) and mammals (otters, river dolphins, platypus) are added to this freshwater-fish total, it becomes clear that as much as one third of all vertebrate species are confined to fresh water. Yet surface freshwater habitats contain only around 0.01% of the world's water and cover only about 0.8% of the Earth's surface (Gleick, 1996). Knowledge of the total diversity of fresh waters is woefully incomplete – particularly among invertebrates and microbes, and especially in tropical latitudes that support most of the world's species. Even vertebrates are incompletely known, including well-studied taxa such as fishes (Stiassny, 2002). Between 1976 and 1994, an average of 309 new fish species, approximately 1% of known fishes, were formally described or resurrected from synonymy each year (Stiassny, 1999) and this trend has continued (Lundberg et al., 2000). Among amphibians, almost 35% of the global total of 5778 species has been described during the last decade (AmphibiaWeb, 2005). Adequate data on the diversity of most invertebrate groups in tropical fresh waters do not exist, but high levels of local endemism and species richness seem typical of several major groups, including decapod crustaceans, molluscs and aquatic insects such as caddisflies and mayflies (Dudgeon, 1999, 2000c ; Benstead et al., 2003; Strayer et al., 2004). Information on microbial biodiversity is fragmentary too, notwithstanding the crucial role of microbes in driving the biogeochemical cycles of the Earth. Most prokaryote taxonomic diversity remains unexplored. Recent genomic analyses (e.g. Zwart et al., 2003) suggest that aquatic microbial biodiversity is considerably higher than inferred from classical, non-molecular evidence. It is likely that the richness of freshwater fungi and microalgae has been likewise underestimated (Johns & Maggs, 1997; Gessner & Van Ryckegem, 2003).

Freshwater Biodiversity

Freshwater biodiversity is the over-riding conservation priority during the International Decade for Action – 'Water for Life' – 2005 to 2015. Fresh water makes up only 0.01% of the World's water and approximately 0.8% of the Earth's surface, yet this tiny fraction of global water supports at least 100 000 species out of approximately 1.8 million – almost 6% of all described species. Inland waters and freshwater biodiversity constitute a valuable natural resource, in economic, cultural, aesthetic, scientific and educational terms. Their conservation and management are critical to the interests of all humans, nations and governments. Yet this precious heritage is in crisis. Fresh waters are experiencing declines in biodiversity far greater than those in the most affected terrestrial ecosystems, and if trends in human demands for water remain unaltered and species losses continue at current rates, the opportunity to conserve much of the remaining biodiversity in fresh water will vanish before the 'Water for Life ' decade ends in 2015. The present paper explores the special features of freshwater habitats and the biodiversity they support that makes them especially vulnerable to human activities. Immediate action is needed where opportunities exist to set aside intact lake and river ecosystems within large protected areas. For most of the global land surface, trade-offs between conservation of freshwater biodiversity and human use of ecosystem goods and services are necessary. We advocate continuing attempts to check species loss but, in many situations, urge adoption of a compromise position of management for biodiversity conservation, ecosystem functioning and resilience, and human livelihoods in order to provide a viable long-term basis for freshwater conservation.

Major Threats to Freshwater Biodiversity

The threats to global freshwater biodiversity can be grouped under five interacting categories: overexploitation; water pollution; flow modification; destruction or degradation of habitat; and invasion by exotic species (e.g. Naiman & Turner, 2000; Jackson et al., 2001; Malmqvist & Rundle, 2002; Postel & Richter, 2003; Revenga et al., 2005). Environmental changes occurring at the global scale, such as nitrogen deposition, warming, and shifts in precipitation and runoff patterns are superimposed upon all of these threat categories (Poff, Brinson & Day, 2002, Galloway et al., 2004). Overexploitation primarily affects vertebrates, mainly fishes, reptiles and some amphibians, whereas the other four threat categories have consequences for all freshwater biodiversity from microbes to mega fauna. Pollution problems are pandemic, and although some industrialized countries have made considerable progress in reducing water pollution from domestic and industrial point sources, threats from excessive nutrient enrichment (Smith, 2003) and other chemicals such as endocrine disrupters are growing (Colburn, Dumanoski & Myers, 1996). Habitat degradation is brought about by an array of interacting factors. It may involve direct effects on the aquatic environment (such as excavation of river sand) or indirect impacts that result from changes within the drainage basin. For example, forest clearance is usually associated with changes in surface runoff and increased river sediment loads that can lead to habitat alterations such as shoreline erosion, smothering of littoral habitats, clogging of river bottoms or floodplain aggradation. Flow modifications are ubiquitous in running waters. They vary in severity and type, but tend to be most aggressive in regions with highly variable flow regimes. This is because humans in these places have the greatest need for flood protection or water storage. That existing dams retain approximately 10, 000 km3 of water, the equivalent of five times the volume of the entire world's rivers (Nilsson & Berggren, 2000), illustrates the global extent of human alteration of river flow. Water impoundment by dams in the Northern Hemisphere is now so great that it has caused measurable geodynamic changes in the Earth's rotation and gravitational field (Chao, 1995). Even some of the world's largest rivers now run dry for part of the year or are likely to do so as a result of large-scale water abstraction (Postel & Richter, 2003). Flow modifications are likely to be exacerbated by global climate change because greater frequency of floods and droughts, and consequent increased water-engineering responses, can be anticipated. Although this matter will not be explored herein, impacts on river biota (fishes, for example) are likely to be severe (e.g. Dudgeon, 2000a). Widespread invasion and deliberate introduction of exotic species adds to the physical and chemical impacts of humans on fresh waters, in part because exotics are most likely to successfully invade fresh waters already modified or degraded by humans (e.g. Bunn & Arthington, 2002; Koehn, 2004). There are many examples of large scale and dramatic effects of exotics on indigenous species (e.g. Nile perch, Lates niloticus, in Lake Victoria, the crayfish plague in Europe, salmonids in Southern Hemisphere lakes and streams), and impacts are projected to increase further (Sala et al., 2000). Indirect impacts can arise from exotic terrestrial plants such as Tamarix spp. (Tamaricaceae), which alter the water regime of riparian soils and affect stream flows in Australia and North America (Tickner et al., 2001).

The particular vulnerability of freshwater biodiversity also reflects the fact that fresh water is a resource for humans that may be extracted, diverted, contained or contaminated in ways that compromise its value as a habitat for organisms. Indeed, some authors now believe it unlikely that there remain a substantial number of water bodies that have not been irreversibly altered from their original state by human activities (Leveque & Balian, 2005). The extent of most freshwater systems is not confined to the wetted perimeter, but includes the catchment from which water and material are drawn. Their position in the landscape (almost always in valley bottoms) makes lakes and rivers receivers of wastes, sediments and pollutants in runoff. This is also true of seas and oceans, but inland water bodies typically lack the volume of open marine waters, limiting their capacity to dilute contaminants or mitigate other impacts.

In addition, in many parts of the world fresh water is subject to severe competition among multiple human stakeholders, to the point that armed conflicts can arise when water supplies are limiting and rivers traverse political boundaries (Poff et al., 2003). There are 263 international rivers, draining 45% of the Earth's land surface. This area supports more than 40% of the global human population is an indication of the scope of the issue (Bernauer, 2002; Postel & Richter, 2003; Clark & King, 2004). In the vast majority of disagreements over multiple uses of water, whether they are international or on a local scale, allocation of water to maintain aquatic biodiversity is largely disregarded (Poff et al., 2003). In China and India, where approximately 55% of the world's large dams are situated (W. C. D., 2000), hardly any consideration has been given to the downstream allocation of water for biodiversity (Poff et al., 2003; Tharme, 2003).

The combined and interacting influences of the five major threat categories have resulted in population declines and range reduction of freshwater biodiversity worldwide. Qualitative data suggest reductions in numerous wetland and water margin vertebrates (19 mammals, 92 birds, 72 reptiles and 44 fish species), while population trends indicate declines averaging 54% among freshwater vertebrates (mainly waterfowl), with a tendency toward higher values in tropical latitudes (Groombridge & Jenkins, 2000; Loh, 2000). Furthermore, 32% of the world's amphibian species now are threatened with extinction, a much higher proportion than threatened birds (12%) or mammals (23%), and 168 species may already be extinct (AmphibiaWeb, 2005). The well-known global decline of amphibians started during the 1950s and 1960s and has continued at the current rate of approximately 2% per year, with more pronounced decreases in tropical streams (Houlahan et al., 2000; Stuart et al., 2004). This is close to the estimate of 2.4% for declines in populations of freshwater vertebrates over the period 1970–1999 (Balmford et al., 2002). These estimates are extremely alarming. Extinction rates of freshwater animals in North America, based on combined data sets for unionid mussels, crayfishes, fishes and amphibians, may even be as much as 4% per decade – five times higher than species losses calculated from any terrestrial habitat (Ricciardi & Rasmussen, 1999). Around 90 species of non-marine turtles occur in this region. Classifications as Critically Endangered (CR), Endangered (EN) and Vulnerable (VU) reflect a dramatic increase in threats due to overexploitation of turtles for food and the traditional Chinese medicine trade, with the consequence that over 80% of the regional fauna is now threatened. Species classified as Data Deficient (DD) are poorly known but perceived to be under threat also (Van Dijk, 2000). These limited data on extinction rates from one continent are believed to be indicative of a global freshwater biodiversity crisis (Abell, 2002). Rates of species loss from fresh waters in non-temperate latitudes are not known with any degree of certainty. They are likely to be high because species richness of many freshwater taxa (e.g. fishes, macrophytes, decapod crustaceans) increases toward the tropics. The drainage basins of many large tropical and subtropical rivers (e.g. the Ganges and Yangtze) are densely populated – with large dams, altered flow patterns and gross pollution from a variety of sources being the inevitable outcomes (e.g. Dudgeon, 2000a, 2002). For larger species in these rivers, the situation is parlous: the Yangtze dolphin is probably the most endangered mammal on Earth (now numbering fewer than 100 individuals ; Dudgeon, 2005), and the Ganges dolphin (Platanista gangetica (Roxburgh)) is 'Endangered' (IUCN, 2003). The crocodilian fauna of the Ganges and Yangtze likewise consists entirely of threatened or highly endangered species. Many other species of water associated reptiles – a primarily tropical group – are gravely threatened (Gibbons et al., 2000; Van Dijk, 2000), most particularly turtles as are large freshwater fishes in most rivers (e.g. Baird et al., 2001; Carolsfeld et al., 2004; Hogan et al., 2004), and many freshwater fish stocks are over-fished to the point of population collapse (e.g. FAO, 2000; Dudgeon, 2002).

Populations of large vertebrates may not be accurate indicators of the status of all of freshwater taxa, but there are grounds for grave concern if their status were reflected in even 5% of the total species complement. To date, however, there has been no comprehensive global analysis of freshwater biodiversity comparable to those recently completed for terrestrial systems (Myers et al., 2000; Olson et al., 2001). Existing data on the population status or extinction rates of freshwater biota are biased in terms of geography, habitat types and taxonomy; most populations and habitats in some regions have not been monitored at all. Even a basic global mapping of inland waters, classified by broad geomorphic categories, is lacking – and there are no global estimates of changes in the extent of lakes, rivers or wetlands (Balmford et al., 2002). Conservation efforts for freshwater biodiversity are constrained by the fact that most of the species in diverse communities are rare (e.g. Sheldon, 1988) and thus their natural histories tend to be poorly known. This means that even when reductions in overall species numbers are predictable, forecasting the identities of the affected taxa is not possible. Furthermore, the unreliability of estimates of species richness in individual river basins (makes it virtually certain that regional national inventories, museum collections and taxonomic knowledge in many parts of the tropics are inadequate to document extinctions, and thus widespread undetected extinctions of inconspicuous species have already taken place (Harrison & Stiassny, 1999; Stiassny, 2002). The problem of species being misidentified, or not represented in collections, or listed incorrectly on protected species lists adds to the uncertainty (Kottelat & Whitten, 1996). One important implication of these various constraints is that, with the exception of a few well-known taxa in a limited number of countries (e.g. Ricciardi & Rasmussen, 1999; Strayer et al., 2004), it is not possible to estimate or accurately project extinction rates of freshwater biodiversity using the approaches applied to terrestrial biota (Dirzo, 2001; Dirzo & Raven, 2003).

Globally, awareness of the need to conserve freshwater biodiversity seems limited. Between 1997 and 2001, only 7% of papers in the leading journal in the field, Conservation Biology, was concerned with freshwater species or habitats (Abell, 2002). Most reported studies from northern temperate latitudes. This negligence is particularly acute in regions where biodiversity is both rich and highly threatened. A mere 0.6% of papers in the conservation biology literature between 1992 and 2001 dealt with freshwater biodiversity in Asia (Dudgeon, 2003b), although this continent supports over half of the global human population, with consequent pressures on inland waters, and a very significant part of the world's biodiversity. Indonesia alone supports about 15% of the word's species, and has more amphibians and dragonflies than any other country (Braatz et al., 1992). The manifest knowledge impediment in Asia and elsewhere in the tropics limits both attempts to quantify the freshwater biodiversity crisis and the ability to alleviate it.

Biodiversity Conservation

A significant challenge to freshwater biodiversity conservation results from the complexity imposed on fresh waters by catchment divides and saltwater barriers. As a result, low gene flow and local radiation lead in the absence of human disturbance to considerable inter drainage variation in biodiversity and high levels of Endemism. Ancient lakes such as Lake Baikal in Siberia and those in the East African Rift Valley support well-known species flocks of endemic crustaceans and fishes, but there are important radiations of cichlids, cyprinids, catfishes and other fishes, as well as frogs, crustaceans and molluscs, elsewhere in Africa and the world. For example, species flocks occur among Cyprinidae in the Philippines, Telmatherinidae on Sulawesi, and Balitoridae in China (Kottelat & Whitten, 1996). Virtually all of these radiations are severely endangered, as the examples from Africa illustrate. At smaller geographic scales there is substantial species turnover among drainage basins and water bodies, and many freshwater species have restricted ranges (e.g. Sheldon, 1988; Pusey & Kennard, 1996; Strayer et al., 2004). These attributes combine with endemism to produce a lack of 'substitutability' among freshwater habitat units. This means that protection of one or a few water bodies cannot preserve all freshwater biodiversity within a region, or even a significant proportion of it. In addition to conflicts arising from the multiple use of water, conservation of freshwater biodiversity is complicated by their landscape position as receivers and the problems posed by high levels of endemism and thus non-substitutability. Other features intrinsic to freshwater environments, especially rivers, also make them vulnerable to human impacts. Rivers are open, directional systems, and elements of their biota range widely using different parts of the habitat at various times during their lives. Fishes and other animals (from shrimps to river dolphins) use different habitats at different times, and longitudinal migrations may be an obligatory component of life histories especially if as in many species migration is associated with breeding. Longitudinal migrations may occur within the river or from river to sea or lake and back or from sea or lake to river and back. Such movements put animals at risk from stresses in various parts of their habitat at different times; long-lived species with low reproductive rates are likely to be the most vulnerable (Carolsfeld et al., 2004). Dams in tropical regions are generally constructed without appropriate fishways or fish passes, or based upon designs that are suitable only for salmonids, and thus they obstruct fish migrations (Roberts, 2001). A dam on the lower course of a river prevents migratory fishes with an obligate marine phase in their life cycle from moving to and from the sea, creating the potential for activities in downstream reaches to impact upstream portions of the river by way of, for example, the nutrient transmission that occurs during spawning migrations of salmon (e.g. Naiman et al., 2002a). Lateral migrations, between inundated floodplains or swamp forest and the main river channel, represent another axis of connectivity important for feeding and breeding in many fishes and other animals (Ward et al., 2002; Carolsfeld et al., 2004; Arthington et al., 2005) that is dramatically altered by human activities.

Terrestrial conservation strategies tend to emphasize areas of high habitat quality that can be bounded and protected. This ' fortress conservation ' is likely to fail for fresh waters (Boon, 2000) and may even be counterproductive (Moss, 2000; Dunn, 2003) for river segments or lakes embedded in unprotected drainage basins unless the boundaries are drawn at a catchment scale, which is virtually never the case. This problem of boundary definition impedes sensible local management of freshwater biodiversity (Baird et al., 2001) because protection of a particular component of river biota (and often habitat) requires control over the upstream drainage network, the surrounding land, the riparian zone, and in the case of migrating aquatic fauna – downstream reaches (Pringle, 2001; Pusey & Arthington, 2003). Conservation action at the catchment scale, involving interconnected landscape units, is needed also for certain terrestrial taxa that undertake seasonal migrations, but the shortcomings inherent in fortress conservation are particularly acute for freshwater biodiversity. The catchment scale is generally appropriate for all types of freshwater management of freshwater habitats (e.g. Pollard & Huxham, 1998; Moss, 2000), and it helps resolve the small-scale but damaging conflicts of interest among competing human demands. However, this approach can be problematic in practice, as relatively large areas of land need to be managed in order to protect relatively small water bodies. A promising approach could involve ecological management that integrates the requirements of terrestrial and freshwater environments. This will complicate the process of establishing appropriate boundaries for protected areas. However, from the freshwater perspective, it would have the added advantage of broadening the historic management approach that has been focused mainly on biodiversity and habitats within river channels, with dependent floodplains and their inhabitants receiving relatively little attention (Kingsford, 2000; Ward et al., 2002). Large animals such as bear, swamp deer, rhinos, and elephants make seasonal use of riparian areas and floodplains for feeding or breeding (Naiman & De´camps, 1997; Dudgeon, 2000b; Naiman, De´camps & McClain, 2005). Maintaining proximity to water is essential for many large animals during the tropical dry season, which can be a period of severe ecological stress for herbivores. Effective preservation of biodiversity associated with freshwater habitats must therefore take account of the year-round habitat use and movements by terrestrial, riparian and amphibiotic fauna (e.g. frogs, water dragons and snakes, platypus, otters, and many water birds), as well as the needs of the strictly aquatic biota. Maintenance of some asemblance of the natural flow variability and the flood/drought cycle of rivers and their floodplains, vernal pools, and water-level fluctuations in wetlands and along lakeshores, also will be essential.

Importance of Freshwater Biodiversity

Freshwater biodiversity provides a broad variety of valuable goods and services for human societies, some of which are irreplaceable (Covich et al., 2004a). The value of this biodiversity has several components: its direct contribution to economic productivity (e.g. fisheries) ; its 'insurance' value in light of unexpected events ; its value as a storehouse of genetic information

; and its value in supporting the provision of ecosystem services (e.g. cleaning water) (Pearce, 1998; Heal, 2000; Covich et al., 2004b). Estimates of the full value of biodiversity need to account for each of these four components; to date, this has not been done. A number of fundamental questions still have to be answered (Loreau et al., 2001), but substantial progress has been made in understanding the effects of biodiversity on the functioning of terrestrial ecosystems (Hooper et al., 2005). However, the precise impacts of biodiversity change will vary with ecosystem type and the processes and properties considered (Giller et al., 2004; Hooper et al., 2005). Although much less is known about fresh waters than terrestrial ecosystems, there is evidence that ecosystem processes can be impacted by changes in biodiversity (Covich et al., 2004a). Invertebrates, for example, play multiple roles in the functioning of rivers (Wallace & Webster, 1996), and the presence of key species (Dangles et al., 2004), magnitude of species richness (Cardinale, Palmer & Collins, 2002; Jonsson & Malmqvist, 2003), and other attributes of communities (e.g. Dangles & Malmqvist, 2004) can affect rates of ecosystem processes. In addition, variability of process rates is likely to be increased when species are lost, even in situations where average rates remain unchanged. In some cases it is possible to predict how different anthropogenic stresses will affect ecosystem functioning (Jonsson et al., 2002), but in most instances insufficient information is available to make informed predictions. Of particular concern is the decline in populations of large freshwater vertebrates to a level whereby they become so scarce that their ecological roles are degraded to an extent that they might as well be extinct. Such functional extinctions, and associated reductions in ecosystem services, have been projected for a variety of land birds (Sekercioglu, Daily & Ehrlich, 2004) and may have already taken place in some freshwater ecosystems. Appreciating the value of freshwater biodiversity is essential to ensure its well-being. It is certain that if scientists are unwilling or unable to place a value on free ecosystem goods and services, then politicians and policy-makers will interpret this as 'zero value'. The resources apt to be protected are those that are appreciated. Water must no longer be a free or cheap resource as it is still treated in most countries (Kingsford, 2000; Clark & King, 2004). Realistic economic valuations of water as a habitat for freshwater biodiversity, and the services that such biodiversity provides, will be an essential driver of any change in societal attitudes (Postel & Carpenter, 1997; Holmlund & Hammer, 1999; Postel & Richter, 2003; Clark & King, 2004).

Inland waters constitute a valuable natural resource, in economic, cultural, aesthetic, scientific and educational terms. Immediate conservation action is needed in some instances where opportunities exist to set aside pristine lake and river systems in large protected areas. Realistically, it must be recognized that there are significant portions of the Earth's surface where it is almost inconceivable that any freshwater resource could be dedicated to the sole purpose of biodiversity conservation, with humans denied access or their use of the resource substantially limited. Even well-protected conservation areas can become focal points for tourism and recreational activities that may reduce habitat quality and biodiversity (Hadwen, Arthington & Mosisch, 2003).Thus, for most of the global land surface, trade-offs between conservation of freshwater biodiversity and human use of ecosystem goods and services are necessary. If science is to be deployed in a manner that will secure commitment to the conservation of freshwater biodiversity from politicians and decision-makers, scientists will have to make some adjustments in attitude (Leveque & Balian, 2005). In particular, reconsideration of what is regarded as acceptable forms of ecosystem management for biodiversity conservation will be required in the wider context of national development policies. We do not advocate abandoning attempts to check species loss but, in many situations, a compromise position of management for biodiversity conservation, ecosystem functioning and resilience, and human livelihoods will provide the most successful long-term basis for freshwater conservation (Moss, 2000). Furthermore, this approach is more likely to be achievable than idealistic prospects of 'win–win' situations between economic development and ecological management practices within which all species can be saved (Redford & Sanderson, 1992), or the alternative and discouraging view that conservation of biodiversity is fundamentally incompatible with economic development (Terborgh, 1999). An apparent lack of common ground between organizations committed to sustaining livelihoods and those concerned with biodiversity conservation might arise from different starting points and prioritisation of goals; if so, such differences must be recognised but they need not imply that attempts to combine the goals of conservation and meeting human needs should be regarded as futile (Adams et al., 2004).

Data are insufficient to estimate accurately loss rates of freshwater biodiversity in many regions. An immediate, coordinated effort to assess global freshwater biodiversity, including identification of major hotspots, is mandated, and should involve partnerships among major non-government organisations, the United Nations, research institutions, and scientific societies. However, the current impediment of insufficient data should not be used as justification for preventing further losses. Nor does the broader community have to wait until all possible information is in hand before taking action. As the current trends in turtles, fishes and other taxa indicate, there are sufficient reliable data to show that the global crisis of freshwater biodiversity is now a calamity. Developing effective conservation and management strategies for freshwater biodiversity requires documenting declines and extinctions and understanding the underlying causes. Implementation of such strategies depends upon effective communication and engagement among scientists, politicians, non-government organizations and local communities (Poff et al., 2003). Pragmatic approaches will be needed to ensure that attempts at communication between freshwater scientists and water resource managers, as well as other stakeholders, contribute to planning and problem solving (Richter et al., 2003) and do not become a dialogue of the deaf. This is a significant challenge as motivations of the broader community may be neither open nor fair. Conservation typically operates in a world where many players are characterized by dishonesty, self-interest, and hostility to nature, and where corporate interests often assume disproportionate importance (Stearns & Stearns, 1999; Meffe, 2001). Emphatically, the importance of freshwater biodiversity to society must be communicated successfully to all. The threats to freshwater biodiversity are becoming sufficiently known among scientists, but are insufficiently incorporated within water development. Those making policy and management decisions affecting freshwater biodiversity and water resources need to apply the relevant scientific information, as far as this is available, and employ robust risk-assessment procedures, monitoring, and adaptive management (Richter et al., 2003; Revenga et al., 2005). Ecologically-sustainable water management will only be achievable if concerns about ecology and biodiversity are treated with the same importance as other goals (such as engineering considerations) when water-resource developments are planned (Richter et al., 2003). This will be a significant advance on the prevailing approach wherein ecological criteria are treated as compliance factors to be evaluated after a water-resource development plan has been completed. A first step in this process would be stipulation of ecosystem flow requirement so that water-resource managers can take account of these throughout the planning process.

CONCLUSIONS

Fresh water is subject to severe competition among multiple human stakeholders, in many regions, and serious conflicts can arise when water supplies are limiting or traverse political boundaries. Conservation of biodiversity is complicated further by the landscape position of rivers and wetlands as ' receivers ' of land use effluents, and the problems posed by endemism, limited geographic ranges and non-substitutability. Protection of freshwater biodiversity is perhaps the ultimate conservation challenge because, to be fully effective, it requires control over the upstream drainage network, the surrounding land, the riparian zone, and – in the case of migrating aquatic fauna – downstream reaches. Such prerequisites are hardly ever met, and will necessitate development of inclusive management partnerships at appropriate (drainage-basin) scales. The complicated issues associated with protected-areas design and management for fresh waters require energetic and imaginative attention from researchers. Water regimes influence aquatic biodiversity via several, inter-related mechanisms operating over a range of spatial and temporal scales. The maintenance of natural variability in flows and water levels is therefore essential to underpin conservation strategies for freshwater biodiversity and habitats. This requires establishing a hydrological regime that mimics natural variability in flows and water levels rather than focusing on minimum levels only. For most freshwater systems and taxa, scientists can – at present – neither estimate the quantities of water that can be extracted nor the temporal changes in flow that can be tolerated. Research on this matter of environmental water allocations is needed urgently. Furthermore, it is essential that provision of flows needed to preserve biodiversity be treated with the same importance as engineering concerns and other goals when water-resource developments are planned.

Fresh water makes up only 0.01% of the World's water and covers only 0.8% of the Earth's surface, yet this tiny fraction of global water supports at least 100 000 species out of approximately 1.75 million – almost 6%. Not surprisingly, considering their landscape position and value as a natural resource, fresh waters are experiencing declines in biodiversity far greater than those in the most affected terrestrial ecosystems. These declines seem to be especially serious in some tropical latitudes, and particularly affect large fishes and other vertebrates.

Freshwater biodiversity is the over-riding conservation priority during the International 'Water for Life' Decade for Action (2005 to 2015) and beyond. Assuming trends in human demands for water remain unaltered and species losses continue at current rates, the opportunity to conserve significant proportions of the remaining biodiversity in fresh water will vanish before the 'Water for Life' decade ends. Threats to global freshwater biodiversity fall into five categories: overexploitation ; water pollution ; flow modification ; destruction or degradation of habitat ; and invasion by exotic species. Their combined and interacting influences on biodiversity are now worldwide, and are exacerbated further by global-scale environmental changes such as nitrogen deposition and climate change. Knowledge of these threats is increasing among scientists but is insufficiently incorporated within water-resource development, and thus requires wider dissemination and emphasis.

Inventories of freshwater biodiversity are incomplete in many parts of the world, especially the tropics, and rates of species loss may be higher than currently estimated. An immediate, coordinated effort to assess global freshwater biodiversity, including major hotspots, should be launched in partnership with major non-government organisations, the United Nations, research institutions and scientific societies. This exercise should take place in parallel with the ongoing development of strategies for the conservation and management of freshwater biodiversity.

Freshwater biodiversity provides a broad variety of valuable goods and services for human societies. Some are irreplaceable. Notwithstanding, there is a paucity of empirical data showing how the value of goods and services derived by retaining habitats in relatively natural conditions compares with that obtained when they are converted for human use. The uses of fresh water, including non consumptive use, underscore the importance of considering the perspectives of a wide range of stakeholders in environmental valuation and in the development of effective conservation policies. Maintenance of biodiversity is a critical test of whether water use and ecosystem modifications are sustainable. Conservation strategies protecting all elements of freshwater biodiversity would guarantee that water use for humans is sustainable while, in contrast, the magnitude of the threat to and loss of biodiversity is an indicator of the extent to which current practices are unsustainable. A mixture of strategies will be essential to preserve freshwater biodiversity in the long term. It must include reserves that protect key, biodiversity-rich water-bodies (especially those with important species radiations) and their catchments, as well as species- or habitat-centred plans that reconcile the protection of biodiversity and societal use of water resources in the context human modified ecosystems. In parallel, scientists must more effectively communicate the importance and value of freshwater biodiversity to stakeholders and policy makers, so as to make certain that all available information on freshwater biodiversity is applied effectively to ensure its conservation.

Ecosystems are conceptual and functional units of study that entail the ecological community together with its abiotic environment. Implicit in the concept of any system, such as an ecosystem, is that of a system boundary which demarcates objects and processes occurring within the system from those occurring outside the system. Furthermore, as open systems, energy–matter fluxes occur across the boundary; these in turn provide the ecosystem with an available source of energy input such as solar radiation and a sink for waste heat. All ecosystems are open systems embedded in an environment from which they receive energy–matter input and discharge energy–matter output. The earth is a non-isolated system. There is almost no exchange of matter with the outer space. To be able to utilize the matter many times during the evolution or from one year and decade to the next, cycling is necessary. Cycling implies that the ecosystem components are linked in an interacting network. The flow of energy from the sun to the ecosystems is also limited. It is important that an ecosystem captures as much sunlight as possible to cover its energy needs. Therefore, ecosystems, with increased biomass, can increase net primary productivity. The development of the life forms that we know from the earth has been possible because the earth has the elements that are needed to build the biochemical compounds that explain the life processes. As ecosystems are valuable commodity, it is important to protect them with all its species and prevent them from the harmful impacts of humans.

REFERENCES

Abell, R. (2002). Conservation biology for the biodiversity crisis: a freshwater follow-up. Conservation Biology 16, 1435–1437.

Adams, W. M., Aveling, R., Brockington, D., Dickson, B., Elliot, J., Hutton, J., Roe, D., Vira, B. &Wolmer,W. (2004). Biodiversity conservation and eradication of poverty. Science 306, 1146–1149.

Amphibiaweb, (2005). AmphibiaWeb species numbers. AmphibiaWeb : Information on Amphibian Biodiversity and Conservation. Berkeley, California, U.S.A. http://amphibiaweb.org/ (accessed 2 April, 2005).

Arthington, A. H., Balcombe, S., Wilson, G., Thoms, M.T. & Marshall, J. (2005). Spatial and temporal variation in fish assemblage structure in isolated waterholes during the 2001 dry season of an arid-zone floodplain river, Cooper Creek, Australia. Marine & Freshwater Research 56, 1–11.

Baird, I. G., Phylavanh, B., Vongsenesouk, B. & Xaiyamanivong, K. (2001). The ecology and conservation of the smallscale croaker Boesemania microlepis (Bleeker 1858–59) in the mainstream Mekong River, southern Laos. Natural History Bulletin of the Siam Society 49, 161–176.

Balmford, A., Bruner, A., Cooper, P., Constanza, R., Farber, S., Green, R. E., Jenkins, M., Jefferiss, P., Jessamy, V., Madden, J., Munro, K., Myers, N., Naeem, S., Paavola, J., Rayment, M., Rosendo, S., Roughgarden, J., Trumoer, K. & Turner, R. K. (2002). Economic reasons for conserving wild nature. Science 297, 950–953.

Benstead, J. P., De Rham, P. H., Gattolliat, J. L., Gibon, F. M., Loiselle, P. V., Sartori, M., Sparks, J. S. & Stiassny, M. L. J. (2003). Conserving Madagascars Freshwater Biodiversity. Bioscience 53, 1101–1111.

Bernauer, T. (2002). Explaining success and failure in international river management. Aquatic Science 64, 1–19.

Berryman, A.A. (1993). Food web connectance and feedback dominance, or does everything really depend on everything else? Oikos 68, 183–185.

Boon, P. J. (2000). The development of integrated methods for assessing river conservation value. Hydrobiologia 422/423, 413–428.

Braatz, S., Davis, G., Shen, S. & Rees, C. (1992). Conserving biological diversity. A strategy for protected areas in the Asia-Pacific Region. World Bank Technical Paper 193, 1–66.

Bunn, S.E. & Arthington, A. H. (2002). Basic principles and ecological consequences of altered flow regimes for aquatic biodiversity. Environmental Management 30, 492–507.

Cardinale, B. J., Palmer, M. A. & Collins, S. L. (2002). Species diversity enhances ecosystem functioning through interspecific facilitation. Nature 415, 426–429.

Carolsfeld, J., Harvey, B., Ross, C. & Baer, A. (2004). Migratory fishes of South America: Biology, Fisheries, and Conservation Status. World Fisheries Trust/ Word Bank/ International Development Research Centre, Washington D.C., U.S.A. and Ottawa, Canada.

Chao, B. F. (1995). Anthropogenic impact on global geodynamics due to reservoir water impoundment. Geophysical Research Letters 22, 3529–3532.

Clark, R. & King, J. (2004). The Water Atlas: Mapping the World's Most Critical Resource. Earthscan/James & James, London,U.K.

Colburn, T., Dumanoski, D. & Myers, J. P. (1996). Our Stolen Future. Dutton, New York, U.S.A.

Covich, A. P., Austen, M. C., Ba¨Rlocher, F., Chauvet, E., Cardinale, B. J., Biles, C. L., Inchausti, P., Dangles, O., Solan, M., Gessner, M. O., Statzner, B. & Moss, B.R. (2004b). The role of biodiversity in the functioning of freshwater and marine benthic ecosystems. BioScience 54, 767–775.

Covich, A. P., Ewel, K. C., Hall, R. O., Giller, P. E., Goedkoop, W. & Merritt, D. M. (2004a). Ecosystem services provided by freshwater benthos. In Sustaining Biodiversity and Ecosystem Services in Soil and Sediments (ed. D. H. Wall), pp. 45–72. Island Press, Washington D.C., U.S.A.

Dangles, O. & Malmqvist, B. (2004). Species richness decomposition relationships depend on species dominance. Ecology Letters 7, 395–402.

Dangles, O., Gessner,M. O., Gue´Rold, F. & Chauvet, E. (2004). Impacts of stream acidification on litter breakdown: implications for assessing ecosystem functioning. Journal of Applied Ecology 41, 365–378.

DeAngelis, D.L. (1980) Energy flow, nutrient cycling and ecosystem resilience. *Ecology*, 61, 764–771.

Dierssen, K. (2000). Ecosystems as states of ecological successions. In: Jørgensen SE, Müller F (eds.), Handbook of Ecosystem Theories and Management. Boca Raton, FL, pp. 427–446.

Dirzo, R. & Raven, P. H. (2003). Global state of biodiversity and loss. Annual Review of Environment and Resources 28, 137–167.

Dirzo, R. (2001). Plant-mammal interactions : lessons for our understanding of nature and implications for biodiversity conservation. In Ecology : Achievement and Challenge (eds. M. C. Press, N. J. Huntly and S. Levin), pp. 319–335. Cambridge University Press, Cambridge, U.K.

Downing, A.L. & Leibold, M.A. (2002) Ecosystem consequences of species richness and composition in pond food webs. *Nature*, 416, 837–840.

Dudgeon, D. (1999). Tropical Asian Streams : Zoobenthos, Ecology and Conservation. Hong Kong University Press, Hong Kong.

Dudgeon, D. (2000a). Large-scale hydrological alterations in tropical Asia: prospects for riverine biodiversity. BioScience 50, 793–806.

Dudgeon, D. (2000b). Riverine wetlands and biodiversity conservation in tropical Asia. In Biodiversity in Wetlands : Assessment, Function and Conservation (eds. B. Gopal, W. J. Junk and J. A. Davis), pp. 35–60. Backhuys Publishers, The Hague, The Netherlands.

Dudgeon, D. (2000c). The ecology of tropical Asian rivers and streams in relation to biodiversity conservation. Annual Review of Ecology & Systematics 31, 239–263.

Dudgeon, D. (2002). Fisheries: pollution and habitat degradation in tropical Asian rivers. Encyclopaedia of Global Environmental Change, Vol. III (ed. I. Douglas), pp. 316–323. John Wiley & Sons, Chichester, U.K.

Dudgeon, D. (2003b). The contribution of scientific information to the conservation and management of freshwater biodiversity in tropical Asia. Hydrobiologia 500, 295–314.

Dudgeon, D. (2005). Last chance to see ...Ex situ conservation and the fate of the baiji. Aquatic Conservation : Marine and Freshwater Ecosystems 15, 105–108.

Dunn, H. (2003). Can conservation assessment criteria developed for terrestrial systems be applied to riverine systems? Aquatic Ecosystem Health and Management 6, 81–95.

Dunne, J.A., Williams, R.J.and Martinez, N.D. (2002). Food-web structure and network theory: The role of connectance and size. Proc. Natl. Acad. Sci. USA 99, 12917–12922.

Engelhardt, K.A.M. & Ritchie, M.E. (2002) The effect of aquatic plant species richness on wetland ecosystem processes. *Ecology*, 83, 2911–2924.

FAO (2000). The State of World Fisheries and Aquaculture – 2000. Fisheries Department, Food & Agriculture Organization (FAO) of the United Nations, Rome, Italy.

Fath, B.D., Jørgensen, S.E., Patten, B.C. and Straškaba, M. (2004). Ecosystem growth and development. BioSystem 77, 213–228.

Galloway, J. N., Dentener, F. J., Capone, D. G., Boyer, E. W., Howarth, R. W., Seitzinger, S. P., Asner, G. P., Cleveland, C. C., Green, P. A., Holland, E. A., Karl, D. M., Michaels, A. F., Porter, J. H., Townsend, A.R. & Vo¨ Ro¨ Smarty, C. J. (2004). Nitrogen cycles: past, present, and future. Biogeochemistry 70, 153–226.

Gessner, M.O. & Van Ryckegem, G. (2003). Water fungi as decomposers in freshwater ecosystems. In Encyclopaedia of Environmental Microbiology (ed. G. Bitton), John Wiley & Sons, New York, U.S.A. (online edition : DOI 10.1002/0471263397. env314).

Gibbons, J. W., Scott, D. E., Ryan, T., Buhlmann, K., Tuberville, T., Greene, J., Mills, T., Leiden, Y., Poppy, S., Winne, C. & Metts, B. (2000). The global decline of reptiles, de´ja‘ vu amphibians. BioScience 50, 653–666.

Giller, P. S., Hillebrand, H., Berninger, U.-G., Gessner,M. O., Hawkins, S., Inchausti, P., Inglis, C., Leslie, H., Malmqvist, B., Monaghan, M., Morin, P. J. & O'mullan, G. (2004). Biodiversity effects on ecosystem functioning: emerging issues and their experimental test in aquatic environments. Oikos 104, 423–431.

Gleick, P. H. (1996).Water resources. In Encyclopedia of Climate and Weather (ed. S. H. Schneider), pp. 817–823. Oxford University Press, New York, USA.

Groombridge, B. & Jenkins, M. (2000). Global Biodiversity. Earth's Living Resources in the 21st Century. World Conservation Monitoring Centre, Cambridge, U.K. (ed. R. D. E. MacPhee), pp. 271–331. Kluwer Academic/ Plenum Publishers, New York, U.S.A.

Gunderson, L.H., Holling, C.S.and Peterson, G. (2000). Resilience in ecological systems. In: Jørgensen SE, Müller F (eds.), Handbook of Ecosystem Theories and Management. Boca Raton, FL, pp. 385–394.

Hadwen, W. L., Arthington, A.H. & Mosisch, T. D. (2003). The impact of tourism on dune lakes on Fraser Island, Australia. Lakes & Reservoirs : Research and Management 8, 15–26.

Hall, S.J. & Raffaelli, D.G. (1993) Food webs: theory and reality. *Advances in Ecological Research*, 24, 187–239.

Hannon, B. (1973). The structure of ecosystems. J. Theor. Biol. 41, 535–546.

Harrison, I. J. & Stiassny, M. L. J. (1999). The quiet crisis. A preliminary listing of the freshwater fishes of the world that are extinct or 'missing in action'. In Extinctions in Near Time

Heal, G. M. (2000). Nature and the Marketplace : Capturing the Value of Ecosystem Services. Island Press, Washington D.C., U.S.A.

Herendeen, R.A. (1981). Energy intensity in ecological and economic systems. J. Theor. Biol. 91, 607–620.

Ho, M.W. and Ulanowicz, R. (2005). Sustainable systems as organisms. BioSystems. 82, 39–51.

Hogan, Z., Moyle, P., May, B., Vander Zanden, J. & Baird, I.(2004). The imperiled giants of the Mekong: ecologists struggle to understand – and protect – Southeast Asias large, migratory catfish. American Scientist 92, 228–237.

Holmlund, C.M. & Hammer, M. (1999). Ecosystem services generated by fish populations. Ecological Economics 29, 253–268.

Hooper, D. U., Chapin, F. S., Ewel, J. J., Hector, A., Inchausti, P., Lavorel, S., Lawton, J. H., Lodge, D. M., Loreau, M., Naeem, S., Schmid, B., Seta¨La, H., Sysmstad, A. J., Vandemeer, J. & Wardle, D. A. (2005). Effects of biodiversity on ecosystem functioning: a consensus of current knowledge. Ecological Monographs 75, 3–35.

Houlahan, J. E., Findlay, C. S., Schmidt, B. R., Meyer, A.H. & Kuzmin, S. L. (2000). Quantitative evidence for global amphibian population declines. Nature 404, 752–755.

IUCN (2003). The 2003 IUCN Red List of Threatened Species. International Union for Conservation of Nature and Natural Resources, Cambridge, U.K. http://www.redlist.org/ (accessed June 1, 2004).

Jackson, R. B., Carpenter, S. R., Dahm, C. N., Mcknight, D. M., Naiman, R. J., Postel, S.L. & Running, S.W. (2001). Water in a changing world. Ecological Applications 11, 1027–1045.

Johns, D.M. & Maggs, C. A. (1997). Species problems in eukaryotic algae: a modern perspective. In Species : the Units of Biodiversity (eds. M. F. Claridge, H. Dawah and M. R. Wilson), pp. 82–107. Chapman & Hall, London, U.K.

Jonsson, M. & Malmqvist, B. (2000) Ecosystem process rate increases with animal species richness: evidence from leaf-eating, aquatic insects. *Oikos*, 89, 519–523.

Jonsson, M. & Malmqvist, B.(2003). Mechanisms behind positive diversity effects on ecosystem functioning : testing the facilitation and interference hypotheses. Oecologia 134, 554–559.

Jonsson, M., Dangles, O., Malmqvist, B. & Gue´Rold, F. (2002). Simulating species loss following perturbation: assessing the effects on process rates. Proceedings of the Royal Society, Series B 269, 1047–1052.

Jørgensen, S.E., Patten, B.C. and Straškraba, M. (2000). Ecosystems emerging: 4 growth. Ecol. Model. 126, 249–284.

Kingsford, R. T. (2000). Ecological impacts of dams, water diversions and river management on floodplain wetlands in Australia. Austral Ecology 25, 109–127.

Knops, J.M.H., Bradley, K.L. & Wedin, D.A. (2002) Mechanisms of plant species impacts on ecosystem nitrogen cycling. *Ecology Letters*, 5, 454–466.

Koehn, J. D. (2004). Carp (Cyprinus carpio) as a powerful invader in Australian waterways. Freshwater Biology 49, 882–894.

Kottelat, M. & Whitten, T. (1996). Freshwater biodiversity in Asia with special reference to fish. World Bank Technical Paper 343, 1–59.

Krause, A.E., Frank, K.A., Mason, D.M., Ulanowicz, R.E. & Taylor, W.W. (2002) Compartments revealed in food-web structure. *Nature*, 426, 282–285.

Le´Ve˜Que, C. & Balian, E. V. (2005). Conservation of freshwater biodiversity: does the real world meet scientific dreams? Hydrobiologia 542, 23–26.

Levine, S.H. (1980). Several measures of trophic structure applicable to complex food webs. J. Theor. Biol. 83, 195–207.

Loreau, M., Naeem, S., Inchausti, P., Bengtsson, J., Grime, J. P., Hector, A., Hooper, D. U., Huston, M. A., Raffaelli, D., Schmid, B., Tilman, D. & Wardle, D. A. (2001). Biodiversity and ecosystem functioning : current knowledge and future challenges. Science 294, 804–808.

Lundberg, G., Kottelat, M., Smith, G. R., Stiassny, M. L. J. & Gill, A. C. (2000). So many fishes, so little time : an overview of recent ichthyological discovery in continental waters. Annals of the Missouri Botanical Gardens 87, 26–62.

Malmqvist, B. & Rundle, S. (2002). Threats to the running water ecosystems of the world. Environmental Conservation 29, 134–153.

Marques, J.C., Nielsen, S.N., Pardal, M.A. and Jørgensen, S.E. (2003). Impact of eutrophication and river management within a framework of ecosystem theories. Ecol. Model. 166, 147–168.

Meffe, G. K. (2001). The context of conservation biology. Conservation Biology 15, 815–816.

Moss, B. (2000). Biodiversity in fresh waters : an issue of species preservation or system functioning ? Environmental Conservation 27, 1–4.

Myers, N., Mittermeier, R., Mittermeier, G. C., Dafonseca, G. A. B. & Kent, J. (2000). Biodiversity hotspots for conservation priorities. Nature 403, 853–858.

Naiman, R. J. & De´Camps, H. (1997). The ecology of interfaces: riparian zones. Annual Review of Ecology and Systematics 28, 621–658.

Naiman, R. J. & Turner, M. G. (2000). A future perspective on North America's freshwater ecosystems. Ecological Applications 10, 958–970.

Naiman, R. J., Bilby, R. E., Schindler, D.E. & Helfield, J.M. (2002a). Pacific salmon, nutrients, and the dynamics of freshwater ecosystems. Ecosystems 5, 399–417.

Naiman, R. J., De´Camps, H. & Mcclain, M. C. (2005). Riparia. Academic Press, San Diego, U.S.A.

Nilsson, C. & Berggren, K. (2000). Alterations of riparian ecosystems caused by river regulation. BioScience 50, 783–792.

Olson, D. M., Dinerstein, E., Wikramanayake, E. D., Burgess, N., Powell, G. V. N., Underwood, E., D'amico, J. A., Strand, H. E., Morrison, J. C., Loucks, C. J., Allnutt, T. F., Ricketts, T. H., Kura, Y., Lamoreux, J. F., Wettengel, W. W., Hedao, P. & Kassem, K. R. (2001). Terrestrial ecoregions of the world : a new map of life on Earth. Bioscience 51, 933–938.

Pearce, D. (1998). Auditing the Earth: the value of the worlds ecosystem services and natural capital. Environment 40, 23–27.

Poff, N. L., Allan, J. D., Palmer, M. A., Hart, D. D., Richter, B. D., Arthington, A. H., Rogers, K. H., Meyer, J.L. & Stanford, J. A. (2003). River flows and water wars: emerging science for environmental decision-making. Frontiers in Ecology and the Environment 1, 298–306.

Poff, N. L., Allan, J. D., Palmer, M. A., Hart, D. D., Richter, B. D , Arthington, A. H., Rogers, K. H., Meyer, J.L. & Stanford, J. A. (2003). River flows and water wars: emerging science for environmental decision-making. Frontiers in Ecology and the Environment 1, 298–306.

Poff, N. L., Brinson, M.M.& Day, J.W. Jr. (2002). Aquatic ecosystems and global climate change. Technical Report, Pew Center on Global Climate Change, Arlington, USA.

Polis, G.A. and Strong, D. (1996) Food web complexity and community dynamics. *American Naturalist*, 147, 813–846.

Pollard, P. & Huxham, M. (1998). The European Water Framework Directive: a new era in the management of aquatic ecosystem health? Aquatic Conservation: Marine and Freshwater Ecosystems 8, 773–792.

Post, D.M., Pace, M.L. and Hairston, N.G. Jr. (2000) Ecosystem size determines food-chain length in lakes. *Nature*, 405, 1047–1049.

Postel, S. & Carpenter, S. (1997). Freshwater ecosystem services. In Nature's Services : Societal Dependence on Ecosystem Services (ed. G. C. Daily), pp. 195–214. Island Press, Washington D.C., U.S.A.

Postel, S. & Richter, B. (2003). Rivers for Life : Managing Water for People and Nature. Island Press, Washington D.C., U.S.A.

Postel, S. & Richter, B. (2003). Rivers for Life : Managing Water for People and Nature. Island Press, Washington D.C., U.S.A.

Pringle, C. M. (2001). Hydrologic connectivity and the management of biological reserves: a global perspective. Ecological Applications 11: 981–998.

Pullin, A.S. (2002). *Conservation Biology*. Cambridge University Press, Cambridge.

Pusey, B. J. & Arthington, A. H. (2003). Importance of the riparian zone to the conservation and management of freshwater fish: a review. Marine and Freshwater Research 54, 1–16.

Pusey, B. J. & Kennard, M. J. (1996). Species richness and geographical variation in assemblage structure of the freshwater fish fauna of the Wet Tropics region of northeastern Queensland. Marine and Freshwater Research 47, 563–573.

Redford, K.H. & Sanderson, S. E. (1992). The brief, barren marriage of biodiversity and sustainability. Bulletin of the Ecological Society of America 73, 36–39.

Revenga, C., Campbell, I., Abell, R., De Villiers, P. & Bryer, M. (2005). Prospects for monitoring freshwater ecosystems towards the 2010 targets. Philosophical Transactions of the Royal Society B 360, 397–413.

Revenga, C., Campbell, I., Abell, R., De Villiers, P. & Bryer, M. (2005). Prospects for monitoring freshwater ecosystems towards the 2010 targets. Philosophical Transactions of the Royal Society B 360, 397–413.

Reynolds, C.S. (1984). The Ecology of Freshwater Phytoplankton. Cambridge University Press, Cambridge, MA, 384 pp.

Ricciardi, A. & Rasmussen, J. B. (1999). Extinction rates of North American freshwater fauna. Conservation Biology 13,220–222.

Richter, B. D.,Matthews, R., Harrison, D. L. & Wigington, R. (2003). Ecologically sustainable water management: managing river flows for ecological integrity. Ecological Applications 13, 206–224.

Roberts, T. R. (2001). On the river of no returns: Thailand's Pak Mun Dam and its fish ladder. Natural History Bulletin of the Siam Society 49, 189–230.

Sala, O. E., Chapin, F. S., Armesto, J. J., Berlow, R., Bloomfield, J., Dirzo, R., Huber-Sanwald, E., Huenneke, L. F., Jackson, R. B., Kinzig, A., Leemans, R., Lodge, D., Mooney, H. A., Oesterheld, M., Poff, N. L., Sykes, M. T., Walker, B. H., Walker, M. & Wall, D. H. (2000). Global biodiversity scenarios for the year 2100. Science 287, 1770–1774.

Sheldon, A. L. (1988). Conservation of stream fishes : patterns of diversity, rarity and risk. Conservation Biology 2, 149–156.

Shugart, H.H. (1998). Terrestrial Ecosystems in Changing Environments. Cambridge University Press, New York, NY, 534 pp.

Simon, K.S. and Townsend, C.R. (2003) The impacts of freshwater invaders at different levels of ecological organisation, with emphasis on ecosystem consequences. *Freshwater Biology*, 48, 982–994.

Smith, V. H. (2003). Eutrophication of freshwater and coastal marine ecosystems – a global problem. Environmental Science and Pollution Research 10, 126–139.

Stearns, B. P. & Stearns, S. C. (1999). Watching, from the Edge of Extinction. Yale University Press, New Haven, U.S.A.

Stiassny, M. L. J. (1999). The medium is the message: freshwater biodiversity in peril. In The Living Planet in Crisis : Biodiversity Science and Policy (eds. J. Cracraft and F. T. Grifo), pp. 53–71. Columbia University Press, New York, U.S.A.

Stiassny, M. L. J. (2002). Conservation of freshwater fish biodiversity: the knowledge impediment. Verhandlungen der Gesellschaft fu¨r Ichthyologie 3, 7–18.

Strayer, D., Downing, J. A., Haag, W. R., King, T. L., Layer, J. B., Newton, T. J. & Nichols, S. J. (2004). Changing perspectives on pearly mussels, North America's most imperiled animals. BioScience 54, 429–439.

Terborgh, J. (1999). Requiem for Nature. Island Press, Washington D.C., U.S.A.

Tharme, R. E. (2003). A global perspective on environmental flow assessment: emerging trends in the development and application of environmental flow methodologies for rivers. River Research & Applications 19, 397–441.

Tickner, D. P., Angold, P. G., Gurnell, A.M. & Owen Mountford, J. (2001). Riparian plant invasions: hydrogeomorphological control and ecological impacts. Progress in Physical Geography 25, 22–52.

Ulanowicz, R.E. and Kay, J.J. (1991). A package for the analysis of ecosystem flow networks. Environ. Software 6, 131–142.

Van Dijk, P. P. (2000). The status of turtles in Asia. In Asian Turtle Trade : Proceedings of a Workshop on Conservation and Trade of Freshwater Turtles and Tortoises in Asia (eds. P. P. Van Dijk, B. I. Stuart and A. G. J. Rhodin), pp. 15–23. Chelonian Research Monographs No. 2, Chelonian Research Foundation, Lunenberg, U.S.A.

W.C.D. (2000). Dams and Development. A New Framework for Decision- Making. The Report of the World Commission on Dams. Earthscan Publications, London, U.K.

Wallace, J.B. & Webster, J. R. (1996). The role of macroinvertebrates in stream ecosystem function. Annual Review of Entomology 41, 115–139.

Ward, J. V., Tockner, K., Arscott, D. B. & Claret, C. (2002). Riverine landscape diversity. Freshwater Biology 47, 517–539.

Zwart, G., Van Hannen, E. J., Kamst-Van Agterveld, M. P., Van Der Gucht, K., Lindstrom, E. S., Van Wichelen, J., Lauridsen, T., Crump, B. C., Han, S. K. & Declerck, S. (2003). Rapid screening for freshwater bacterial groups by using reverse line blot hybridization. Applied and Environmental Microbiology 69, 5875–5883.

Toxic Effect of Mercury—Exposure in Nile Tilapia *(Oreochromis niloticus)*

— Hussein A. Kaoud, Egypt

ABSTRACT

The effect of mercury (Hg) toxicity, its impact on histopathological changes, the median lethal concentration (LC_{50}-96 h) to Nile tilapia, Oreochromis niloticus, *were investigated through semi-static acute toxicity test developed with mercury chloride ($HgCl_2$).). Fingerlings (4.45±0.31 cm and 2.35 ±0.18g) were kept during 96 hours in 5-liter glass aquaria, according to the following mercury concentrations, set up in three replicates: 0.00 (control 0.05, 0.10, 0.20, 0.30, and 0.40 mg Hg L^{-1}. The value of LC_{50}-96h was estimated in 0.300 mg Hg L^{-1}. This study indicated that:1) Hg poisoning caused structural damage in the fish organs*

Keywords: *Mercury; Histopathology;* Oreochromis niloticus

INTRODUCTION

Chemicals derived from agricultural operations (pesticides and herbicides) and industrial effluents, such as metals, ultimately find their way into a variety of different water bodies and can produce a range of toxic effects in aquatic organisms, ranging from alterations to a single cell, up to changes in whole populations (Bernet et al., 1999; Al-Kahtani, 2009)

The accumulation of toxic metals to hazardous levels in aquatic biota has become a problem of increasing concern. Excessive pollution of surface waters could lead to health hazards in man, either through drinking of water and/or consumption of fish (Mathis and Cummings, 1973).

Mercury (Hg) is one of the most toxic heavy metals in our environment including the lithosphere, hydrosphere, atmosphere and biosphere (Barbosa *et al.*, 2001). The toxic effects of heavy metals have been reviewed, including bioaccumulations (Adami *et al.*, 2002; Waqar, 2006). Heavy metals are surrounded with great care and special importance due to their highly toxic effects on fish as they affect survivability, growth and reproduction.

A series of complex chemical transformations allows the three-oxidation states of Hg cycle in the environment (Barbosa et al., 2001). In the zero oxidation state (Hg0), mercury exists in its metallic form; vapor is the most abundant form (98%). The mercurous and mercuric states are the two higher oxidation states where the mercury atom has lost one (Hg+) or two electrons (Hg2+), respectively; methyl mercury is the most important form of mercury in terms of toxicity and health effects from environmental exposures (Jackson, 1997; Goyer and Clarsksom, 2001; Castro-Gonzalez and Mendez-Armentab,2008).

Pollution of aquatic environments with metals is common worldwide and, under certain environmental conditions, aquatic fauna may concentrate large amounts of some metals from the water in their tissues. Metals are potentially harmful to most organisms even in very low concentrations and have been reported as hazardous environmental pollutants that may bioconcentrate in aquatic organisms.

In the present study, short -term bioassays were designed to evaluate the effect of mercury in water and bioaccumulation in fish tissues due to mercury exposure of Nile tilapia, Oreochromus *niloticus*).

MATERIALS AND METHODS

Fish Culture Management

Healthy *Oreochromis niloticus* fingerlings were collected in Marsh 2010, from ponds of the Central Laboratory for Aquaculture Research at Abbassa, Abo-Hammad, and Sharkia, Egypt (belonging to a single population) .They were collected locally and confined to large plastic aquaria bearing tap water for up to 7 days in the laboratory for acclimation.

Mercury Chloride

Technical grade mercury chloride (99% purity) was obtained from El-Nasr Chemical Company (Cairo, Egypt) and prepared in aquatic solution to provide the required concentrations of mercury. Control test without mercury was performed.

Determination of LC_{50}

Acute Toxicity Assays

The stock solution (370 mg Hg L^{-1}) was prepared by dissolving a calculated quantity of active ingredient (0.5 g $HgCl_2$ in 1,000 mL of dechlorinated tap water). A series of five concentrations of Hg was prepared by adding a calculated volume from the stocky solution into test containers, considering the equivalent on mercury (Hg). Therefore, nominal concentrations were:

0.05, 0.10, 0.20, 0.30, and 0.40 mg Hg L^{-1}. One container was kept as unexposed control group. Test was carried out with three simultaneous replicates. No food was supplied during the experiment. Test solutions were replaced by fresh ones of the same respecti-ve concentrations every 24 h until 96 h of testing, according to the renewal method recommended in APHA (1998).

The bioassay was conducted in Marsh 2010, Laboratory, Department of Veterinary Hygiene and Management, Faculty of Veterinary Medicine, Cairo University, with controlled conditions of water temperature (26.30±2.25 °C) and photoperiod (10L: 14D cycle). The used fish species was Nile tilapia, *Oreochromis niloticus*. Fingerlings with a mean weight of 2.35 ±0.18 g and mean total length of 4.45±0.31 cm. The acclimatization period was of 7 days, in a 50-L glass aquarium. During this period, fish were fed a dry commercial food (pellets with 25% of crude protein). Afterwards, fingerlings were transferred to 5-L glass aquaria, which were internally covered with a plastic film to prevent contamination by residues from previous experi-ments. Plastic film was also placed on the top of the aquarium to prevent evaporation. Air pumps and individual air stone diffusers provided aeration. The experiment was carried out at a stocking density of 10 fish/aquarium.

Mortalities were recorded at 24, 48, 72 and 96 h of exposure, and dead fish were removed regularly from the test solutions. The data obtained were statistically analyzed using the Trimmed Spe-arman Karber method (Hamilton *et al.,* 1977) for estimating the median lethal concentration (LC_{50}), and 1/10 of the LC_{50}-96 h (30 µg Hg L^{-1}) was taken as the safe Hg concentration (Sprague, 1971).

RESULTS

Histopathological Alterations

The histopathology of different Tilapia tissues revealed that there are several histopathological changes in different Tilapia organs as shown in figures.

In one hand, fish exposed to 1\10 LC50 of mercury (30 µg L^{-1}) for 7 days, a total of 40, 60, 30, 15 and 25% respectively of fishes showed extensive pathological lesions in their gills, liver, intestine, muscles and kidneys, Table.2.

The observed lesions in the gills of experimental groups were mucus coagulation and accumulation of cellular debris in the epithelium of lamellae and inter-lamellar regions, hemorrhage, lamellar edema, hyperplasia, epithelial cell necrosis and congestion (Fig.3 and 4).

Liver of tilapia treated with mercury showed degeneration of the hepatocytes with nuclear pyknosis in the majority of the cells, hepatocellular vacuolation with Kupffer cell activation as well as the accumulation of the metal binding proteins in their nuclei. Intravascular hemolysis is seen in blood vessels and sinusoids with necrosed hepatocytes (Fig.5).

Muscular tissues degeneration in muscle bundles with aggregations of inflammatory cells (leucocytic infiltration) between them with focal areas of necrosis , atrophy and edema of muscle bundles as well as splitting of muscle fibers and hyalinized muscles tissue were seen (Fig.6).

Intestine Intestine of tilapia treated with cadmium showing necrosed mucosa, sub-mucosal hemorrhage, muscle fibers were loosely arranged with the degeneration of sub-mucosal tissue and each villus facing the lumen showed cell degeneration and the cells did not show distinct nuclei and cytoplasmic boundaries. There was a distortion of basement membrane of the villi and blood vessel, and lymphocytes were fully distorted and there was a degeneration of columnar epithelium of the intestine (Fig.7).

Kidney showed hydropic swelling of the renal tubules, sometimes with pyknotic nuclei and many necrotic areas as well as swollen proximal epithelial cells with necrotic nuclei (Fig.8).

Discussion

The value of LC_{50} determined for Nile tilapia *(Oreochromis niloticus)* in the present study, according to the different exposure times, is shown in Table 2. The 96 h LC_{50} value (the simple graphic method) is 0.30 mg $CdCl_2$ L^{-1}.

The LC_{50}-96h, determined in the present study was relatively higher to those reported by Ishikawa et al. (2007) and Kaoud & Mekawy (2011) for Nile tilapia ,*Oriochromis niloticus*are (22.0 and 24..0 mg·L^{-1}, respectively). The LC50-96h was compared with the results from other studies developed on mercury toxicity to fish, Table, 3.

In one hand, the LC_{50}-96h, determined in the present study was 0.30 mg Hg L^{-1}. Ishikawa *et al.* (2007) reported LC50-96h of 0.220 mg Hg L^{-1} in small sized *Tilapia Oreochromis ni-loticus* while Kaoud and Mekawy (2011) observed LC50 -96h as 0.240 mg Hg L^{-1} for *Tilapia Oreochromis ni-loticus.*

On the other hand, the higher values obtained by Ramamurthi et al. (1982) for *Tilapia mossambicus* may be attributed to some differences in standard techniques that were adopted in their experiments such as the larger size of the test-organisms (Ishikawa et al., 2007; Buhl ,1997 and Boening ,2000),. The acute toxicity of waterborne heavy metals on aquatic organisms is highly variable even among phylogenetically closely related species and depends on metal speciation, being the free ions (WHO, 1992).

Histopathological biomarkers have been largely used in fish to identify and evaluate the toxic effects of pollutants exposure (Rabitto *et al.*, 2005; Oliveira Ribeiro *et al.*, 2006). The presence of necrosis is in fact one of the most visible damages in tissues affected by a pollutant (Rabitto *et al.*, 2005). According to Manahan (1991) the occurrence of necrosis is also a consequence of enzymatic inhibition, damages in the cellular membrane integrity, and disturbances in the synthesis of proteins and carbohydrate metabolism.

Pandey *et al.* (1994) described alteration in liver and intestine of *Liza parsia* exposed to $HgCl_2$ (0.2 mg Hg L^{-1}) for 15 days. Similarly, Oliveira-Ribeiro *et al.* (2002) reported serious injuries in gill and olfactory epithelium of *Sal velinus alpinus* exposed to 0.15 mg Hg L^{-1}. According to Allen (1994), the exposure of *Orechromis aureus* to 0.5 mg Hg L^{-1} caused a raise in the number of leucocyte and erythrocyte within 24 hours. Gill and Pant (1985) also related hematological anomalies in *Barbus conchonius* exposed to 0.18 mg Hg L-1 in acute test.

Dias et al., (2007) described alteration in spleen, heart, and brain due to the effects of the mercury chloride toxicity on tilapia ,*Oreochromis niloticus* (0.02 mg$L^{-1,}$ 0.002 mg L-1, and 0.0002 mg L-1 after 3, 7, 10 and 14 days of exposure).

Hg Bioaccumulation

The highest bioaccumulation of mercury was observed in the organs mainly implicated in metal intoxication and so it was higher in the liver followed by muscles.

Liver: Mercury hardly traced in the liver of the control fish, as well as at the lowest concentration the mean residue was 0.048±0.013 µg g^{-1} while in fish exposed to Hg only, the mean of accumulated quantity was 5.860±0.22 µg g^{-1}, Table 3.

Muscles: In the liver of the control fish the mean residue was 0.029±0.007 µg g^{-1} while in fish exposed to Hg only, the mean of accumulated quantity was 1.576±0.22 µg g^{-1} (Table 3).

Table 9.1: Median Lethal Concentration (LC_{50}) of mercury in Nile tilapia, *Oreochromis niloticus*

Exposure Time (hour)	LC50 (mg Hg L^{-1})	95% ConfidentLimit (mg Hg L^{-1})^{1})
24	0.58	0.48 – 0.58
48	0.47	0.41 – 0.53
72	0.37	0.30 – 0.42
96	0.30	0.32 – 0.28

Table 9.2: Acute Toxicity of Mercury in Tilapia Species

Reference	Species	LC50-96h (Hg mg L^{-1})
Present study	*Oreochromis niloticus*	0.300
Ramamurthi et al. (1982)	*Tilapia mossambicus*	0.739
Ishikawa *et al.* (2007)	*Oreochromis niloticus*	0.220
Kaoud & Mekawy (2011)	*Oreochromis niloticus*	0.240

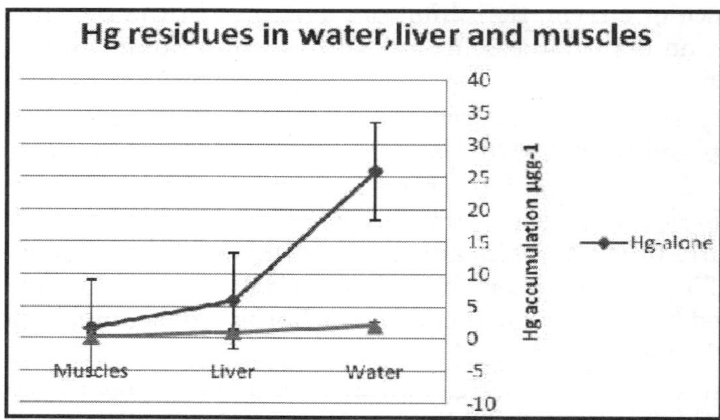

Fig. 9.1: Mercury (Hg) residue in water (µg Hg L^{-1}), liver and muscles (µg Hg g^{-1} dry weigh) of Nile tilapia *(O. niloticus)* exposed to Hg. Lesions %

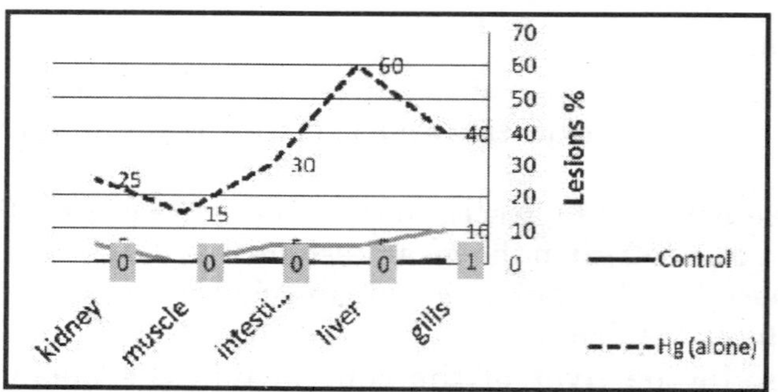

Fig. 9.2: Prevalence (%) of lesions recorded on the gill, liver, intestine, muscles and kidney of grass carp in short-term bath with mercuric chloride and prevalence of lesions in each group

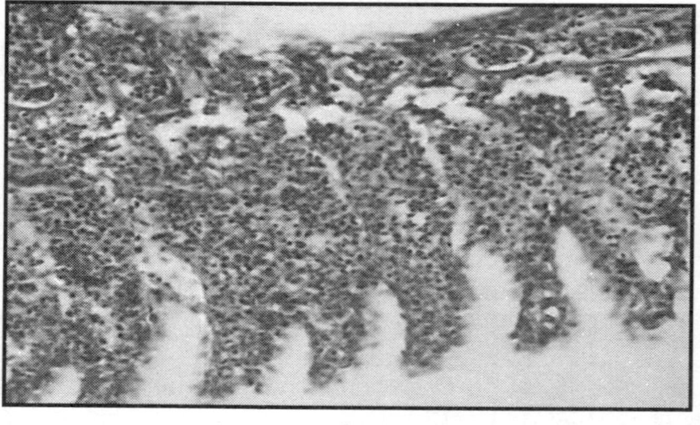

A

9.3: A-Tilapia's gill filament showing lamellar hyperplasia and fusion of secondary gill lamellae. (H & E, 400 X)

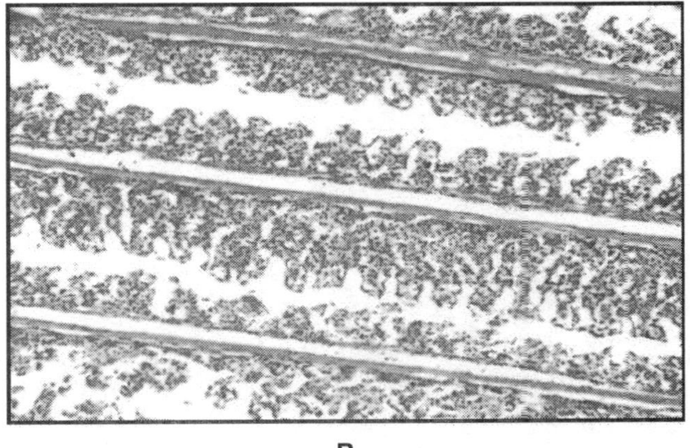

B

Fig. 9.3: B: Tilapia's gill filament showing lamellar hyperplasia associated with lamellar edema (H & E, 200 X)

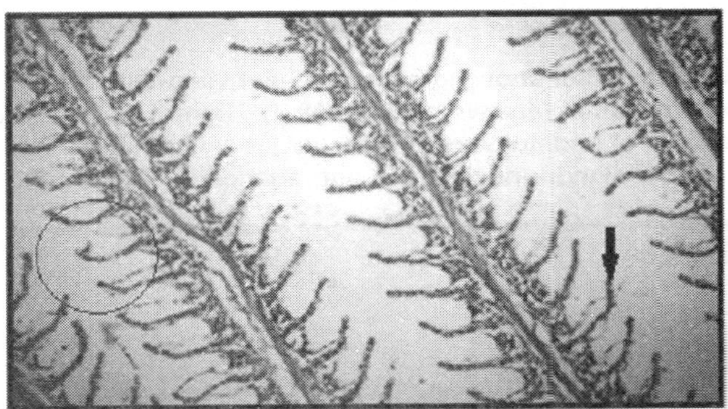

Fig. 9.4: Necrosis of epithelial cells and destruction of secondary lamellae (arrow) (H&E×400)

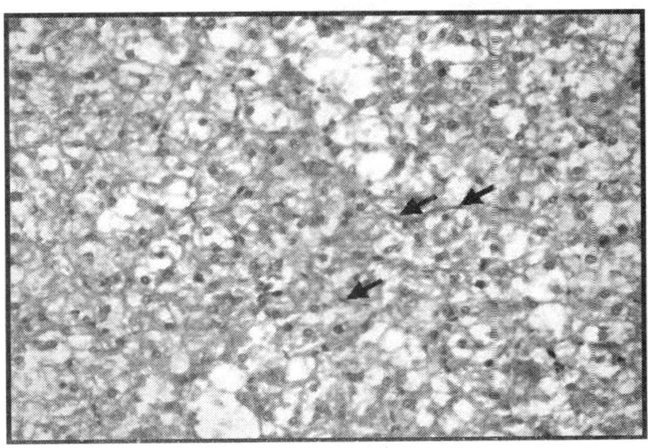

A

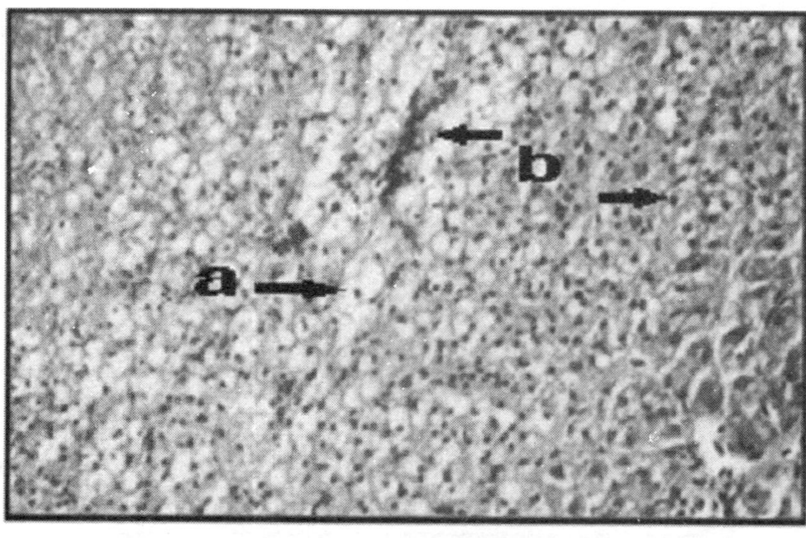

B

Fig. 9.5 (A-B): Left: liver showing hepatocellular vacuolation and necrosis with Kupffer cell activation (arrows) (H & E 400 X). Right: Liver showing vacuolar degeneration of hepatocytes (a) with individual hepatocellular necrosis and focal mononuclear cell aggregation (b) (H & E, 400 X)

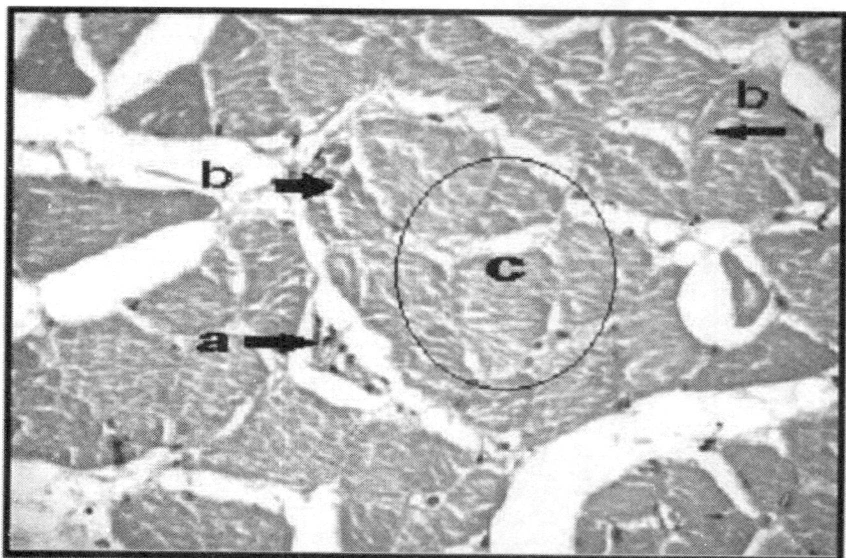

Fig.9.6: Degeneration in muscle bundles with aggregations of inflammatory cells (leucocytic infiltration) between them (a) with focal areas of necrosis (b), atrophy and edema of muscle bundles (c) as well as splitting of muscle fibers and hyalinized muscles tissue(H & E, 400 X)

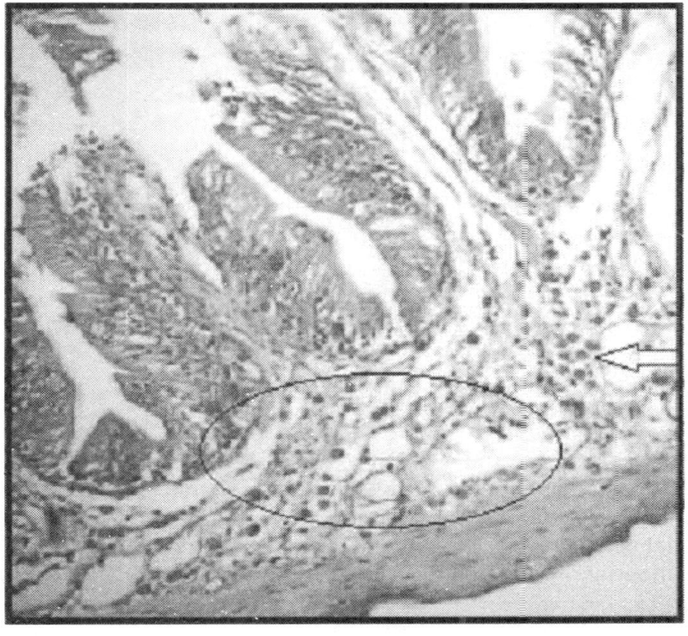

A

B

Fig. 9.7 (A-B): Left: Intestine of tilapia treated with mercury showing necrosed mucosa (n), sub mucosal hemorrhage (arrow) (H & E, X 200). Right: Intestine of tilapia treated with mercury showing higher power of the previous lesion (H & E, X 400)

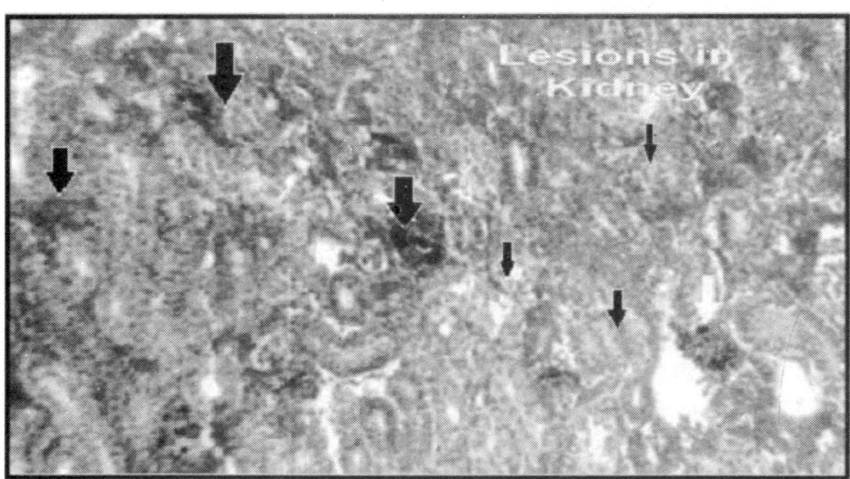

Fig. 9.8: Kidney showed hydropic swelling of the renal tubules, sometimes with pyknotic nuclei and many necrotic areas as well as swollen proximal epithelial cells with necrotic nuclei (Narrow arrows). More number of melano macrophage centres MMC (Wide arrows) (H & E, X 200)

REFERENCES

Adami G. M., Barbieri P., Fabiani M., Piselli S., Predonzani, S., Reisenhofer E., (2002): Levels of cadmium and zinc in hepatopancreas of reared *Mytilus galloprovincialis* from the Gulf of Trieste (Italy). Chemosphere, 48 (7), 671 – 677.

Al-Kahtani M A (2009): Accumulation of Heavy Metals in Tilapia Fish (*Oreochromis niloticus*) from Al-Khadoud Spring, Al-Hassa, Saudi Arabia. American Journal of Applied Sciences 6 (12): 2024-2029.

Allen, P. (1994): Changes in the haematological profile of the cichlid *Oreochromis aureaus* (Steindachner) during acute inorganic mercury intoxication. *Comp. Biochem. Physiol., 108C(1):* 117-121

American Public Health Association (APHA) (1998): Standard methods for the examination of water and wastewater. 20th ed. American Public Health Association, Washington, DC.

Barbosa A.C., Jardim W., Dorea J.G., Fosberg B., Souza J., (2001): Hair mercury speciation as a function of gender, age and body mass index in inhabitants of the Negro River basin, Amazon, Brazil. Arch Environ Contam Toxicol 2001; 40: 439–44.

Bernet, D., H. Schmidt, W. Meier, P. Burkhardt- Hol and T. Wahli, (1999): Histopathology in fish: Proposal for a protocol to assess aquatic pollution. J. Fish Dis., 22: 25-34. DOI: 10.1046/j.1365-2761.1999.00134.x

Boening, D.W. (2000): Ecological effects, transport, and fate of mercury: A General Review. *Chemosphere, 40:* 1335-1351.

Buhl, K.J. (1997): Relative sensitivity of three endangered Þ shes, Colorado SquawÞ sh, Bonytail, and Razorback Sucker, to selected metal pollutants. *Ecotoxicol. Environ. Safety, 37*: 186-192.

Castro-Gonzalez M.I. ; Mendez-Armentab, M. (2008): Heavy metals: Implications associated to fish consumption. Environmental Toxicology and Pharmacology 26 : 263–271.

Chang, J.S., Law, R. and Chang, C.C. (1997): Biosorption of lead, copper and cadmium by biomass of *Pseudomonas aeruginosa* PU 21. Water Res. 31: 1651-1658.

Dias D.C , Maiorino F.C; Ranzani-Paiva m.T. , ishikawa N.M, Lombardi J.V., Ferreira J.R., França F.M., Cláudia Maris Ferreira C.M. (2007) : Histopathological evaluation of the spleen, heart, and brain of the tilapia *Oreochromis niloticus* (linn aeus, 1758) exposed to mercury chlo ride. Bol. Inst. Pesca Sao Paulo]. Vol. 33, no. 2, pp. 213-220.

Desi I, Nagymajtenyi L, Schuiz H. (1998): Behavioural and neurotoxicological changes caused by cadmium treatment of rats during development. Journal of Applied Toxicology 18: 63-70.

Eccles, H. (1999): Treatment of metal-contaminated wastes: why select a biological process? TIBTECH. 17: 162-165.

Gill, T.S. and Pant, J.C. (1985): Mercury-induced blood anomalies in the freshwater teleost. *Water, Air and Soil Pollution., 24:* 165-171.

Goyer, R.A., Clarsksom, W.T., (2001): Toxic effects of metals. In: Klaassen, C.D. (Ed.), Casarett and Doull's Toxicology. The basic Science of Poisons. McGraw-Hill, New York, pp. 811–867.

Hamilton, M.A.; Russo, R.C.; Thurston, R.V. (1977): Trimmed Spearman-Karber method for estimating median lethal concentrations in toxicity bioassays. *Environ Sci. Technol., 11:* 714-719.

Ishikawa N M 1; Maria JosÈ Tavares Ranzani-Paiva M J T, Julio Vicente Lombardi J V (2007): Acute toxicity of mercury ($HgCl_2$) to Nile Tilapia, *Oreochromis niloticus, B. Inst. Pesca*, São Paulo, *33*(1): 99 – 104.

Jackson, T.A., (1997):Long-range atmospheric transport of mercury to ecosystems, and the importance of anthropogenic emissions—a critical review and evaluation of the published evidence. Environ. Rev. 5, 99–120.

Kuyucak, N. and Volesky, B. (1989): The mechanism of cobalt biosorption. Biotech. Bioeng. 33: 823-831.

Lee, Y.K. (1997) :Commercial production of microalgae in the Asia-Pacific rim. J. Appl. Phycol. 9: 403-411.

Manahan, S. E. (1991): Water Pollution Environment Chemistry, first ed. Lewis Publishers, London

Oliveira-Ribeiro, C.A.; Belger, L.; Pelletier, E.; Rouleau, C.(2002): Histopathological evidence of inorganic mercury and methylmercury toxicity in the Arctic charr *(Salvelinus alpinus). Environmental Research, 90:* 217-225.

Rabitto, I.S., Alves Costa, J.R.M., Silva de Assis, H.C., Pelletier, E., Akaishi, F.M., Anjos, A., Randi, M.A.F. & Oliveira, R. (2005): Effects of dietary Pb(II) and tributylin an neotropical fish *Hoplias malabarius*: Histopathological and biochemical findings. *Ecotoxicology and Environmental Safety* 60, 147-156.

Sprague, J.B. (1971): Measurement of pollutant toxicity to fish. III. Sublethal effects and safe concentrations. *Water Res., 3:* 793-821.

Waqar A., (2006): Levels of selected heavy metals in Tuna fish. Arab. J. Sci. Eng., 31 (1A), 89–92.

Wetlands—A Fragile Ecosystem

Its Prospectus, Conservation and Management Strategies and Action Plan in Indian Scenario

—Dharmendra Kumar Meena, India
—Kanti Meena, India
—A.K. Prusty, India
—Pronob Das, India
—Satendra Kumar, India
—D. Panda, India
—Md.Shahbaz Akhtar, India
—B.K. Behera, India

ABSTRACT

Wetland ecosystem diversity and the provision of its services depend on the frequency, quantity and quality of water flowing into, retained in, or flowing from the ecosystem. Wetlands are biodiversity-rich and important as habitats for species that depend on water and for those which share aquatic and terrestrial ecosystems. Being varied and dynamic, they support a great many forms of life. Water is the driving force in wetlands. Water's chemical and physical properties, water regime and biota influence their development and characteristics. Plants and animals form a characteristic biocenosis adapted to the wetland, and particularly to the soil and water conditions. The term is used for aquatic ecosystems, e.g. lakes, rivers or lagoons, but is more common for marshes, peatlands, floodplains and coastal mudflats. Although wetlands are great impotent from economic point of view, are under threats so it is must to conserve and manange these econotones for their environment friendly and sustainable use and existence. Of the purpose various strategies, legal framework action plan are review and most relevant are discussed in this review. This will ignite a deep and keen interest among the researcher to take of this new area of biodiversity into most priority basis.

Key words: *Ecosystem, biocenosis, wetland, biodiversity, floodplain, environment friendly, sustainable*

INTRODUCTION

Wetlands are dynamic ecosystems, where water accumulates for at least part of the year and are among the most precious natural resources on earth. Wetlands are defined as "areas of marsh, fen, peat land or water, whether natural or artificial, permanent or temporary, with water that is static or flowing, fresh, brackish or salt, including areas of marine water, the depth of which at low tide does not exceeds six meters". In addition, it "may include riparian and coastal zones adjacent to the wetlands, and islands or bodies of marine water not deeper than six meters at low tide lying within wetlands". The area covered by wetlands on Earth is roughly 12% of the land surface that is about 12.8 million sq km. They support high levels of biological diversity and are, after tropical rain forests, among the richest ecosystems on Earth, providing essential life support for much of humanity, as well as for several other species. The area of wetlands in India (excluding rivers) is estimated at 58,286,000 ha, or 18.4% of the country's surface area (Cheriyan, 2002). Most of these are directly or indirectly linked to rivers. These wetlands provide a wealth of biological resources and fisheries in the country.

Floodplain Wetlands

Floodplains are the flat land bordering rivers, which are subjected to periodic flooding from rivers, which tend to be most expansive along the lower reaches of rivers. Hence, 'floodplain wetlands' are wetlands associated with rivers and streams along their floodplains. They may be generally connected to the principal rivers and or receive backflow from the rivers during floods or from the catchments, following monsoon rains. Floodplain Wetlands in India cover an estimated area of 2,00,000 ha (Sugunan, 1995), and are a common feature of the Indian landscape, especially along the Ganga and Brahmaputra river systems in the north and northeastern regions of the country. The floodplain wetlands located in different parts of India are locally known as beel, chaur, maun, boar, hoar, pat, etc. Those floodplain wetlands, which are connected to their parent river are open type and those have no connection are closed type. These water bodies exhibit enormous diversity in size and shape, according to their origins and geographical location, physical structure and chemical composition. They are important fishery resource in India, especially in states like Assam, West Bengal, Bihar and Manipur, where thousands of poor fishers depend on these water bodies for daily livelihood.

The Ramsar Convention on Wetlands

Wetlands were among the first ecosys-tems internationally recognized as be-ing threatened due to human activities and deserving particular consideration. The Convention on Wetlands was de-veloped as an intergovernmental treaty and signed in 1971 in the Iranian city of Ramsar, and is thus commonly known as the Ramsar Convention. Focusing on conservation and wise use of wet-lands and their species, it was the first of the global environmental treaties. To date it has provided the framework for national action and international co-operation aimed at conservation and sustainable development of wetlands and their resources (Beltram 2005).

Accordingly, the Convention broadly defines wetlands as "areas of marsh, fen, peatland or water, whether natu-ral or artificial, permanent or tempo-rary, with water that is static or flow-ing, fresh, brackish or salt, including areas of marine water the depth of which at low tide does not exceed six metres (Article 1). Wetlands include a number of different habitats and are a part of hydrological systems of surface and underground waters. The purpose of the Convention is con-servation of all wetlands as part of their catchment areas by maintaining their vital functions, properties and pro-cesses to deliver ecosystem services. Functionally, wetlands are connected to and cannot be separated from deep water or terrestrial ecosystems. There-fore the Convention (Article 2) states that the definition of wetlands should also include lakes, rivers, or in other words, standing and running waters and riparian ecosystems.

The Ramsar Convention defines the importance of wetlands according to their ecological, botanical, zoological, limnological and hydrological proper-ties (Article 2.2). "Wetlands of Inter-national Importance" (Ramsar Sites) are sites designated under the Ramsar Convention on Wetlands and represent those wetland areas within a country, or areas shared between two or more countries, that are important interna-tionally, but also nationally and locally. Criteria for inclusion in the List fall into two groups: 1-sites containing repre-sentative, rare or unique wetland types; 2 - sites of international importance for conserving biological diversity. Ramsar sites are designated "To develop and maintain an international network of wetlands which are important for the conservation of global biological diversity and for sustaining human life through the maintenance of their ecosystem components, processes and services." (Resolution IX.1, Annex B) To date, Ramsar sites have covered a number of different habitat types based on Ramsar Classification System, which includes 42 categories grouped into marine and coastal wetlands, inland wetlands and human-made wetlands. Presently (November 2006), there are over 1630 wetland sites, totaling nearly 146 million hectares, designated for inclusion in the Ramsar List of Wetlands of International Importance in the 153 Contracting Country Parties to the Convention. The figure is a relatively small yet crucial portion of all estimated wetland areas. Wetlands are located at all latitudes and altitudes, but the data on their extent differ according to availability as well as the definition used. According to some recent data, wetland ecosystems (including lakes, rivers, marshes and coastal regions to a depth of 6 meters at low tide) are estimated to cover more than 1280 million hectares, an area

33% larger than the United States and 3 times larger than the EU. However, many wetland types are under-represented and there are some geographic regions in particular where further data are needed.

Although to date wetlands have been recognised for their biodiversity values and the critical ecosystem services they deliver for the well-being of hu-man communities (such as fish and fibre, water supply, water purification, climate regulation, flood regulation, coastal protection, recreational op-portunities and, increasingly, tour-ism), they are still among the most threatened ecosystems globally and in Slovenia. More than 50% of spe-cific types of wetlands in parts of North America, Europe, Australia and New Zealand were destroyed during the twentieth century, and many others in different parts of the world degraded. The primary indirect drivers of degra-dation and loss of inland and coastal wetlands have typically been popula-tion growth and increasing economic development. The primary direct driv-ers of degradation and loss include infrastructure development, land con-version, water withdrawal, eutrophica-tion and pollution, overharvesting and overexploitation, and the introduction of invasive alien species (Millennium Ecosystem Assessment, 2005).

In addition to designation of Ramsar sites, technical and policy guidelines have been developed by the Conven-tion to assist countries in preparing their national wetland policies based on these principles (Ramsar Toolkit). However, action at regional, national and local levels, including appropriate management of the whole catchment area (of both surface water and ground water), and the "wise use", that is, sus-tainable development of wetlands at the national level and through interna-tional cooperation are essential for the conservation of dynamic and unstable wetland ecosystems.

Status of Wetland in Indian Scenario

The eastern and northeastern India is conspicuous in having vast stretches of floodplain wetlands extending over 2,02,213 ha. The state of West Bengal has more than 150 beels, spread across the districts of Nadia, 24 Parganas, Cooch-Behar, Hooghly, Murshidabad, Malda and Midnapore, covering an effective area of 42,500 ha (Sugunan and Mukhopadhyaya, 1995), which is about 22% of the total freshwater area of the state. Thus the beels are an important natural resource playing a vital role in the fisheries, rural economy and environment of the state. The area of these beels range from 2 to 600 ha, however most of them are between 20-25 ha in area (Vinci and Mitra, 2000) Assam has 1392 beels spread over 1,00,000 ha. This includes 322 beels along the river Barak (Yadava, 1989). The beels associated with the river Brahmaputra and its tributaries is estimated at 94,500 ha. Floodplain wetlands in Bihar (locally called chaur) are spread over 40,000 ha, along the Gantak and Koshi river basins, on the northern part of the state. There are 16 chaurs in Bihar. The area of these chaurs ranges from

4 ha (Mahisath chaur) to 600 ha (Larail chaur) as reported by Sinha and Jha (1997) and Jha and Chandra (1977). Other important chaurs of the state are Dabadih (100 ha) and Kamaldha (300 ha). Small floodplain wetland and marshes in Manipur are locally known as pats. The important of these are Pumlenpat (3500 ha), Kharungpat (2000 ha), Ikoppat (2000 ha), Takmu (500 ha), Withou (270 ha), Leinganpat (270 ha), Khullakpat (300 ha), Sanapat (52 ha) and Utrapat (41 ha) besides those associated with the Loktak floodplain lake. According to Forest Survey of India, mangroves cover an additional 6,740 sq km. Their major concentrations are Sunderbans, Andaman, and Nicobar Islands, which hold 80% of the country's mangroves. The rest are in Orissa, Andhra Pradesh, Tamilnadu, Karnataka, Maharashtra, Gujarat, and Goa.

Wetlands have been drained and transformed due to anthropogenic activities, like unplanned urban and agricultural development, industries, road construction, impoundments, resource extraction, and dredge disposal, causing substantial economic and ecological losses in the long term. They occupy about 58.2 million hectares, of which 40.9 million hectares are under paddy cultivation. About 3.6 million hectares are suitable for fish culture. Approximately 2.9 million hectares are under capture fisheries (brackish and freshwater). Mangroves, estuaries, and backwaters occupy 0.4, 3.9, and 3.5 million hectares respectively. Man-made impoundments constitute 3 million hectares. Nearly 28,000 km are under rivers, including main tributaries and canals. Canal and irrigation channels constitute another 113,000 km. In India, out of an estimated 4.1 m ha (excluding irrigated agricultural lands,rivers, and streams) of wetlands, 1.5 m ha are natural, while 2.6 m ha are manmade. The coastal wetlands occupy an estimated 6,750 sq km, and are largely dominated by mangrove vegetation.

Global Scenario of Wetlands

The earth, two-thirds of which is covered by water, looks like a blue planet-the planet of water-from space (Clarke, 1994). The world's lakes and rivers are probably the planet's most important freshwater resources. But the amount of fresh water covers only 2.53% of the earth's water. On the earth's surface, fresh water is the habitat of a large number of species. These aquatic organisms and the ecosystem in which they live represent a substantial sector of the earth's biological diversity.

It is interesting to know that there are nearly 14 x 10^8 cubic km of water on the planet, of which more than 97.5% is in the oceans, which covers 71% of the earth's surface. Wetlands are estimated to occupy nearly 6.4% of the earth's surface. Of those wetlands, nearly 30% is made up of bogs, 26% fens, 20% swamps, and 15% flood plains. Of the earth's fresh water, 69.6% is locked up in the continental ice, 30.1% in underground aquifers, and 0.26% in rivers and lakes. In particular, lakes are found to occupy less than 0.007% of world's fresh water (Clarke, 1994).

Utility of Wetlands

Wetlands are among the most productive ecosystems. They directly or indirectly support millions of people and provide goods and services to them. Various goods and services provided by wetlands are as follows:

I. Support all life forms through extensive food webs
II. Habitat to aquatic flora and fauna, as well as numerous species of birds, including migratory species.
III. Filtration of sediments and nutrients from surface water
IV. Nutrients recycling
V. Water purification
VI. Floods mitigation
VII. Maintenance of stream flow
VIII. Ground water recharging
IX. Provide drinking water, fish, fodder, fuel, etc
X. Control rate of runoff in urban areas
XI. Buffer shorelines against erosion
XII. Comprise an important resource for sustainable tourism, recreation and cultural heritage
XIII. Stabilization of local climate
XIV. Source of livelihood to local people
XV. Genetic reservoir for various species of plants (especially rice)

Rationale of being Wetlands so Lucrative

I. **Plant and wild life habitat:** They are habitat for diverse range of animals, including birds, frogs, invertebrates and fish species as well as aquatic plants and various tree species.
II. **Nursery and breeding grounds:** Provide important breeding and nursery areas for large range of organisms.
III. **Catchment water quality:** Wetlands improve the water quality downstream. As water passes through the wetland it slows down allowing the sediments to settle; the weeds and vegetation too filter water, absorb nutrients and pollutants to certain extent.
IV. **Nutrient recycling:** Wetlands are highly productive ecosystems because of their ability to retain and recycle precious nutrients.
V. **Flood mitigation:** They detain floodwaters or runoff, reducing downstream flood sparks which could otherwise cause erosion and damage.
VI. **Scientific data:** They are storehouses of knowledge about past ecological communities and climatic sequences.
VII. **Ground water recharge:** They help ground water recharge by holding rain and runoff water.

VIII. **Recreation:** Bird watching, sport fishing, swimming, water sports, etc.

IX. **Socio cultural importance:** Settlement of human habitations near or around wetlands, folklore associated with wetlands, rituals, food and nutritional security of people, livelihood, grazing areas, forestry areas, areas for agriculture, etc.

According to a report on the economic value of wetlands, 'The Economic Values of the World's Wetlands' 2004, WWF International, the services and resources provided by the 12.8 million sq km of global wetlands are economically valued to the tune of US $ 70 billion per year. Asian wetlands are the highest valued, at US $ 1.8 billion per year. "The lower the wetland area, the higher is their average value", says the report. The annual economic value of global wetlands as assessed by the WWF, is given in Table 1. A realistic estimate of the economic values of the wetlands in India, is, however, not available as yet. In India the value of wetlands are considered in terms of their biological wealth, fishery, water holding, agricultural importance etc. No attempt is made so far to equate their value in economic terms. This may perhaps be the reason for the low priority given at political and planning levels to the conservation and sustainable use of wetlands.

Wetlands Loss and Degradation

Wetlands are estimated to occupy around 8.6 million sq km (6.4 %) of the earth's surface, out of which about 4.8 million sq km are found in the tropics and sub-tropics. This estimation was compared with estimates in the 19th century and it was found that approximately 50% of the world's wetlands have been lost in the past century alone. The major activities responsible for wetlands loss are urbanization, drainage for agriculture, and water system regulation (Shine & de Klemm, 1999).Environmental impacts on wetlands may be grouped into five main categories: loss of wetland area, changes to water regime, changes in water quality, overexploitation of wetland products, and introduction of exotic or alien species.

These quality and quantity declinations, have contributed to the decline in the biological diversity of flora and fauna, migratory birds, and productivity of wetland systems. Simultaneously, several thousand species have become extinct, and fish, timber, medicinal plants, water transport, and water supply are over exploited. The Wildlife Institute of India's survey reveals that they are disappearing at a rate of 2% to 3% every year.

Though accurate results on wetland loss in India are not available, the Wildlife Institute of India's survey reveals that 70-80% of individual fresh water marshes and lakes in the Gangetic flood plains have been lost in the last five decades. Indian mangrove areas have decreased by half from 700,000 ha in 1987 to 453,000 ha in 1995.

Factors for Threatening the Wetlands

Dense human population in catchments, urbanisation, and various anthropogenic activities has resulted in over exploitation of wetland resources, leading to degradation in their quality and quantity. Now, there is increasing concern to conserve and restore perishing wetlands and endangered habitats to achieve ecological sustainability.

Some of the major threats to wetlands are as given below:

I. Urbanization-increasing developmental pressure for residential, industrial and commercial facilities.

II. Anthropogenic activities-unplanned urban and agricultural development, industries, road construction, impoundment, resource extraction and dredge disposal

III. Agricultural Activities- conversion of wetlands for paddy fields; construction of a large number of reservoirs, canals and dams; diversion of streams and rivers to provide for irrigation

IV. Deforestation-removal of vegetation in the catchment leading to soil erosion and siltation

V. Pollution-unrestricted dumping of sewage, solid wastes and toxic chemicals from industries and households

VI. Salinization-over withdrawal of groundwater has led to salinization

VII. Aquaculture-pisciculture and aquaculture ponds

VIII. Introduced Species-exotic introduced plant species such as Water Hyacinth and Salvinia clog waterways and compete with native vegetation

IX. Climate change-increased air temperature; shifts in precipitation; increased frequency of storms, droughts, and floods; increased atmospheric carbon dioxide concentration; and sea level rise.

Scope for Management of Floodplain Wetlands in India

Floodplain wetland needs to be managed for protection in good condition, rehabilitate degraded wetlands where feasible, and support appreciation of wetlands by:

I. Protecting wetland biodiversity, functions and services;

II. Protecting social and economic benefits of wetlands;

III. Providing flow regimes that mimic natural conditions, where possible;

IV. Providing wetlands with water of appropriate volume and quality;

V. Limiting further fragmentation and reconnecting wetland systems;

VI. Preventing or limiting catchment activities that impact upon wetlands;

VII. Protecting the cultural heritage and spiritual significance of wetlands;

VIII. Rewarding wetland managers who improve the condition of wetlands; and

IX. Promoting the importance of wetlands to the community.

While management modes may vary according to the aspect of wetlands to be managed, I would like to high light the means to manage the fisheries of floodplain wetlands, as they along with reservoirs are the future of inland fisheries development in India.

I. Fish production

Floodplain wetlands vary in size and shape, and extend of riverine connection and they offer tremendous scope for expanding both capture and culture fisheries. On an average the fish production rates in floodplain wetlands of Ganga and Brahmaputra river systems range between 160 kg ha^{-1} $year^{-1}$ (Bihar) to 210 kg ha^{-1} $year^{-1}$ (Assam and West Bengal). However through scientific management the fish production from these water bodies can be increased several folds. For this there are several management mods, which are described below.

II. Capture fishery

Floodplain wetlands that retain their riverine connection for a reasonably long period of time are typical continuum of rivers, where the management strategy can be essentially the capture fishery norms followed for the riverine fisheries. The basic approach may be to allow recruitment of fishes by conserving and protecting the brooders and juveniles. In order to ensure recruitment the following parameters need to be taken in to consideration. Identification and protection of breeding grounds, allowing free migration of brooders and juveniles from beel to river and vice versa and protection of brood stock and juveniles are the main options. The management strategies to be followed are increasing the minimum mesh size at capture to stop juvenile fishing, increase or decrease fishing effort, observe closed seasons to protect brooders, strict adherence to minimum size at capture, diversify fishing gear, if required, for species and size specific fishing, selective augmentation of stock when needed.

III. Culture-based fishery

The main constraint in optimizing fish yield from closed floodplain wetlands is their derelict and weed choked nature. The basic strategy here is stocking and recapture. Floodplain wetlands are rich in nutrients and fish food organisms, which enable the stocked fishes to grow to support a fishery. The growth of fishes will be faster. In culture-based fishery the growth is dependent on stocking density and survival is dependent on size of the stocked fish. The right species stocked at right size at the right density and their recapture at right size is the determining factors of yield. These need to be decided as part of ecosystem oriented management.

IV. *Capture and Culture-based Fisheries*

There are management systems, which combine the norms of capture/culture-based fisheries and culture fisheries. In this system, the marginal areas of wetlands are cordoned off for culture fishery either in ponds or in pens and the central portion (wetland proper) is left for capture fisheries, as shown in the following figure. Under this system, a series of small ponds created along the periphery of the lake, which is leased out to entrepreneurs for fish farming. Some of these act as nurseries to rear the seed for both aquaculture and stocking in the wetland. When culture based fishery is practiced the connecting channel used to be blocked using wire mesh to prevent the stocked fishes from escaping and the water inflow and out flow is regulated through a sluice installed at the mouth of the connecting channel.

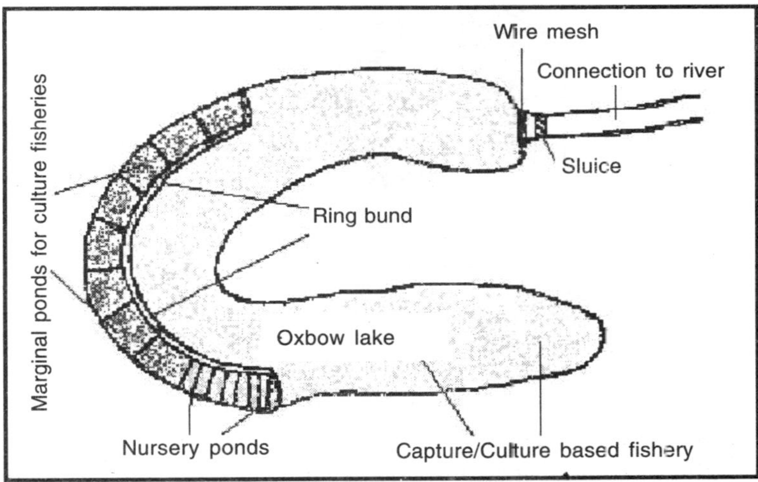

V. *Integrated management*

As some of the floodplain wetlands also serve as bird sanctuaries, national parks and reserves of biodiversity, areas of recreation, there used to be several environmental issues to mitigate. These wetlands are also used for navigation, irrigation, jute retting, collection of edible aquatic plants and animals as well as birds. Each activity affects other uses. Therefore a plan has been developed to integrate the many uses of the water bodies with a holistic approach. This example refers to a plan drawn for a floodplain wetland in West Bengal, India, as shown in the following figure, which has a swampy southern portion and a relatively deep northern portion, where the connection to a river existed. The integration plan envisaged were developing agriculture and aquaculture in the southern portion, while leaving the northern part for capture and culture based fisheries. A dike separated the two segments of the wetland and water flow to agriculture and aquaculture areas in the southern segment can be regulated through canals. The central marshy portion of the southern segment was left intact for harboring birds that used to frequent the area.

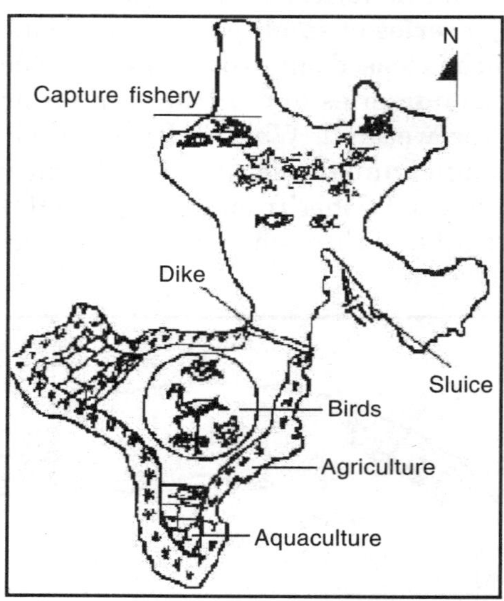

VI. Fishery options

Species management is a very important tool in floodplain wetland fishery management. This can be achieved through the various options of species enhancement described below.

(a) Fishery based on Indian major carps

The wetlands, especially the closed ones, can be developed as culture based fisheries as their fishery depends on stocking. The main species being stocked are those of Indian major carps. These are fast growing species and effective in utilizing the available food niches.

(b) Other indigenous fishes

Anabas testudineus, Clarias batrachus, Ompok spp. murrels, Amblypharyngodon mola, Gudusia chapra, Puntius spp. are a few candidate species on which a fishery can be developed. The low yield rates of these species, compared to that of major carps, can be compensated with the high price of indigenous species and the biodiversity gains can be considered as bonus.

(c) Ornamental fishes

Explorations in these water bodies in the past revealed that apart from food fishes, they also harbor several fish species, which are smaller, attractive and can be considered ornamental. These revelations coupled with the ever-growing demand for aquarium fishes provide ample scope for augmenting the economic return from these water bodies. Available information suggest the existence of 45 species belonging to 16 families in the floodplain wetlands of Assam and 63 species belonging to 23 families in West Bengal, with potential for aquarium purposes.

VII. Pen and cage culture

Manageable portions of the wetlands are cordoned of in pens to stock high value species and can be managed on the line of culture fishery. This is good for closed, weed chocked and unproductive wetlands. The Central Inland Fisheries Research Institute has identified culture of fishes and prawns in enclosures or 'pens' of manageable size and area, erected in the marginal areas of these water bodies as effective management tool for realizing additional fish production and income for the poor fishers, who depend on the wetlands for their daily livelihood. A production of 1,308 kg ha^{-1} of fresh water prawn Macrobrachium rosenbergii, in three months, was obtained from pens and the return on investment was 29.5%. Low cost materials like bamboo, cane, wooden logs etc. are used for putting up of pens. There are also immense potential for cage culture of fast growing fishes.

VIII. Management of livelihood issues

Livelihood comprises a set of economic activities undertaken by the members of households, which in the context of floodplain wetlands include fishing, agriculture, labour, small business, etc. Out of these, one or two constitute the major source of livelihood and others becoming supporting sources. In floodplain wetlands the main livelihood is fishing. The degree of dependence varies from sole dependence to fishing as subsidiary income. The involvement of people also varies from catching fish, net making, marketing, preparation of boat, etc. There, fore the issues on livelihood comprises all these functions undertaken by the fishers and all people depend up on fisheries in one way or other. These issues too need to be addressed while drawing up a plan for floodplain wetland management involving the fishers and other stakeholders.

WETLAND MANAGEMENT

Regulatory Framework for Wetland Management

As of now there is no specific legal framework for wetland conservation, management and their wise use. Draft regulatory framework for conservation and management of wetlands is being finalized to be notified under the Environment (Protection) Act, 1986.At present conservation and wise use of wetlands is being ensured through following legal instruments:

I. Legislations-Indian Forest Act, 1927; Forest (Conservation) Act, 1980; Wildlife (Protection) Act, 1972; Air (Prevention and Control of Pollution) Act, 1974; Water (Prevention and Control of Pollution) Act, 1974; Water Cess Act, 1977;Environment (Protection) Act, 1986; Biological Diversity Act, 2002; Coastal
II. Regulation Zone Notification, 1991; and their respective amendments.
III. Policies-National Environment Policy, 2006; National Conservation Strategy and Policy Statement on Environment and Development, 1992; National Forest Policy, 1988.
IV. Plans-National Biodiversity Action Plan, 2008
V. National Wetlands Conservation Programme

The Government of India has been implementing the National Wetlands Conservation Programme (NWCP) in close collaboration with the State/UT Governments since the year 1985-86. Under the programme, 115 wetlands have been identified till now by the Ministry which require urgent conservation and management interventions.

Wetland Management, Conservation, Restoration Strategies and Action Plan

Management is the manipulation of an ecosystem to ensure maintenance of all functions and characteristics of the specific wetland type. The loss or impairment of a wetland ecosystem is usually accompanied by irreversible loss in both the valuable environmental functions and amenities important to the society (Zentner, 1988). Appropriate management and restoration mechanisms need to be implemented in order to regain and protect the physical, chemical, and biological integrity of wetland ecosystems. In this context, a detailed study of wetland management and socio-economic implications is required from biological and hydrological perspectives.

Mostly , in urban centers, environmental pressures on wetlands are created by human activities (changing land use in the watershed area, pollution from point and non-point sources, soil compaction, loss in interconnectivity, and solid waste dumping, and so forth), which affect their natural functions. Protecting and preserving their functions proves to be incredibly complex, as it involves building a partnership among various agencies, working in co-ordination, and addressing the common goal of minimizing human-induced changes that affect the hydrology, biogeochemical fluxes and the quality of these lakes. The problems of wetlands can be broadly summarized as:

I. Hydrologic alterations, which include changes in the hydrologic structure and functioning of a wetland by direct surface drainage, de-watering by consumptive use of surface water inflows, unregulated draw down of unconfined aquifer from either groundwater withdrawal or by stream channelization for various human activities.

II. Increased sedimentation, nutrient, organic matter, metals, pathogen, and other water pollutant loading from both storm water runoff (non-point source) and wastewater discharges (point source).

III. Atmospheric deposition of pollutants into these lakes mainly by the vehicular and industrial pollution both from within the cities and from the suburban industrial complexes.

IV. Introduction or change in characteristic wetland flora and fauna (exotic) as a result of change in the adjacent land uses deliberately or naturally changing the water quality, and so forth.

The overexploitation of wetlands in many cities of India are evident, as it is used for disposing untreated sewage, runoff from urban and agricultural areas, changed land use within the watershed, and so forth. All these unplanned short-sighted anthropogenic activities have resulted in rendering the ecosystem integrity in peril. Deteriorating water quality due to pollution has also led to the spawning of mosquitoes in the absence of predators, such as Gambusia affinis, and killifishes (Fundulus spp.), which prey on mosquito larvae (Buchsbaum, 1994). It has been suggested that an Integrated Pest Management approach involving bio-regulation could possibly control mosquitoes rather than draining wetlands.

A wetland management program generally involves activities to protect, restore, manipulate, and provide for functions and values emphasizing both quality and acreage by advocating their sustainable usage (Walters, 1986). Management of wetland ecosystems require intense monitoring and increased interaction and co-operation among various agencies such as state departments concerned with the environment, soil, agriculture, forestry, urban planning and development, natural resource management; public interest groups; citizen's groups; research institutions; and policy makers

Such management goals should not only involve buffering wetlands from any direct human pressures that could affect their normal functions, but also in maintaining important natural processes operating on them that may be altered by human activities. Wetland management has to be an integrated approach in terms of planning, execution, and monitoring, requiring effective knowledge on a range of subjects from ecology, hydrology, economics, watershed management, and local expertise, people, planners and decision makers. All these would help in understanding wetlands better and evolve a more comprehensive and long-term conservation and management strategies. Some of the suggested strategies in this regard are:

1. The management strategies should involve protection of wetlands by regulating inputs, using water quality standards (WQS) promulgated for wetlands and such inland surface waters to promote their normal functioning from the ecosystem perspective, while still deriving economic benefits by sustainable usage.
2. Urban wetlands provide multiple values for suburban and city dwellers (Castelle, Johnson, & Conolly, 1994). The capacity of a functional urban wetland in flood control, aquatic life support, and as pollution sink implies a greater degree of protection. These wetlands provide a resource base for people dependent on them. When dealing with such common resources, some of the important factors to be considered for developing a management strategy are described below.
   - I. It is an immediate need to create a database on the wetland types, morphological, hydrological, and biodiversity data surrounding land use, hydrogeology, surface water quality, and socio-economic dependence. Such a database would highlight the stress these systems are subjected to in the given context.
   - II. Involve institutions, colleges, and regulating bodies in conducting regular water quality monitoring of surface water, groundwater, and biological samples. Such programs help in providing technical support and information, which aid in understanding these systems better and formulating a comprehensive restoration, conservation, and management program.
   - III. Development of a water quality database, accessible to all users, for analyzing and disseminating information. This can be achieved through:
     - (*a*) Exchanging data across departments involved in the program to allow easy accessibility to regularly and continuously monitored data;
     - (*b*) Updating technical guidance and water quality maps at regular intervals and indicating quality determinant parameters;
     - (*c*) Analyzing and discussing case studies of water quality issues;
     - (*d*) Providing spatial, temporal, and non-spatial water quality database systems.
   - IV. Correct non-point source pollution problems and administer the Pollution Prevention Program through environmental awareness programs.

V. Creating buffer zones for wetland protection, limiting anthropogenic activities around the demarcated corridor of the wetland, could revive their natural functioning. The criteria for determining adequate buffer zone size to protect wetlands and other aquatic resources depend on the following (Castelle, et al. 1994):
   I. Identifying the functional values by evaluating resources generated by wetlands in terms of their economic costs,
   II. Identifying the magnitude and the source of disturbance, adjacent land use, and project the possible impact of such stress in the long term,
   III. Identifying catchment characteristics-vegetation density and structural complexity, soil condition and factors.

VI. A fully formed functional In-buffer must consider the magnitude of the identified problems, the resource to be protected, and the function it has to perform. Such a buffer zone could consist of diverse vegetation along the perimeter of the water body, preferably an indigenous species, serving as a trap for the sediments, nutrients, metals and other pollutants, and reducing human impacts by limiting easy access and acting as a barrier to invasion of weeds and other stress inducing activities (Stockdale, 1991).

VII. Wetlands require collaborated research involving natural, social, and inter-disciplinary study aimed at understanding the various components, such as monitoring of water quality, socio-economic dependency, biodiversity, and other activities, as an indispensable tool for formulating long term conservation strategies (Kiran & Ramachandra, 1999). This requires multidisciplinary-trained professionals who can spread the understanding of wetland importance at local schools, colleges, and research institutions by initiating educational programs aimed at raising the levels of public awareness and comprehension of aquatic ecosystem restoration, goals, and methods.

   Actively participating schools and colleges in the vicinity of the waterbodies may value the opportunity to provide hands-on environmental education which could entail setting up laboratory facilities at the site. Regular monitoring of waterbodies (with permanent laboratory facilities) would provide vital inputs for conservation and management.

VIII. An interagency regulatory body comprising personnel from departments involved in urban planning and resource management (Forest department, Fisheries, Horticulture, Agriculture, and so forth), and from regulatory bodies such as Pollution Control Board, local citizen groups, research organizations, and NGO's, would help in evolving effective wetland programs. These programs would cover significant components of the watershed, and need a coordinated effort from all agencies and organizations involved in activities that affect the health of wetland ecosystems directly or indirectly.

Restoration means reestablishment of pre-disturbance aquatic functions and the related physical, chemical, and biological characteristics (Cairns, 1988; Lewis, 1989) with the objective of emulating a natural and a self regulating/perpetuating system that is integrated ecologically with the landscape and the functions the wetlands perform. The goals for any restoration program should be realistic and tailored to individual regions, specific to the problems of degradation, and based on the level of dependence. The restoration program should mandate all aspects of the ecosystems, including habitat restoration, elimination of undesirable species, and restoration of native species, from the ecosystem perspective with a holistic approach designed at watershed level, rather than isolated manipulation of individual elements. This often requires reconstruction of the physical conditions-chemical adjustment of the soil and water, biological manipulation, reintroduction of native flora and fauna.

Restoration goals, objectives, performance indicators (indicates the revival or success of restoration project), monitoring, and assessment program should be viably planned so that project designers; planners, biologists, and evaluators have a clear understanding. Monitoring of restoration endeavors should include both structural (state) and functional (process) attributes. Monitoring of attributes at population, community, ecosystem, and landscape level is appropriate in this regard.

Restoration strategy developed in collaboration with the government, researchers, stakeholders at all levels, and NGO's should:

I. Set principles for establishing priorities and decision making.

II. Prioritize goals, assessment, and monitoring strategies based on specific roles they perform, level of dependency and type of problems faced by them.

III. Foster innovative financing and use of land and water programs for better and sustainable usage of wetland resources.

It is important to give priority to repairing those systems that would become extinct without any intervention. Prioritizing systems for repair requires that a framework be developed categorizing the level of interventions (National Research Council, Committee on Restoration of Aquatic Ecosystems, 1992). These categories should be based on:

I. Wetlands that could recover without any intervention.

II. Wetlands that could be restored close to their former condition to serve their earlier functions, considering cost involved, technical review of the restoration plan, and based on the goals and objectives set.

III. Wetlands that are not restorable to any agreeable viably

CONCLUSION

In conclusion, it is important to stress the critical role of wetlands in delivering ecosystem services and their particular contribution to the rich biodiversity of Slovenia. These ecosystems will con-tinue to deliver their services and sup-port life as long as humans use them wisely. Ensuring the future of wetlands and their services requires maintaining the quantity and quality of the natural water regimes on which they depend, and the frequency, amounts and timing of water flows. The Ramsar Conven-tion's "wise use" concept of the 1970s promoted the need for a cross-sectoral approach and integrated management of wetland ecosystems. The year 2007 will mark 20 years of the Brundtland Report defining the concept of sustain-able development. Now, using the Millennium Ecosystem Assessment conceptual framework, wise use is still the leading concept for maintaining the ecological character of wetlands in the context of sustainable development. It will ensure the delivery of ecosystem services to support human well-being within Ramsar sites and within their catchment areas as well.

Table 10.1: The annual economic value (figures are rounded off) of global wetlands (in million US $)

Regions	Mangroves	Unvegetated sediment	Salt/brackish marshes	Freshwater marshes	Freshwater woodlands
North America	30	551	30	2.00	64
Latin America	8	105	3	0.50	6
Europe	0	268	12	0.30	20
Asia	28	1618	24	0.03	150
Africa	85	159	2	0.30	10
Australia	35	148	2	1.00	84
Total	**186**	**2849**	**73**	**4.13**	**334**

Source: 'The Economic Values of the World's Wetlands, 2004', WWF International.

REFERENCES

Beltram, G., 2005. Use Wetlands Wisely. In: Nature's Capital and the Millennium Development Goals. Our Planet, UNEP.

Buchsbaum, R. (1994). Management of coastal marshes. In D. M. Kent (Ed.), Applied wetlands science and technology (pp. 331). Boca Raton, FL.: CRC Press.

Cairns, J. (Ed.). (1988). Rehabilitating damaged ecosystms. Boca Raton, FL: CRC Press.

Castelle, A. J., Johnson, A. W., & Conolly, C. (1994). Wetland and stream buffer size requirements: A review. Journal of Environmental Quality, 23(5), 878-882.

Clarke, R. (1994). The pollution of lakes and reservoirs (UNEP environment library, no.12). Nairobi, Kenya: United Nations Environment Programme.

Cheriyan George, 2002. Wetland conservation for ecological health. Deccan Herald (www.deccanherald.com), Tuesday, November 19: 1-2.

Jha, B. C. and Chandra, K. 1977. Kusheshwarsthan chaur (North Bihar), status and prospects for fisheries development. Billetin No. 71. Central Inland Capture Fisheries Research Institute. 15 p.

Kiran, R., & Ramachandra, T. V. (1999 March). Status of wetlands in Bangalore and its conservation aspects. ENVIS Journal of Human Settlements, 16-24.

Lewis, R. R. III. (1989). Creation and restoration of coastal plain wetlands in Florida. In J. A. Kusler, & M. E. Kentula (Eds.), Wetland creation and restoration: The status of the science (US EPA/7600/3-89/038) (vol. 1, pp. 73-102). Corvallis, OR: U.S. Environmental Protection Agency, Environmental Research Laboratory.

Sugunan, V. V. 1995a. Floodplain lakes- a fisheries perspective. In Howes, J. R. (ed) Conservation and sustainable use of floodplain wetlands. Asian Wetlands Bureau, Kula Lumpur. 123 p.

Sinha, M. and Jha, B. C. 1997. Ecology and fisheries of ox-bow lakes (maun) of North Bihar- A threatened ecosystem. Bulletin No. 74. Central Inland Capture Fisheries Research Institute. 65 p.

Shine, C., & de Klemm, C. (1999). Wetlands, water, and the law: Using law to advance wetland conservation and wise use (IUCN environmental policy and law paper no. 38). Gland, Switzerland: IUCN.

Stockdale, E. (1991). Fresh water wetlands, urban storm water and non point source pollution control: A literature review & annotated bibliography. Olympia, WA: Washington Department of Ecology.

Sugunan, V. V. and Mukhopadhyaya, M. K. 1995. Conservation and sustainable use of floodplain wetlands: case studies of Bandardaha and Beloon beels. pp 67-71. In Howes, J. R. (ed) Conservation and sustainable use of floodplain wetlands. Asian Wetlands Bureau, Kula Lumpur.

Vinci, G. K. and Mitra, K. 2000. Environmental issues and sustainable fish production from floodplain lakes of Ganga basin. pp 67-75. In Sinha,M., Jha, B, C. and Khan, M,. A. (eds) Environmental Impact Assessment of Inland Waters for Sustainable Fisheries Management and Conservation of Biodiversity. Central Inland Capture Fisheries Research Institute, Barrackpore.

Walters, C. J. (1986). Adaptive management of renewable resources. New York: Macmillan.

Yadava, Y. S. 1989. Beel fishery resources in Northeast India. Bulletin No. 63. Central Inland Fisheries Research Institute. pp 8-14.

Zentner, J. (1988). Wetland restoration in urbanized areas: Examples from coastal California. In J. A. Kusler, S. Daly, & G. Brooks (Eds.), urban wetlands: Proceedings of the National Wetland Symposium, June 26-29, 1988, Oakland, California. Berne, NY: Association of Wetland Managers.

Index

F